Australia's First Campaign

The Capture Of German New Guinea, 1914

Robert Stevenson

16pt

Copyright Page from the Original Book

© Copyright Army History Unit
Campbell Park Offices (CP2-5-166)
Canberra ACT 2600
AUSTRALIA
(02) 6266 4248
(02) 6266 4044 - fax
Copyright 2020 © Commonwealth of Australia

First published 2021

This book is copyright. Apart from any fair dealing for the purposes of private study, research, criticism or review as permitted under the Copyright Act, no part may be reproduced, stored in a retrieval system or transmitted in any form or by any means, electronic, mechanical, photocopying, recording or otherwise, without written permission.

The views expressed in this publication are those of the author(s) and not necessarily those of the Australian Army or the Department of Defence. The Commonwealth of Australia will not be legally responsible in contract, tort or otherwise for any statement made in this publication.

All inquiries should be made to the publishers.
Big Sky Publishing Pty Ltd
PO Box 303, Newport, NSW 2106, Australia
Phone: 1300 364 611
Fax: (61 2) 9918 2396
Email: info@bigskypublishing.com.au
Web: www.bigskypublishing.com.au

 A catalogue record for this book is available from the National Library of Australia

Cover design and typesetting by Think Productions, Melbourne

Front cover and title page: Soldiers of the Australian Naval and Military Expeditionary Force in New Guinea, 1914 (T.J. Rodoni Collection, University of Newcastle, ARODGN_0247).

Back cover background: German prisoners of war and civilian internees, Sydney, 1914 (SPC-A).
Top: *Politzeitruppen* being trained after the outbreak of war (AWM A02544).
Centre: The reception of the Australian fleet, Sydney Harbour, 4 October 1914 (SPC-A).
Bottom: Naval 12-pounder breech-loading gun (AWM P06162.001).

TABLE OF CONTENTS

SERIES INTRODUCTION	ii
ACKNOWLEDGEMENTS	iv
MEASUREMENTS	vii
PLACE NAMES	viii
ABBREVIATIONS	x
PROLOGUE	xii
INTRODUCTION	xix
CHAPTER 1: PEACEFUL PENETRATION	1
CHAPTER 2: THE REALISATION OF AMBITIOUS HOPES	51
CHAPTER 3: A GREAT AND URGENT IMPERIAL SERVICE	87
CHAPTER 4: OPENING MOVES	162
CHAPTER 5: DAY OF BATTLE	236
CHAPTER 6: NO MORE 'UM KAISER	315
CHAPTER 7: AN AFFAIR OF CONTINUOUS GOOD LUCK?	358
EPILOGUE	387
APPENDIX 1: CHRONOLOGY	403
APPENDIX 2: NAVAL AND MILITARY RANKS	410
APPENDIX 3: AUSTRALIAN ORDER OF BATTLE	413
APPENDIX 4: GERMAN ORDER OF BATTLE	417
APPENDIX 5: COLONEL WILLIAM HOLMES' APPRECIATION OF THE SITUATION	419
APPENDIX 6: ANMEF OPERATION ORDER NUMBER 1	424
APPENDIX 7: TERMS OF CAPITULATION OF GERMAN NEW GUINEA	426
APPENDIX 8: THE BATTLEFIELD TODAY	432
SELECT BIBLIOGRAPHY	451
BACK COVER MATERIAL	456

Index

In memory of
Warrant Officer Class One O.S. 'Ocker' Stevenson, OAM (1939—2016) and Professor Jeffrey Grey (1959—2016)

SERIES INTRODUCTION

In 2004, the then Chief of Army's Strategic Advisory group, the Australian Army's senior generals, established a scheme to promote the study and understanding of military history within the Army. The focus was the Army's future generation of leaders and, from this, the Campaign Series was created. The series is intended to complement the Army's other history publications which are academically rigorous and referenced.

The Campaign Series focuses on leadership, command, strategy, tactics and personal experiences of war. Each title within the series includes extensive visual sources of information—maps, including specifically prepared maps in colour and 3D, commissioned artwork, photographs and graphics.

Covering major campaigns and battles, as well as those less known, the Australian Army History Unit's Campaign Series provides a significant contribution to the history of the Australian Army and an excellent

introduction to its campaigns and battles.
Tim Gellel
Head, Australian Army History Unit

ACKNOWLEDGEMENTS

Many individuals have contributed to this publication. Researching *Australia's First Campaign* took me across Australia and north to the islands that were once part of the German Empire. In Papua New Guinea (PNG), Mr Munden Bray from the Rabaul Historical Society kindly showed me through the society's museum and provided local knowledge on East New Britain. Melinda Sutherland and Greg Belford extended their special brand of hospitality in Port Moresby on the transit back from New Britain.

In Australia, the staffs of the Australian War Memorial (AWM), the National Archives of Australia (NAA) and the state libraries of New South Wales and Queensland were invariably friendly and helpful. Mr Kel Pearce, formerly of the Commonwealth War Graves Commission, provided background information on the Rabaul (Bita Paka) War Cemetery. Mr John Perryman, Director Strategic and Historical Studies at the Sea Power Centre—Australia (SPC-A), facilitated my access to the centre's holdings and authorised the use of many of the photographic images reproduced in this volume. Mr Chris Dale granted permission to use the Klewitz family photograph of Lieutenant Carl Klewitz, which appears on his German colonial uniforms website. The University of Newcastle provided Thomas Rodoni's photograph from its Rodoni Archive, which appears on the front cover of this volume. Dr Rhys Crawley generously shared the fruits of his research in the Admiralty records at The National Archives in London. Mr John Land, curator of the Australian Army Infantry Museum (AAIM) at Singleton, assisted with the identification of the British and German small arms and provided photographs of those weapons. My fellow 'history tragics', Ian Finlayson and Ric Pelvin, read the manuscript and saved me from a number of errors, as well as providing additional insights. All remaining faults and errors however, are mine.

As the first among equals, I owe the greatest debt to the Australian Army History Unit (AAHU). The AAHU supported the project through the Army

Research Grants Scheme, providing me with the opportunity to travel to New Britain and conduct field research in 2016. My gratitude also extends to the AAHU's team of experts who have added so much to the finished product: Captain Anne Giles and Ms Sophie Jerapetritis for the project direction, Nick Anderson for the handy advice for a first-time campaigner, Corporal Kyla Morris for the maps, Cathy McCullagh for her editing and Denny Neave and the talented Big Sky Publishing team for the typesetting and book design. Finally, I owe much gratitude to my wife Rose for giving up her annual leave to accompany me to PNG, where she stomped through more muddy jungle and later provided her professional insights when proofreading the manuscript. I am grateful for the opportunity to tell the important story of the Australian military's first campaign and to contribute to the Australian Army Campaign Series.

MEASUREMENTS

	Imperial	Metric
Length	1 inch	25.4 millimetres
	1 foot = 12 inches	0.305 metres
	1 yard = 3 feet	0.91 metre
	1 mile = 5280 feet or 1760 yards	1.61 kilometres
	1 nautical mile = 6076 feet	1.852 kilometres
Weight	1 pound	0.45 kilograms
	14 pounds = 1 stone	6.35 kilograms
	1 imperial or long ton = 2240 pounds	1.016 metric tonnes/1016 kilograms
Speed	1 knot = 1 nautical mile per hour	0.514 metres per second

PLACE NAMES

Name in 1914	Current	Remarks
Admiralitäts-Inseln	Admiralty Islands	
Bismarck-Archipel	Bismarck Archipelago	
Bougainville-Insel	Bougainville Island	
Karolinen	Carolines	
Deutsch-Kiautschou	Jiaozhou Bay	
Deutsch-Neuguinea		German New Guinea
Herbertshöhe	Kokopo	
Kaiser Wilhelmsland		North-east New Guinea
Marianen	Marianas	
Marschall-Inseln	Marshall Islands	
Neu-Mecklenburg	New Ireland	
Nue-Pommern	New Britain	
Pelew Islands	Palau	
Pleasant Island	Nauru	
Ponape	Pohnpei	
Nördliche Salomon-Inseln	Autonomous Bougainville	Northern Solomon Islands
Simpsonhafen	Simpson Harbour	
Truk	Chuuk Lagoon	

| Tsingtao | Qingdao |

ABBREVIATIONS

AAHU	Australian Army History Unit
AAIM	Australian Army Infantry Museum, Singleton
AIF	Australian Imperial Force
ANMEF	Australian Naval and Military Expeditionary Force
AWM	Australian War Memorial
CMG	Companion of the Most Distinguished Order of Saint Michael and Saint George
CNF	Commonwealth Naval Forces
CO	Commanding Officer of a ship or unit
DSO	Distinguished Service Order
HMS	His Majesty's Ship
HMAS	His Majesty's Australian Ship
KCB	Knight Commander of the Most Honourable Oder of the Bath
KCMG	Knight Commander of the Most Distinguished Order of Saint Michael and Saint George
KCVO	Knight Commander of the Royal Victorian Order
KGS	Imperial Government Ship (Kaiserliches Gouvernement Schiff)
LC	Library of Congress
MC	Military Cross
NAA	National Archives of Australia
MID	Mention/ed in Despatches

NCO/s	non-commissioned officer/s
NLA	National Library of Australia
OC	Officer Commanding a sub-unit
PMO	Principal Medical Officer
P&O	Peninsula and Orient
RAN	Royal Australian Navy
RANR	Royal Australian Naval Reserve
RN	Royal Navy
RNR	Royal Naval Reserve
SLQ	State Library of Queensland
SLSA	State Library of South Australia
SMS	His Majesty's Ship (Seiner Majestät Schiff)
SPC-A	Sea Power Centre—Australia
SS	Steam Ship
VC	Victoria Cross
VD	Volunteer Decoration

PROLOGUE

It was a hot, humid tropical day. The temperature swiftly climbed as the sun rose in the sky, a white orb beating down mercilessly on the vibrant, emerald jungle. Beneath the thick, interlocking layers of foliage it was quiet and dark, but any relief offered by the shade of the towering, languid trees was negated by the intense heat trapped beneath the canopy, where no air stirred. Long gone were the wispy palms of the breeze-fanned beach. Inland it was like a giant, green-hued stokehold. Manoeuvring through the shadows, a small column of tawny-clothed men shouldered their way through the verdant growth, like ships ploughing through the sea. Their advance was quiet except for the unavoidable sounds of rustling leaves and clawing vines dragged across cloth and the occasional muttered curse as thorns tore at exposed skin. The column wove in and out seeking the path of least resistance; when the closely matted scrub became too thick, the men turned back towards the road and skirted along the verge until a new path could be found. From the blinding light that beat down on the dusty road, they quickly disappeared again into the steamy, subdued semi-twilight of the jungle shadows.

Fighting the suffocating heat and claustrophobic bush, the men struggled to stay alert, vigilant for a foe who might be anywhere ahead or behind or, indeed, nowhere near them. They weren't sure whether they were heading in the right direction and, even if they were, there remained the unanswered question—would the enemy fight? Offshore they had been told to expect no resistance. Onshore such advice was less reassuring. The only local information they had received until now was provided by a nervous Chinese storekeeper they had apprehended after landing from the destroyer that morning. Rousted out of his store near the bay, he claimed their goal was just a couple of miles inland along the powdery dirt road they now paralleled.

Scrutinising the thick foliage, straining to see through to what lay beyond, their leader peered searchingly to the left trying to discern any distant patch of unfiltered light that would disclose the ribbon of road along which the rest of the party was trailing. Petty Officer George Palmer might well have wondered what had brought him to this strange place. Born at Chelmsford in Essex, England, in 1879, he had gone to sea as a boy and later migrated to Australia. He served a short stint in South Africa in 1902 with the Australian forces before returning to the Antipodes for discharge. Taking up residence in Parkville, Victoria, he joined the Royal Australian Naval Reserve. Soon after the declaration of war in August 1914 he had heeded the clarion call for naval volunteers to join a force destined to serve in some undisclosed location overseas. Signing on for six months' full-time service at Williamstown, he and the other sailors caught the overnight train to Sydney where they joined the rest of the contingent and boarded their auxiliary cruiser turned transport, His Majesty's Australian Ship (HMAS) *Berrima,* for the voyage that turned out to be north to the islands of German

XV

New Guinea. A month later, the excitement had worn off for the 35-year-old master mariner and here he was, cast ashore in this foetid hell.

He blinked as perspiration trickled off his forehead, rolling over his brow to slip into his eyes which stung with the salt. His vision blurred and he was forced to wipe his face for what seemed the hundredth time, his hands leaving wet, muddy prints on the wooden stock of his trusty Lee-Enfield rifle. He gave an involuntary shiver as more brine ran down the line of his spine, soaking a uniform already darkened with sweat. After years in the navy he was used to thinking of life at sea as wet work, but sneaking around in this miserable, clammy world was worse. It was utterly bewildering for a sailor suddenly turned soldier. The jungle was a strange place and he couldn't wait to get back to the ship and away from this stinking green inferno.

Just when he thought it couldn't get any worse they hit another bad patch of scrub. He and Able Seaman Leslie Eastman were forced to lead the party to starboard, drifting deeper into the bush and away from the track, further slowing their progress. Once around the worst of it, he pulled hard to port aiming to find the road again. As they angled back, Palmer surveyed the next obstacle barring their way.

He paused mid-step and froze as his heart seemed to skip a beat, before sucking in a deep breath of the pungent, dusty air. Through the tangle of knotted vegetation, about 30 yards ahead, he spotted a group of natives, perhaps 20 in all, with a European. This man was using hand signals and motioning to the natives to keep quiet and remain under cover. Further to port he spied another group, two 'whites' and another 'black' half-hidden, who were facing away from him, intently watching the road from the deep shadows of the jungle fringe. The whites appeared to be uniformly dressed in khaki with slouch hats, although he really had no idea what a German soldier should look like. They and the blacks were certainly armed, and it was obvious that they were lying in wait for the main body of the Australian party moving along the track, unaware of their silent spectators. Despite the earlier reports, it was now clear that the Germans were not going to just give up, they were there to fight.

In a swift, fluid action, Palmer shouldered his rifle, took aim and fired. The detonation shattered the quite morning, scattering the Germans and their Melanesian auxiliaries. There followed a ragged volley of return fire accompanied instantaneously by the vicious crack of bullets flying overhead, ripping the high leaves into jungle-green confetti.

Palmer's bullet hit the first German in the hand, knocking his rifle from his grasp. Although stunned, Sergeant Major Maurice Mauderer fumbled to draw his sidearm. But when he glanced up he realised that the tawny strangers had a bead on him and the range was point-blank. He cried out, offering to surrender, calling to his captors in accented English that he was wounded. He turned and yelled to his men to stop firing. As the two figures advanced on him, the soldier glanced down at his shattered hand, a bloody mess of torn tissue and shattered bone. He began to tremble with shock and the realisation that he was now a prisoner of the cursed British. On the dusty road to Bita Paka the battle for German New Guinea had begun.

INTRODUCTION

Few Australians have ever heard of Bita Paka (also written as Bitapaka) and not one in a thousand would be able to locate it with any accuracy within the Bismarck Archipelago. Even providing the hint that it lies near Kokopo, today the capital of East New Britain, would probably not be of much assistance. While this may be understandable given that the locale is a tiny pinprick in the vast Pacific and its main feature a cemetery, such geographical ignorance is a tangible reflection of a widespread lack of knowledge in Australia of its long involvement with its nearest neighbour. Since 1975, when the mandated territory of New Guinea and the Australian External Territory of Papua were granted independence as the new Independent State of Papua New Guinea, few Australians have paid much attention to the island nation aside from a handful of those with government, academic, humanitarian or business interests. The bulk of Australians have only a vague awareness that Papua had first been claimed by the colony of Queensland in 1883 before becoming an Australian-administered territory in 1906, while New Guinea was forcibly acquired by the Commonwealth in 1914 (see Chronology at Appendix 1). Nor are many aware that Australians lost their lives seizing that territory. While just about every Australian knows something of Kokoda and the so-called 'Battle for Australia' in 1942, few appreciate why that later generation of diggers came to be fighting there, on what was Australian soil.

On 11 September 1914, an English-born naval reservist fired the first Australian shot in battle during the Great War. Petty Officer George Robert Palmer initiated Australia's first action along a dusty road on the tip of the Gazelle Peninsula. Fighting in thick bush against a hidden and fleeting enemy, he and a handful of mostly untried sailors and novice soldiers fought a short, vicious action that left six of their number dead and another four wounded. As a result of that single action, less than a week later all of

German New Guinea was surrendered and Australia achieved a long-cherished goal of ridding the islands to its near north of a hostile power. Back home, nobody knew of the momentous events as radio communications were slow and unreliable. Besides, the country was preoccupied with the recent federal election triggered by the nation's first double dissolution of both houses of parliament, not to mention the great battles being fought along the frontiers of Europe thousands of kilometres away. On that day, the front page of the *Sydney Morning Herald* contained a brief summary of the latest bulletins on the fighting in France and advice that Prime Minister Joseph Cook, the leader of the defeated Australian Liberal Party, had tendered his resignation to the Governor-General. Alongside the political news lay an article reminding the well-heeled ladies of Sydney's eastern suburbs of the necessity for white gloves to be worn at the forthcoming Randwick horse races. Not until page eight was there any mention of affairs in the Pacific and only then to announce that the naval authorities had advised that all was well aboard the navy's new flagship HMAS *Australia,* although its whereabouts were a strict secret. Ominously, an adjacent article announced the arrival of the Japanese collier *Fukoko Maru* at Newcastle where the crew reported having coaled two German cruisers at the Caroline Islands on 5 August—the very day Britain declared war on Germany.

Reports of the fighting and losses on New Britain were only published three days after the action. When the news was made public the nation rejoiced at its first victory. The politicians who despatched the force, now out of government and some out of a job, were partially consoled by the reflected glory of the achievement. For many Australian-born Britons, it was doubly sweet as, simultaneously, the local German threat was removed and Australia gained a substantial sea-land buffer between its thinly populated northern shores and Asia's teeming millions just over the horizon. In one day the young country grabbed some 240,000 square kilometres of overseas territory, or slightly more than the total land mass of the state of Victoria. The nation's new status within the British Empire as a sub-imperial power was strengthened and celebrated, though in half a dozen homes the heady news was stifled as families came to grips with the sudden and unexpected death of a loved one. Not for the first time (nor last), the nation celebrated its military prowess publicly while, behind closed doors and drawn curtains, mothers and fathers sat alone and quietly wept for their sons who had paid the ultimate price.

For such a small-scale action, Bita Paka nonetheless occupies a pivotal place in Australian history. This skirmish ushered in a new era in Australian foreign affairs and international relations. It provided the cause for Australia's politicians to later assert themselves on the world stage, demanding an independent voice among the premiers of the old world. In 1919 the leader of the Commonwealth, which was not yet two decades old, would argue and win the right to retain the territory seized from its enemy. This claim would be advanced on behalf of

Australia's 60,000 war dead, the first of whom fell near Bita Paka. Brazenly, and in the face of world opinion and against the wishes of their imperial benefactor, Australia's political leaders would place their country's interests first, thrusting Australia's territorial boundaries forward to the very edge of the Equator and giving Australians a stronger reason to look out over the seas that girded the nation, rather than focussing inland on the interior of their half-conquered continent.

From a military standpoint, Bita Paka is likewise crucial in the development of an independent Australian defence force. The joint naval and military affair, the first of its kind for the Royal Australian Navy (RAN) and the Australian Army, was the first operation planned and executed by the uniformed services of the Commonwealth of Australia. The mixed naval and army brigade that fought the action—officially the Australian Naval and Military Expeditionary Force (ANMEF)—was the first Australian joint navy-army formation. Seven months before Gallipoli, the ANMEF became the first

Australian force to see overseas action in the Great War, its personnel suffered the first battle casualties, including the first navy and army fatalities, they inflicted the first casualties on the enemy, and its members were awarded the first decorations for gallantry. The operation can also lay claim to a number of other Australian 'firsts': Australian amphibious landing; RAN shore bombardment; Australian bayonet charge of the Great War; and deployment of Australian service nurses. Moreover it remains a campaign shrouded in mystery and controversy, witnessing the first loss of an RAN warship, the Australian services' first war crimes, and a battle in which up to a third of the Australian casualties were probably inflicted by friendly fire rather than the enemy. More pointedly, the capture of New Guinea was the only campaign of the Great War that can rightly claim to have served Australian strategic interests in a direct and tangible way.

Beyond the battlefield, the performance of Colonel William Holmes, the commander of the ANMEF, is of more than passing interest. The 51-year-old citizen-soldier not only raised and led Australia's first land formation to see battle, he was the first Australian officer to negotiate the surrender of a uniformed enemy force, the first to take formal control of an enemy colony, and he formed and headed Australia's first overseas military government. He did all this without substantial guidance and few resources. In spite of these achievements, his name is largely unknown and his reputation has been eclipsed by his contemporary, John Monash. Had Holmes survived however, he might well have commanded the Australian Corps in 1918 and it would be his image adorning the Australian 100 dollar note today.

Despite its significance, the New Guinea campaign of 1914 has not been well served historically. This is a pity as there is a great deal to be learned from Australia's first and only independent operation of the Great War, although in fairness the widespread apathy towards the campaign is easily understood. Operations in the Pacific were small scale, the fighting over in a few days, and the events were peripheral to the great powers. In a world war characterised by vast and bloody battles and expansive campaigns, the swift seizure of a handful of Pacific islands, at a relatively low cost, was always going to be overshadowed by later events, particularly Gallipoli, which still holds a fascination that has not dimmed with time. Hence it is not surprising that histories of the Great War, including those focussed on Australia's participation, generally dismiss Germany's demise in the Pacific in a few lines.

On the other hand, the success of the Australian operations in August and September 1914, coupled with the parallel deployments by British, New Zealand and Japanese forces, quickly thwarted the Kaiser's pre-war plans to turn the Pacific into a theatre of war. A strategy to disrupt Australasian maritime trade across the Asia-Pacific region was quickly stymied and Germany's operational options snuffed out. Today, with the benefit of hindsight, the early string of Allied successes looks like a foregone conclusion, but the failure of Britain to deal equally swiftly with other German colonial outposts, particularly in German East Africa, demonstrates that matters could have been different.

Before delving into the New Guinea campaign, it is necessary to explain several terms and practices employed throughout this volume to ensure common understanding. The first of the terms are those designators used to describe war and its complex facets. The terms 'strategy', 'operations' and 'tactics' are often employed (and misemployed) with little regard to their meaning. Each refers to a particular level of war. Strategy, or the strategic level of war, embraces the 'big picture', the arena that is the concern of politicians and senior military commanders at the highest echelons, where the objectives of the war are set, national power is harnessed to achieve those objectives, and decisions are made on how military force is to be employed. During the Great War, the government of the United Kingdom of Great Britain and Ireland directed the

British Empire's strategy. Australia and the other self-governing dominions (Canada, Newfoundland, New Zealand and South Africa) merely played a supporting role. Indeed the operations in New Guinea only occurred because the British government requested Australian assistance through the office of the Australian GovernorGeneral, as business was done in those days. Although the dominion governments did not play a day-to-day role in the formulation of imperial strategy, this should not be interpreted as implying that they had no influence at this level. As we shall see, the outcome of the New Guinea campaign was largely determined by strategic policy decisions of successive Australian governments in the years between Federation in 1901 and the outbreak of war in 1914.

The operational level of war is a relatively recent addition to the lexicon of military terminology. The idea that there was another level of war sandwiched between strategy and tactics evolved slowly with the growth of armed forces and the expansion of warfare both physically and intellectually. While not in use at the time of the New Guinea operations, it is a useful term for explaining how the war in the Pacific was waged because it refers to the conduct of campaigns that serve as the link between higher strategy and the battles fought by tactical commanders. At the behest of Britain, Australia's senior political and military leadership tasked its naval and military commanders with achieving a strategic objective—the occupation of Germany's Pacific colonies and the severing of German strategic communications. It was those operational commanders who developed the plan to accomplish that objective. The operation to seize New Guinea, while small in scale, was a discrete campaign and it was conducted as a joint operation (in those days described as a combined operation) in that it involved the close cooperation and coordination of both navy and army forces.

At their most fundamental level, wars are fought on the battlefield. In New Guinea, the battle began with the first shot fired by a tired, frightened naval petty officer, and thereafter the two sides fought each other in a close quarters and sometimes vicious fight. Active operations concluded 10 days later when the remaining German forces surrendered. For all its limited scale and short duration, the fighting tested the leadership and tactics of an untried force and determined the fate of New Guinea for the next 60 years. Although each of the levels of war is discrete, their relationships are symbiotic since each influences the others in often unexpected and unforeseeable ways, with battlefield outcomes shaped as much by strategic and operational factors as the tactics of junior commanders and skill of individual soldiers.

Military ranks are a field that can be mystifying for the uninitiated. This is especially so because different countries employ different systems and, even within a single nation, the various uniformed services often employ separate designations for equivalent ranks; indeed, in some cases, there is no corresponding rank. For instance, in British Commonwealth countries, a naval captain is the equivalent of an army colonel, while a captain in the army is the equivalent of a naval lieutenant. To assist in deciphering ranks, a simplified table of British navy and army ranks, as they were employed in 1914, along with their closest German equivalents, is provided at Appendix 2. German military ranks, when first cited in the text, are given as their nearest British equivalent, with the German version italicised within parentheses, for example, Captain of Cavalry (*Rittmeister*). Ranks given in the text are those held by the individual at the time rather than the highest rank achieved.

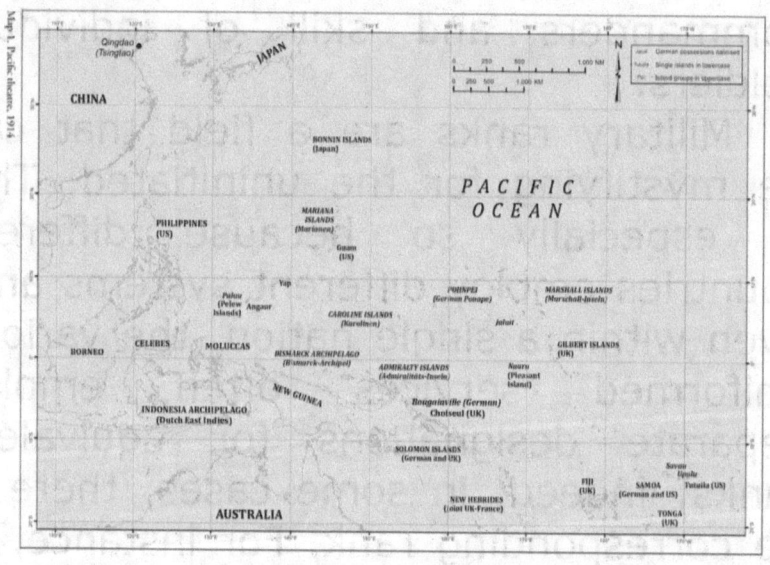

Naval and military organisation is a further subject in which confusion can occur. In 1914 the warships of the RAN formed an independent task group known as a 'fleet unit'. Fleet units were capable of independent action as a self-contained squadron, or the squadron or elements of it could operate as part of a larger fleet. Led by the battle cruiser HMAS *Australia*, the RAN squadron comprised three light cruisers (HMAS *Encounter, Melbourne* and *Sydney*), a destroyer flotilla of three River class torpedo boat destroyers (HMAS *Parramatta, Yarra* and *Warrego*), and a pair of E class submarines (*AE1* and *AE2*). The Australian land formation employed in New Guinea was the ANMEF, a 2000-strong joint brigade of naval and army troops comprising three battalions. All battalions were divided into companies, which were the battalion's tactical sub-units. Army companies were around 100 strong, while the naval companies were about half that size. Appendix 3 provides the Australian order of battle for the campaign.

Arrayed against the Australian expedition was Germany's powerful East Asiatic Squadron. This squadron comprised two armoured cruisers, His Majesty's Ships (*Seiner Majestät Schiff*—SMS) *Scharnhorst* and *Gneisenau*, three light cruisers (SMS *Emden, Leipzig* and *Nürnberg*), the aged sloop SMS *Cormoran*, and various auxiliary cruisers, gunboats and support vessels. German land forces were an amalgam of recently mobilised German army reservists and Melanesian policemen divided into geographical commands. Appendix 4 provides the German order of battle.

On the eve of war, Britain, France, Germany, the Netherlands, Portugal and the United States all possessed territories in the Asia-Pacific region, while Japan cast its eyes covetously west to China and south at the existing empires of the European powers. Many of the Pacific colonies had titles that will be unfamiliar to non-specialists today, while other locations have different names from those employed during the colonial era. For instance, when Germany claimed the islands that today comprise the Bismarck Archipelago, they ignored the previous British name of the New Britannia Archipelago and, rather ironically, retitled it in honour of the German chancellor who promoted German hegemony in Europe at the expense of acquiring overseas possessions. To make it easier for the reader, current geographic titles are employed throughout the text with any former name enclosed in parentheses (and italicised if German)—for example, New Britain (*Nue-Pommern*) and Pohnpei (Ponape).

The extensive Imperial German Pacific Protectorates in the western Pacific, known as German New Guinea (*Deutsch-Neuguinea*), consisted of two administrative divisions. The first was the Island Territory, north of the Equator, comprising the island groups of the Carolines (*Karolinen*) including Yap; Palau (Pelew Islands); the Marianas (*Marianen*) except for Guam, which was United States territory; the Marshall Islands (*Marschall-Inseln*); and the island of Nauru, which was also known as Pleasant Island. The second administrative division was the Old Protectorate, south of the Equator, encompassing the north-eastern sector of the island of New Guinea (*Kaiser Wilhelmsland*) along with the islands of the Bismarck Archipelago (*Bismarck-Archipel*) including New Britain (*Neu-Pommern*), New Ireland (*Neu-Mecklenburg*) and the Admiralty Islands (*Admiralitäts-Inseln*); and the Northern Solomon Islands (*Nördliche Salomon-Inseln*), which included Buka and Bougainville Island (*Bougainville-Insel*). In the eastern Pacific was the separate colony of German Samoa (*Deutsch-Samoa*). On the outbreak of war in August 1914 these colonies formed a barrier to Australia's north and east where German encroachment into the South Seas appeared to be aimed directly at Britain's Pacific dominions. What follows is the story of how Australia dealt with the German threat on its northern doorstep.

CHAPTER 1

PEACEFUL PENETRATION

Australia's history from the time of European occupation is dominated by concerns over security. In the era of the British Empire, Australian security assurance was provided by the collective umbrella of imperial defence and underwritten by the global dominance of the Royal Navy (RN). While the United Kingdom's Westminster government maintained worldwide interests, its security focus was primarily directed towards India and Europe as it sought to maintain a balance of power among its colonial competitors. With every shift in this balance, threats (real and imagined) emerged and, like a rock dropped in a pool, sent ripples out across the oceans to lap on the shores of Britain's far-off territories. Hence the century following the European settlement of Australia was wracked by a succession of invasion scares beginning with Napoleonic France (1799—1815), shifting to Tsarist Russia during the Crimean War (1853—56), switching to imperial Japan after its victory in the Russo-Japanese War (1904—05) and finally settling on Wilhelmine Germany with its intrusion into the Pacific seeking what it believed was its rightful place in the sun.

Blanche Bay, New Britain. This pre-war photograph was taken from the high ground below the volcano 'North Daughter' and looks south across Blanche Bay towards the entrance to the bay. Rabaul township is on the left. The German warships SMS Scharnhorst, Gneisenau, Nürnberg and Leipzig, which were on their annual cruise of the Pacific, lie at anchor in Simpson Harbour. The two heights on the left are the volcano 'Mother' (far left) and an older crater. 'South Daughter' lies hidden behind 'Mother' (AWM H18475).

Germans first became active traders in the Pacific in the mid-nineteenth century. A commercial base was founded at Samoa in 1857 and, within 10 years, the first German-owned copra plantation was established. In the 1870s further trading bases sprang up in the Bismarck Archipelago and the Marshall and Gilbert islands. Intent on protecting German trading interests and taking advantage of British diplomatic weakness, the German government claimed German New Guinea as a protectorate in 1884. The Marshall Islands and the northern Solomon Islands were annexed in 1885. From that time the colony was administered under imperial charters by the German New Guinea Company (*Deutsche Neuguinea-Kompagnie*) in the manner of the old British and Dutch East India companies, although with less success. In 1899 the German government stepped in and agreed to take over the administration of the protectorate and a Governor was appointed, based at Kokopo (*Herbertshöhe*) at the northern end of New Britain. In 1910 the capital of the colony was moved from Kokopo to nearby Rabaul, on the northern shores of Blanche Bay overlooking the magnificent Simpson Harbour (*Simpsonhafen*).

In the early 1900s German attempts to gain leverage in contested colonial regions acquired the label 'peaceful penetration' in the British press. While the term was used as early as 1903, it became increasingly popular during the First Moroccan Crisis (1905—06). In Australia the term was adopted to describe aggressive German economic activity across the Pacific. Although the Germans chose not to fortify their Pacific territories, it was recognised that Rabaul possessed the finest harbour in the region and Australians saw it as a potential haven for raiding naval cruisers in time of war.

British submarine telegraph cable. This particular cable was cut by SMS Nürnberg as Germany attempted to disrupt British strategic communications in 1914 and is now in the RAN historical collection and on display at the Naval Heritage Centre at Garden Island in Sydney (author image).

As German economic interests grew in the Pacific so too did its naval presence. In 1897 Germany seized the fortified port of Qingdao (Tsingtao) in Shandong Province from China and in the following year was granted the Jiaozhou Bay concession (*Deutsch-Kiautschou*) which covered the surrounding area. There it established a permanent garrison and naval headquarters for its local fleet. By 1914 the powerful East Asiatic Squadron was based at Qingdao, comprising two modern armoured cruisers and a number of light cruisers. German pre-war plans revolved around this squadron and its ability to wage war on Britain's maritime commerce that plied the trade routes criss-crossing the Indian and Pacific oceans. The squadron posed no significant direct invasion threat to Australia or New Zealand, at least while Britain maintained its position of naval supremacy, and such a situation only improved with the Anglo-Japanese Alliance of 1902. Germany however, did have plans to attack Australasian merchant shipping and port facilities, believing that it was feasible and such a strategy could be successful. To support these plans the German Admiralty established an extensive spy network across the Pacific, including in Australia, and its agents provided German planners with information on Australia's defences, trade and communications.

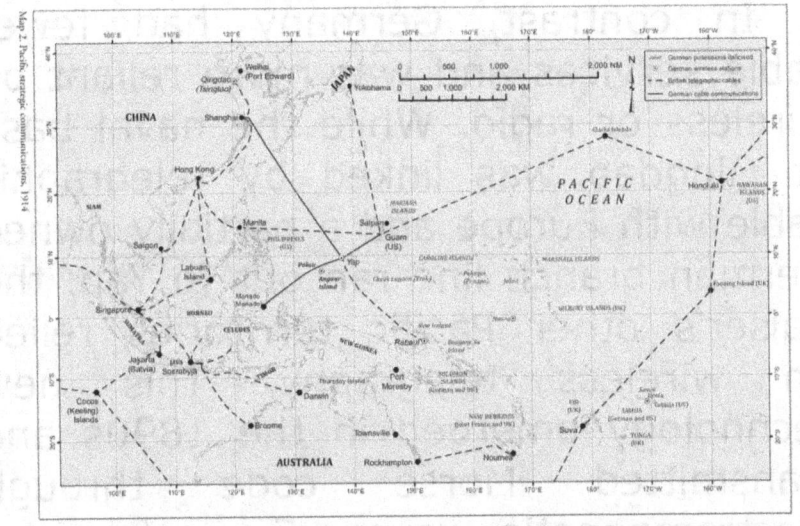

Overseas territories had strategic value, providing both communications links and logistics infrastructure for naval lines of communication. They were particularly important to maritime powers such as Britain whose prosperity and very survival depended on the free flow of trade. Similarly, Australia and New Zealand were both trading nations which were part of the British Empire's global trade network. To link its network of territories and trade partners, Britain maintained a global system of submarine telegraph cables that spanned the world's oceans as part of its 'all Red Line'. These were the satellites of their day.

In contrast, Germany had fewer cable services and was more reliant on wireless or radio. While the naval base at Qingdao was linked by telegraphic cable with Europe and a partially owned German branch line ran out to Yap, the Kaiser's other Pacific territories relied on wireless telegraphy. This new technology emerged in the 1890s and transmitted Morse code through electromagnetic waves. Europe's naval powers were among the first to recognise the potential of wireless, as the technology would allow them to coordinate their ships' movements around the globe in a way not previously possible. Germany led the way with its four Brandenburg class pre-dreadnoughts, which were completed between 1893 and 1894, becoming the first battleships to be fitted with wireless communications. By 1909 all 90 German warships of the High Seas Fleet were wireless equipped. The Royal Navy followed, with HMS *Hector* the first British warship to have wireless telegraphy fitted in 1899.

Even though the technology was little more than a decade old, by the time war broke out in 1914 all navies relied on wireless to transmit orders to distant fleets and vessels, whether combatants or merchant marine. While many merchant ships still used simple crystal receivers or crude magnetic-wire sets with a range of only a few hundred kilometres, modern warships were equipped with more capable equipment, and the most powerful ground stations, with their elaborately constructed antenna arrays, could transmit up to 8000 kilometres. By 1914 Germany had built, or was in the process of completing, wireless stations to link its imperial territories with Qingdao. These stations were located at Bita Paka on New Britain, at Apia on Samoa, on Yap, and on Nauru, creating a communications chain across the Pacific. The stations enabled Germany to control its warships and, in the event of war, radio interception would provide intelligence on the movement of friendly and enemy shipping.

Bita Paka wireless station, New Britain, 1914. Bita Paka formed part of Germany's global wireless network and its web extended deep into the southern oceans. Construction of the station by the German Telefunken company commenced in July 1914 but the station's masts had not been fully completed by September. Even so, the site was functioning with an improvised antenna. This photograph shows the station after it was completed by the Australian military administration. At the time of occupation the wireless masts were lying on the ground, not having been erected. The buildings at the base of the masts include an engine room, operation room and store (AWM J03099).

While wireless offered many advantages over fixed submarine cables by providing mobile and relatively fast communications between ships in close proximity, the new technology had its limitations. Early wireless was particularly vulnerable to both climatic and electromagnetic interference in addition to the usual problems of human error in transmission and receipt, and encoding and decoding. For instance, radio messages sent from HMAS *Australia* sailing off New Guinea might have to be relayed through one or more of the Australian fixed wireless stations at Port Moresby, Thursday Island, Cooktown, Townsville and Brisbane to reach the Naval Board in Melbourne. Interference caused by poor weather or atmospheric conditions, and hold-ups in the retransmission of messages between sites, could impose significant delays. In some cases, during the New Guinea campaign, it took more than a week for a wireless message despatched from the islands to be delivered to Australia's southern capital.

Aside from communications, the other immediate strategic commodity necessary to sustain warships was fuel. Today fuel oil is the lifeline of non-nuclear fleets, in 1914 it was coal. Warships and merchantmen of the era were mostly coal-fired steamships requiring regular refuelling, either by colliers at sea or in port. Fast-moving warships were particularly greedy and a few examples will serve to illustrate this point. On the outbreak of war, HMAS *Australia* was sent zigzagging across the Pacific on a series of missions. In the three months between 1 August and 31 October the Australian flagship sailed 16,353 nautical miles, requiring re-coaling 11 times and consuming more than 15,000 tons which, depending on the quality of the coal, was consumed at a rate of between 10 and 20 tons per hour. Extra speed could be coaxed from the engines when they burned coal sprayed with oil, but at a full speed of 25 knots, *Australia* would eat up 500 tons a day. Even with a hold capacity of some 3200 tons of coal and 820 tons of oil, there were limits to the flagship's endurance.

Refuelling HMAS Australia at sea. The ship on the left is a collier and is unloading sacks of coal which are then wheeled below by the crew to the ship's bunkers. The ship on the right is an oiler. Whether at sea or in port, coaling involved the entire ship's crew, including officers, to ensure refuelling was completed as quickly as possible. It was a back-breaking and indescribably dirty job (AWM P02646.002).

In comparison, *Australia's* main opponents, SMS *Scharnhorst* and *Gneisenau*, each had a maximum storage capacity of 2000 tons of coal. At 10 knots these ships burned 100 tons a day and could steam for 20 days. At 20 knots the figures were 500 tons a day and four days. However, no captain wished his reserves to dwindle too low and it was a general rule in all navies to keep bunkers at least half full at all times, dictating that ships of this class needed coaling every eight to nine days. This meant either entering a friendly (or neutral) port for replenishment or rendezvousing at sea with supply vessels. Such logistical considerations limited the operational options of all fleet commanders, especially in an expansive theatre such as the Pacific.

SMS Scharnhorst and Gneisenau, the core of Germany's East Asiatic Squadron (AWM EN0042).

Logistics was a key consideration for Vice Admiral (*Vizeadmiral*) Maximilian von Spee, commander of Germany's

East Asiatic Squadron. His flagship was *Scharnhorst*, a 12,985-ton armoured cruiser built at the Blohm & Voss shipyard in Hamburg as the lead vessel of the two-ship Scharnhorst class. *Scharnhorst* was laid down in 1905, launched in 1906, commissioned into service in 1907 and assigned to the East Asiatic Squadron in 1911. The ship's primary armament consisted of eight 21-centimetre guns, its secondary armament combined six 15-centimetre guns and eighteen 8.8-centimetre guns, and it had four 44-centimetre submerged torpedo tubes. The ship had a top speed of around 23 knots.

Gneisenau was the second warship of the Scharnhorst class. The vessel was laid down in 1904 at the A.G. Weser dockyard in Bremen, launched in 1906, commissioned in 1908 and then assigned to the East Asiatic Squadron. In terms of displacement, speed and armament, *Gneisenau* was identical to her sister, while both ships were manned by long-serving crews who maintained a high reputation for seamanship and gunnery.

Supporting Spee's major combatants were the light cruisers *Emden, Nürnberg* and *Leipzig*. Although each belonged to a different class, they all carried the same main armament of ten 10.5-centimetre guns and two 45-centimetre torpedo tubes, and had top speeds of between 22 and 25 knots. They were ideal commerce raiders and were well suited to implement Germany's naval strategy in the Indo-Pacific region. But whether the squadron was able to achieve Germany's strategic objectives rested largely on the shoulders of Spee and he faced Britain's response to the raider threat in the form of the battle cruiser *Australia*.

Despite the strength of Spee's squadron there was a distinct fracture between Germany's strategic ends and the operational means to prosecute its planned campaign. This disparity is most clearly evident in the mismatch between the ships assigned to Spee and the tasks he was expected to execute in wartime. The German naval staff correctly anticipated that Spee might be cut off on the other side of the globe once war was declared and so they granted him complete liberty of action. In deciding how to employ his squadron, he had to consider where he could hit the enemy hardest, while surviving as long as possible. He had two broad alternatives. He could break up his squadron and scatter his ships, allowing each to wage a private war, or he could keep his ships together as a 'fleet in being'. The second option would force his opponent to marshal considerable assets to hunt for him and, given the size of the theatre, locating him would be like trying to find the proverbial needle in a haystack. By evading detection, Spee might even have an opportunity to fight an enemy squadron in a conventional fleet-on-fleet action where his skills and those of his squadron might be tested.

VICE ADMIRAL MAXIMILIAN VON SPEE

COMMANDING EAST ASIATIC SQUADRON

Admiral Maximilian von Spee, circa 1910 after his promotion to rear admiral (LC-B2-3311-4).

Maximilian Johannes Maria Hubertus Reichsgraf von Spee (1861—1914) was born in Copenhagen, Denmark, and raised in the Rhineland of Germany before joining the Imperial German Navy (*Kaiserliche Marine*) in 1878. He saw considerable colonial service in his early career, including on a gunboat in German West Africa in the 1880s and with the East Africa Squadron in the late 1890s, before seeing action in China during the Boxer Rebellion (1900—01). Later he held various commands as well as senior staff positions relating to weapons development, before being appointed Chief of Staff of the North Sea Command in 1908 and being promoted rear admiral (*konteradmiral*) in 1910.

In 1912 he was given command of the East Asiatic Squadron and promoted to the rank of vice admiral (*vizeadmiral*) the following year.

In June 1914 Spee was about to begin a cruise to German New Guinea. *Scharnhorst* and *Gneisenau* first proceeded to Nagasaki, Japan, where they coaled in preparation for the voyage. While on the way to Chuuk Lagoon (Truk) in the Caroline Islands, Spee received news of the assassination of Archduke Franz Ferdinand. On 17 July Spee arrived in Ponape in the Carolines where he remained while tensions in Europe steadily mounted. With access to the German land-based radio network, Spee learned of the Austro-Hungarian declaration of war on Serbia on 28 July, followed shortly after by Russian mobilisation against Austria-Hungary. On 31 July, word came that the German ultimatum demanding Russia demobilise its armies was set to expire. Spee summoned his scattered light cruisers and ordered the squadron to prepare for war.

With the outbreak of war Spee was in a quandary over what to do. Pre-war German Admiralty plans directed him to attack enemy commerce and troop convoys. Although reluctant to fully embrace this strategy by dispersing his squadron, he did have some success, unleashing the light cruiser SMS *Emden* to hunt alone in the Indian Ocean and allowing the auxiliary cruisers SMS *Cormoran* and *Prinz Eitel Fredrich* to prowl Australian waters. However, the Admiral was wary of Allied naval strength, particularly the battle cruiser HMAS *Australia*. Even before the outbreak of hostilities Spee declared his hand, airing his fears in a letter to his wife in which he declared that *Australia* 'by itself, is an adversary so much stronger than our squadron that one would be bound to avoid it.'

The problem for Spee was that armoured cruisers comprised the heart of his squadron. While these big, powerful ships were designed for fleet actions, they were ill-suited to commerce raiding. Paired with them were his light cruisers, warships superbly designed for commerce operations. The light cruisers could catch and sink any merchantman in the world and they could outrun all but the newest battle cruisers. The armoured cruisers, however, were each more than three times as heavy as his light cruisers, with a crew over twice as large, and they burned too much coal. If the naval staff in Berlin had thought more carefully about their plans for commerce warfare, then some additional light cruisers and auxiliary cruisers would have been more useful than Spee's two larger warships. A further factor that shaped Spee's appreciation of the situation was the consideration that, if he scattered his ships, they might do considerable damage in the short term, but ultimately each would be hunted down or run out of coal and ammunition. On the other hand, if he kept his ships together, the squadron had a better chance of surviving if he encountered a British squadron and he might even be able to fight his way back to Germany. The danger with this option was that, by operating together, the squadron might achieve little against Allied trade and still be destroyed if it encountered a superior force.

Spee eventually opted for the 'fleet in being' option whereby he kept the bulk of his squadron intact, while keeping the Allies guessing as to his whereabouts. This approach forced the British to retain significant assets in the Pacific to try to hunt him down and prompted them to approach Japan for assistance in Chinese waters. When Japan agreed—and then promptly declared war on 23 August—the balance tipped against Spee, triggering his decision to take the bulk of the East Asiatic Squadron and try to fight his way back to Germany. He aimed to do this by sailing east across the Pacific, rounding Cape Horn and then turning north for the run across the South Atlantic and North Atlantic oceans. It was a risky plan, but the Admiral was not willing to lose the pride of Germany's overseas fleet in commerce raiding where it was likely that his ships would be lost one by one. He preferred to take his chances on the high seas in a fleet action where his tactics and the quality of his ships and crew could be tested in the time-honoured naval way. He was gambling not only with his reputation, but also the lives of his two sons who had followed their father into the navy and were serving aboard *Gneisenau* and *Nürnberg*.

German naval officers of Scharnhorst and Gneisenau. Spee (fifth from the right) stands with his captains and senior officers. While the ships of the East Asiatic Squadron were individually outclassed by their Australian opponents, German professionalism was of a high order and the result of any showdown between the two squadrons would be determined as much by the skilful handling of the ships and the commander's tactics, as by weight of shell and range of guns (AWM EN0046).

Although there was a divergence between Spee's strategic direction from Berlin and the technical capabilities of the squadron he commanded, his squadron had a reputation for excellence. Both his major ships had been in active commission for over two years and were manned by picked crews who were renowned for their gunnery. Their capacity would be ably demonstrated in later battles where superior German optics and skilful long-range gunnery proved disconcertingly accurate. While Spee fretted over a showdown with *Australia*, an outcome between the two squadrons under the right conditions might not have been a foregone conclusion as there were more factors at play in fleet actions than superficial appearances of ship size, speed and guns.

If Spee posed a clear and present danger to Britain's Pacific dominions, Germany's position on land was bleak. While German territorial claims and economic interests in the Pacific were significant, its European population remained small. Aside from a mostly assimilated and loyal expatriate population in Australia, there were only a few thousand German subjects scattered across the Pacific. On 1 January 1914 the estimated non-indigenous population of German New Guinea was just 1640, comprising 1224 males and 416 females. Of the adult males, 1163 were missionaries, 227 were settlers and planters, 192 were artisans (mostly Japanese), 188 were merchants and traders, 135 government officials, and 78 were seamen. The Melanesian population was estimated at 789,000. Civilian demography was reflected in the size and nature of the German security forces.

Unlike Germany's African territories, which boasted permanent colonial protectorate troops (*Schutztruppe*), in the Pacific the only concentration of regular troops was the *3rd Marine Battalion* (*III. Seebataillon*) belonging to the Qingdao garrison in China. In fact Germany placed little emphasis on the land defence of its Pacific territories because of the remoteness of the islands and the inherent difficulties of defending such distant and scattered colonies. While Britain continued to 'rule the waves', resources funnelled into defending German colonies from European opponents were regarded as wasted and so security was focussed predominantly on internal threats.

The main German garrisons in the Pacific comprised locally recruited indigenous police (*polizeitruppe*) commanded by a handful of seconded European officers and non-commissioned officers (NCOs). The first *polizeitruppe* was recruited by the German New Guinea Company at Finschhafen in 1887 and comprised just one German officer, two German NCOs and 24 Melanesian police-soldiers (*polizei-soldaten*). The troop operated on a part-time basis with military training restricted to two hours each morning followed by plantation duties for the remainder of the working day. They mobilised for full-time service only in the event of an emergency. A second part-time troop was raised at Kokopo in 1894.

When the Colonial Ministry relieved the New Guinea Company of its governmental responsibilities in 1899, Berlin assumed responsibility for the *polizeitruppe*. As the new administration gradually opened district offices across the colony, a full-time *polizeitruppe* unit was assigned to each and, by 1900, their number had risen to 100. The detachments were led by their civilian district officers until German police NCOs (*polizeimeister*) with military backgrounds could be recruited to take command. *Polizeimeister* operated under the command of the district officers as no overall command structure existed.

Polizeitruppen, German New Guinea, 1909. This pre-war photograph shows an early police detachment armed with Mauser Model 1871 rifles (Gewehr 71). The uniform consists of a peaked cap and dark red lap-lap/sarong, with a brown leather belt with a box-type ammunition pouch (NAA A57, A5).

In the first decade of the new century the *polizeitruppe* expanded rapidly. By 1910 the number of *polizeitruppen* had grown to 11 Europeans and 690 Melanesians. Although much larger, the force was still scattered across the districts and it was difficult to mobilise men for deployment outside their area. To overcome this limitation the Governor of New Guinea, Dr Albert Hahl, initiated a three-year program to improve the efficiency of the force. Central to that task was the creation of a 250-man Police Expeditionary Force (*Polizei Expeditionstruppe*) which was to be self-contained, centrally controlled and capable of deployment whenever and wherever needed. The first contingent of the *Polizei Expeditionstruppe,* comprising 120 men, was raised at Rabaul in June 1911. To assist Hahl a specially recruited regular Prussian Army officer, Lieutenant (*Oberleutnant*) Albert Prey from the *58th Infantry Regiment* (*3rd Posen*), was sent to Rabaul to command the *polizeitruppe.* By 1913 Prey's force, including the embryonic *Polizei Expeditionstruppe,* numbered 893.

Modest growth continued in the final year before the outbreak of war. By 1914 the peacetime strength of the *polizeitruppe* across Germany's 'Island Territory' and 'Old Protectorate' amounted to 32 Europeans and 932 Melanesians, distributed as follows: German New Guinea 670, East Carolines 122, West Carolines 71, Marianas 30, and the Marshall Islands 39. In addition, 12 *polizeitruppe* were serving as customs and harbour police. When Prey's tour concluded, he was replaced by two seconded army officers, Captain of Cavalry (*Rittmeister*) Carl von Klewitz and Lieutenant (*Oberleutnant*) Georg Mayer. Klewitz and Mayer arrived at Rabaul in March 1914.

Klewitz and Mayer most likely carried the internalised attitudes and prejudices of the Wilhelmine officer corps. The 'von' in Klewitz's name is typical of the predilection of the German Army for aristocratic officers. The absence of the honorific from Mayer's name might indicate that he was one of the newer bourgeois class of officer since, by the outbreak of the Great War, 70% of all German officers were commoners;

however this is unlikely since both officers belonged to the cavalry and the mounted branch was one of several prestigious military bodies that remained closed to officers of commoner background. Whatever their respective social pedigrees, Klewitz and Mayer would have been expected to uphold the conservative, politically right wing, anti-liberal attitudes of their peers.

In serving in the Pacific, the pair joined a small, self-selected group who volunteered for imperial duty across the German Empire. Among German officers more applicants sought colonial service than could be accommodated and there were long waiting lists for foreign assignments. This remained so despite the relatively modest status of the *Schutztruppe* within Wilhelmine Germany's military pecking order. The reasons officers sought overseas service varied with the individual. The highly principled probably saw themselves as patriotic representatives of the Kaiser and the vanguard of German *kultur,* the warriors sought independent command and the possibility of action, adventurers were attracted to exotic and far-flung locales, the scandal-ridden sought refuge to avoid being forced from the army, while more liberal officers sought escape from the strictures of a conservative military hierarchy. Whatever their motivations, Klewitz and Mayer arrived in New Guinea just as Governor Hahl returned to Germany and, in his absence, Deputy Governor Eduard Haber became Acting Governor.

CAPTAIN CARL VON KLEWITZ
COMMANDER *POLIZEITRUPPE*, GERMAN NEW GUINEA

Lieutenant Carl Klewitz dressed in the uniform of a south-west African Schutztruppe officer before his departure for Namibia in 1904 (Klewitz family).

Carl von Klewitz (1881—1945) joined the *Württemberg Army* as a cavalry ensign in 1898, beginning his service with the *25th Wurttemberg Dragoons*. By 1900 he had been promoted second lieutenant (*leutnant*) before he was transferred to the south-west African *Schutztruppe* in 1904, seeing action during the Herero Rebellion (1904-07). The Herero Rebellion was provoked by oppressive German colonial rule in what is now Namibia, causing the indigenous population to rise in revolt. The conflict rapidly escalated and, following several reverses, the Germans rushed in reinforcements, eventually deploying some 21,000 troops. Herero resistance was ruthlessly crushed, the survivors scattered and many died of starvation and thirst as they attempted to flee. Around 12,000 of the remaining Herero and Nama peoples were forced to surrender and were placed in concentration camps. In the four-year campaign it is estimated that some 60,000 to 80,000 Herero and Nama were killed, which amounted to approximately 80% of the Herero population of Namibia. In 1905 Klewitz was awarded the Prussian Order of the Crown 4th Class with Swords and the Württemberg Military Service Order, along with the honorific title 'von' for his Namibian service.

Namibia provided Klewitz with a taste of operational service and, although in 1906 he returned to the *25th Württemberg Dragoons*, colonial duty called him back to south-west Africa in the following year. In 1912 he returned home, having been promoted to lieutenant (*oberleutnant*) in 1910. In 1913, now a seasoned campaigner, he was seconded to the Colonial Office and in January 1914 sent to command the German New Guinea *Polizeitruppe,* again being promoted, this time to captain of cavalry (*rittmeister*).

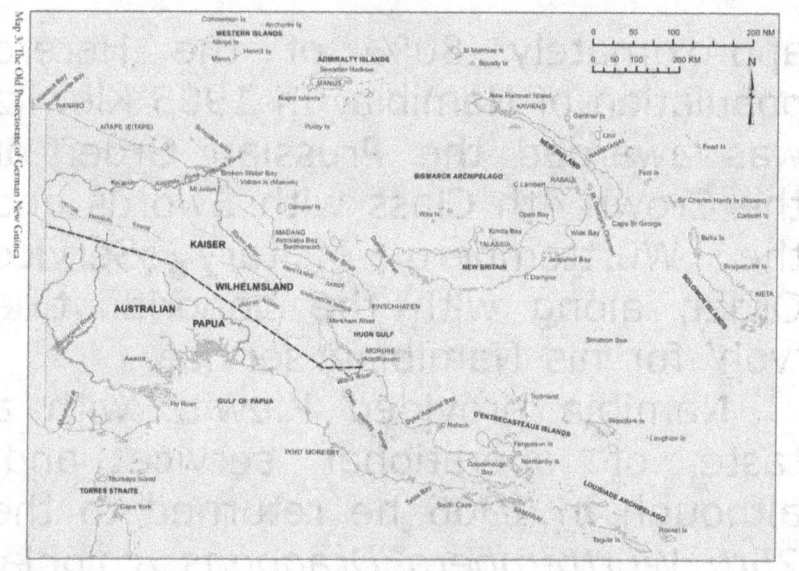

Despite the change in civil leadership, Klewitz and Mayer quickly began work. They had much to learn and do, little realising that they had only five months before war would erupt. Klewitz was appointed *Polizeimeister* with overall responsibility for the 17 German police NCOs and 670 *polizeitruppen* in German New Guinea, most of whom were divided between the nine government stations scattered across the Old Protectorate. Those available in the vicinity of Rabaul totalled 240, including the budding *Polizei Expeditionstruppe* of 125 police-soldiers. Mayer took command of this force.

German police training in musketry, 1914. Despite efforts to improve training it was reported that the police were generally poor shots (AWM A02545).

The work of improving the force was pushed ahead even though progress remained painfully slow. Not surprisingly, the remote district commanders were reluctant to send their best men to Rabaul for the expeditionary force, naturally preferring to keep them close by to meet local needs. So, notwithstanding the pair's best efforts, individual training standards remained low. Marksmanship in particular was substandard and it was later reported that the police could only hit targets at close range. Klewitz subsequently recounted that, of his available troops in September 1914, around 50 had more than six months' training, 70 had four months and the remainder less than a month, having joined after hostilities were declared.

Polizeitruppe officers and NCOs maintained a generally uniform appearance. They are most often portrayed in contemporary photographs wearing issue or privately purchased tropical helmets or slouch hats with either a khaki or white tunic and trousers, or a combination of both. The Melanesian *polizeitruppen* were less uniform in appearance, although most wore the issue dark red lap-lap or loincloth and a dark khaki peaked cap with red headband or straw slouch hat. Personal equipment was limited to a leather belt with one or two ammunition pouches and a bayonet. Canvas shoulder knapsacks were carried for expeditions but footwear was not common. Existing flexibility over constabulary dress was further exacerbated by the introduction of variations after the declaration of war to distinguish 'military' from 'non-military' sections of the force. The military forces mobilised to defend the protectorate were to consist of all German reservists and the *polizeisoldaten* of the *Polizei Expeditionstruppe*. Members of this body were to wear green armbands or military headdress with an imperial cockade. The bulk of the *polizeitruppen* however, were designated non-military and were supposed to wear white armbands and white cap-covers. These minor variations in dress, unknown to the Australians at the time, would make it difficult to distinguish *polizeisoldaten* from *polizeitruppen,* especially in the heat of battle.

A German reservist in New Britain in 1914. He is armed with a 7.92-millimetre Model 1898 Mauser rifle and is wearing the loosely standard uniform adopted by the German troops, comprising trousers, tunic, long leather boots, slouch hat and a leather belt with cartridge case. In addition to a rifle, a number of officers and NCOs carried various semi-automatic pistols or revolvers as side arms (AWM A02546).

When war was declared Haber was authorised to call up for military service all men belonging to the reserves. Given the low number of German nationals in the islands, it is not surprising that, when the available reservists reported at Rabaul, Haber could muster just seven reserve officers and 52 NCOs and soldiers. This reinforcement gave Klewitz a total force of 61 Germans and some 240 police troops to defend the capital and nearby Bita Paka radio station.

The Rabaul gun, one of the two 7.85-centimetre Krupp field guns (Feldkanone C73) held at Rabaul. The guns were captured by the ANMEF on 11 September 1914 and became the first enemy ordnance captured by Australian forces in the Great War. Today the Rabaul gun is held in the RAN historical collection and is on display at the Naval Heritage Centre, Garden Island (author image).

Haber's other military resources were pathetically limited. The colony had not been prepared for defence so there were no fixed defences nor were there any sea mines to protect the harbour. There were two field guns available at Rabaul, both 7.85-centimetre (6-pounder) Krupp field guns dating from around 1889. The pair had been sent to New Guinea in 1910 and, although capable of field use, they were without limbers and only had blank ammunition for firing ceremonial salutes. In addition to the field guns, the Germans also possessed two 37-millimetre Hotchkiss Revolving Cannon (*3.7-zentimeter maschinenkanone*), but neither was available for the defence of Rabaul.

Although the German campaign plan would be decided by the Acting Governor, who had legal authority over the security forces, Haber had no military experience and relied on Klewitz for military advice. In essence there were three broad options open to the Germans. First, they could immediately surrender to any Allied force that appeared. Second, they could choose to defend the seat of government and its facilities, particularly the wireless station at Bita Paka, hopefully inflicting casualties on the invaders, and extend resistance in order to secure a better negotiating position if eventually forced to surrender. Third, they could withdraw the government and radio station inland and plan a guerrilla campaign, hoping to hold out long enough for a relief force to arrive or for Germany to win the war in Europe.

37MM HOTCHKISS REVOLVING CANNON

A 37-millimetre Hotchkiss Revolving Cannon, one of two such guns available to the German New Guinea garrison in 1914. This particular weapon (Serial No 2 1881) was mounted on the deck of the German government yacht Komet. Today the cannon is held in the RAN historical collection (author image).

The Hotchkiss Revolving Cannon had five 37-millimetre barrels and was capable of firing 68 rounds per minute at an effective range of 1800 metres. Each feed magazine held 10 rounds and weighed approximately eight kilograms. The weapon was operated by a crew of two—a gunner and a loader. The larger calibre and longer range of these weapons necessitated exploding projectiles so the crew could adequately judge range. Such a requirement dictated a shell weight of at least 400 grams as that was the lightest exploding shell allowed under the laws of war. Hence the Hotchkiss fired a 450-gram or 1-pound shell.

Despite the potency of these weapons, neither of the German guns was available for the defence of Rabaul. One of the guns was on the German survey ship SMS *Planet* when it sailed from Rabaul for the German communications hub at Yap on 1

August. It was lost when the Japanese occupied the island on 7 October 1914. The other gun was at Madang (*Friedrich Wilhelmshafen*) on the north coast of New Guinea and, with the declaration of hostilities, this gun was mounted on the deck of the German Imperial Government Ship (*Kaiserliches Gouvernement Schiff* or KGS) *Komet*. After conveying Acting Governor Haber from Madang back to Rabaul, *Komet* served in the waters around New Britain until it and its cannon were captured in a joint RAN-ANMEF operation on 11 October 1914.

The first option was not acceptable from a diplomatic point of view and, in any case, the Acting Governor later claimed not to have the authority to surrender the territories. It was also clear that an immediate surrender would undermine Germany's position in any redistribution of colonies in the aftermath of the war. The second option could only work against small landing parties rather than a large occupation force since the Germans lacked the numbers and weapons to mount a sustained conventional defence. The third option was only feasible if Haber and his military commander had the stomach for a long campaign and planned well in advance to stockpile the necessary provisions, ammunition and weapons to allow them to mount a prolonged resistance.

Although militarily attractive, a guerrilla campaign was the most difficult option to implement and carried the greatest risk for the Acting Governor. Not only would it entail hardship for the local populace, it was only feasible if the German commanders were ruthless and the Melanesian police and carriers remained loyal in a drawn-out fight. Haber also had to balance his desire to hold out and the danger this option posed for the civilian population (German and Melanesian). An extended campaign would inevitably lead to hardened attitudes on both sides and could spark reprisals or the internment of the German civilians who remained behind. The spectre of the Boer War and the British concentration camp system would have been a significant factor in Haber's decision-making.

Polizeitruppen being trained after the outbreak of war. The troops confronting the ANMEF at Rabaul amounted to two regular army officers, 52 German reservists and 240 indigenous polizeisoldaten. The officer wearing the white tropical tunic and sun helmet (second from the right) is Lieutenant Georg Mayer, Klewitz's deputy and commander of the Polizei Expeditionstruppe (AWM A02544).

RIFLE, MAUSER 7.92MM GEWEHR 98, MODEL 1898

The *polizeitruppen* in the Pacific had been issued a variety of rifles during its short history including the Mauser Model 1871 (*Gewehr* 71) and the Model 1888 commission rifle (*Gewehr* 88). By 1914 the main long arm of the German forces was the 7.92mm Model 1898 Mauser rifle (*Gewehr* 98) and photographic evidence suggests this was the main long arm of the New Britain garrison. The *Gewehr* 98 used a Mauser bolt action and was a magazine-fed, smokeless-powder rifle, with a maximum range of 3735 metres, although its effective battlefield range was around 500 metres. In New Guinea, thick vegetation usually precluded long engagements and, while a number of Australian accounts refer to the ANMEF coming under sniper fire, it is clear that the *polizeisoldaten* were not trained in that role and the inexperienced recipients were only reporting the fire of lone riflemen rather than specialist marksmen. Although the overall quality of German musketry was low, given the conditions on New Britain such a limitation was less significant since the terrain and vegetation meant that the fighting was mostly at close range.

The *Gewehr* 98 weighed 4.09 kilograms with an empty magazine and fired the 1905 7.92 x 57-millimetre Mauser *S Patrone* round, featuring a pointed bullet rather than the older, round-nose M/88 pattern cartridge. The rifle's bolt action was simple and yet exceedingly strong and was its most notable feature. The Mauser's main tactical disadvantages in New Guinea were its length and rate of fire. At 125 centimetres, the *Gewehr* 98 was slightly longer than the British Lee-Enfield and the German rifle easily tangled in thick vegetation, while the muzzle could become clogged with debris if the firer was not careful when taking cover. In addition, the Mauser action, while strong, was not as fast as the Lee-Enfield and the *Gewehr* 98's rate of fire was restricted by its five-round internal clip-loaded magazine. For these reasons the *Gewehr* 98 proved a less than ideal weapon in the hands of the *polizeitruppen*.

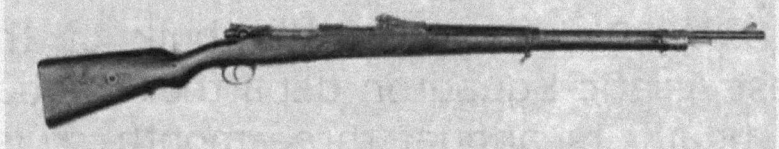

7.92mm Model 1898 Mauser rifle (AAIM).

As for Klewitz, he was a professional officer and undoubtedly personal honour demanded that he fight hard for the Fatherland. Both Klewitz and Mayer were schooled in the German Army's doctrine of decisive battle. The battle of annihilation—*Vernichtungsschlacht*—despite its apocalyptic ring, was a term that did not mean literal extermination. Rather, the concept involved the comprehensive defeat—physical and psychological—of the enemy at all levels, from the lowliest soldier to the commander-in-chief. It meant breaking both the will and capacity for continued resistance through a single hammer blow, delivered with surprise and with as much violence as could be mustered. In attempting to achieve this, Klewitz had some significant advantages in that he could choose where and when to strike, his men were acclimatised, and they knew the ground in a way his opponents did not.

On 20 June 1914 the bulk of the East Asiatic Squadron departed Qingdao to begin its annual three-month cruise of the Pacific to wave the German flag.

On 31 July SMS *Emden* followed as Captain Karl von Muller was anxious to avoid being caught in port by the British naval squadron stationed at nearby Weihai (Port Edward) if war broke out. When war was declared on 5 August, Spee was at Pohnpei (Ponape) in the Carolines group with *Scharnhorst, Gneisenau,* the supply ship *Titania* and Japanese collier *Fukoku Maru,* while his other warships were scattered. *Nürnberg* was sailing from North America to join Spee. *Leipzig* was en route to Mexico to replace *Nürnberg*. *Emden,* having returned to Qingdao with the auxiliary cruiser SMS *Prinz Eitel Fredrich,* had already been active. On 3 August, after the Russian declaration of war, Muller captured the Steam Ship (SS) *Ryazan,* a German-built Russian merchant ship. *Ryazan* was quickly refitted at Qingdao as an auxiliary cruiser with armament taken from the immobilised sloop *Cormoran* and commissioned as the new SMS *Cormoran*. With Britain's declaration of war, Spee ordered a concentration of all available ships at Pagan Island in the Marianas archipelago.

To the south, in New Guinea, the only naval assets available to Haber were the survey ship SMS *Planet* and the government yacht KGS *Komet*. As war loomed *Planet* was despatched to Yap carrying one of the 37-millimetre Revolving Cannon. The vessel was eventually scuttled at the entrance to the harbour on 7 October to avoid capture by Japanese naval forces. Meanwhile, *Komet* was at Morobe (*Adolfhaven*) on the north coast of New Guinea having taken the Acting Governor there on a tour of inspection. On the night of 6 August the Bita Paka station picked up a message indicating that war had been declared between Britain and Germany. In the absence of the Acting Governor, German officials at Rabaul prepared the colony for war.

CHAPTER 2

THE REALISATION OF AMBITIOUS HOPES

In the countdown to war in 1914 Australia's political leaders vied with one another to demonstrate the strength of their commitment to the British Empire. Joseph Cook, the outgoing Prime Minister, while addressing an election meeting at Horsham in the wheat belt of Victoria, declared on 31 July that if war broke out, 'I want to make it quite clear that all our resources in Australia are in the Empire and for the Empire, and for the preservation and security of the Empire.' Andrew Fisher, the leader of the Australian Labor Party, went further. At a meeting in Coolac, Victoria, on the same day he offered an unreserved commitment: 'Should the worst happen after everything has been done that honour will permit, Australia will stand beside our own to help defend her to our last man and last shilling.' Those offers were not empty political rhetoric.

Beginning with the passage of the *Defence Act 1903,* defence preparations had received bipartisan support in the decade before the war. Successive Australian governments began planning and then implemented policies which established an independent 'blue water' navy, created an army based on universal compulsory training, laid the foundations for a military aviation service, and established a range of industries and training institutions necessary to sustain an Australian defence force. These initiatives were driven by many, although three men stand out—George Pearce, William Creswell and James Legge.

The fact that Australia had a navy and army in 1914 was not an inevitable product of Federation, nor was it a foregone conclusion that Australians would support the enormous outlay and commitment necessary to create an independent defence force. These decisions and resultant action occurred because of the foresight of Australia's political and military leaders. Recognising that Australian prosperity and independence leveraged off the collective security umbrella provided by the British Empire, Australians realised that they had an obligation to contribute to the mutual demands of imperial defence while providing for their own local needs.

In 1914 Australia was a trading nation, its wealth based on trade in what was an increasingly globalised world. In the years immediately prior to the outbreak of war there were clear signs that the Australian economy was emerging from a lengthy period of economic recession and stagnation that had lasted almost 20 years. This long depression had been a great shock to contemporaries. Australia had enjoyed sustained, rapid economic growth almost without interruption from the discovery of gold in 1851 until the end of the 1880s. Wool, wheat and gold were the basis of a highly successful export-oriented economy that gave Australians the highest per capita income in the world. This was followed by almost two decades of economic contraction as drought, falling export prices and bank closures wiped away earlier gains and the economy proved slow to recover. Part of the reason for the sluggish revival was the dependence on British capital which dried up when Australia became a less attractive investment option. The other factor was Australia's heavy dependence on Britain as its primary market. In 1900 more than 60% of Australia's exports went to Britain and any interruption to this trade would be devastating for the recovering Australian economy.

SENATOR GEORGE PEARCE
AUSTRALIAN MINISTER FOR DEFENCE

Senator George Pearce, Australian Minister for Defence in 1914. When he left parliament in 1938, Pearce had served as a senator for 37 years and three months, a record term, and his total service as a minister was 24 years and seven months, also a record in the Australian parliament. Pearce was appointed a Knight Commander of the Royal Victorian Order (KCVO) in 1927 (AWM 306781).

George Foster Pearce (1870-1952) served four terms as Minister for Defence (1908-09, 1910-13, 1914-21, 1932-34). To this day he retains the record as the longest serving Australian Defence Minister. He was born in South Australia and educated at a public school until aged 11, then worked on farms and later became a carpenter before losing his job in the depression of 1891. He moved to Western Australia where in 1893 he helped found the Progressive Political League, a precursor to the West Australian branch of the Australian Labor Party. Self-educated in politics and economics, in 1901 he was elected to the first Commonwealth parliament as a senator for Western Australia. He narrowly missed being appointed to the first Labor Cabinet in 1904. In 1908 he was appointed

Minister for Defence in the Cabinet of Andrew Fisher.

Today it is difficult to see how a politician like Pearce could rise or even survive in politics. He was not a breezy popularist nor was he a 'man for all seasons'. Pearce was dour rather than electric, competent rather than charismatic, hard working rather than attention seeking, and yet this self-made, humble man was instrumental in shepherding a number of strategic policy reforms to fruition in the half-decade before war broke out. It was Pearce who pushed forward with the introduction of compulsory service for all Australian males; with a change of heart in Britain and on the foundations laid by former Prime Minister Alfred Deakin, he helped establish a RAN fleet unit; he oversaw the foundation of the Royal Australian Naval College at Jervis Bay and the Royal Military College, Duntroon; and he was instrumental in developing local defence industries for small arms, clothing and equipment production.

Without these bold, expensive and long-term programs, the New Guinea campaign could not have been fought. It was in large measure due to Pearce's foresight and hard work that the ANMEF could be raised, equipped and despatched in little more than a week.

In 1907 the commander of the Commonwealth Naval Forces (CNF), Captain William Creswell, wrote a memorandum to the Prime Minister, Alfred Deakin, outlining the dangers of German expansionism. Creswell believed the Kaiser's visit to Tangiers in 1905, which precipitated the First Moroccan Crisis, was designed to secure a German counterpoise to Gibraltar, 'the desire to acquire a good point of observation ... and overlook the Cape route.' Further east, Germany's assistance in the construction of the Hejaz Railway could place an Ottoman army in Egypt, 'rendering quite conceivable the closing of the [Suez] Canal, and severance of our line of communication.' More specifically, German attempts to establish a foothold in Persia through the Berlin-Baghdad railway project and various schemes in Asia Minor were 'all directed to effect a through line to the East as a direct communication with Germany's Eastern possessions.'

Rear Admiral Sir William Rooke Creswell, KCMG, RAN (1852-1933), father of the RAN. This photograph was taken in 1914 when Creswell was First Naval Member of the Australian Commonwealth Naval Board. In 1919 he was appointed a Knight Commander of the Most Excellent Order of the British Empire and in 1922 he was promoted to vice admiral (SPC-A).

It was for these reasons that Creswell championed the creation of an Australian fleet for the defence of the Commonwealth and its interests. Parliamentary debate on the subject demonstrated that Creswell was not alone in seeking the establishment of an Australian navy. He was quickly becoming regarded as the nation's chief spokesman on naval matters and in February 1904 the government appointed him to the newly created position of Naval Officer Commanding CNF. Through frequent changes of Defence Minister, Creswell consistently pressured and argued for new ships and increased manpower for the navy. He firmly believed that local naval forces were essential to open careers in which Australians could render the service necessary for the country to contribute to imperial naval strategy.

At first Creswell urged the creation of a torpedo boat destroyer force for local protection of ports and coastal trade but found himself criticised by British naval authorities who dismissed his views as having no strategic justification. Despite this, he continued to press for a local navy and eventually secured the support of Deakin. At Creswell's urging the nationalist Prime Minister sent a message to the Admiralty proposing that Australia provide a thousand seamen and purchase submarines or destroyers. Although nothing came of the proposal as the Admiralty remained ambivalent on the subject, in February 1909 the Fisher government ordered three destroyers to be built in Britain.

The reception of the Australian fleet, Sydney Harbour, 4 October 1913. The ship in the foreground is HMAS Australia, which is standing off the RAN base at Garden Island. The light cruisers Sydney and Melbourne are behind Australia (SPC-A).

The 1909 Imperial Defence Conference in London saw a change in British attitude as alarm grew over the rapid increase in German naval power. Pushing a considerably expanded plan, the Admiralty now reversed its opposition to a native fleet, proposing Australia acquire a new type of all-big-gun armoured cruiser (later designated a battle cruiser of the Dreadnought type), three high-speed scout cruisers or 'satellites', six destroyers and three submarines to comprise a fleet unit. The fleet would operate under national control in peacetime but revert to Admiralty control in the event of war. Deakin and Pearce seized the opportunity and, pressing forward with this plan, they quickly placed an order for the construction of the new vessels in Britain.

In 1913 Australia's ambitious plans to create a home-grown navy finally came to fruition. Rear Admiral George Patey, a long-serving British naval officer, was appointed the first Rear Admiral Commanding His Majesty's Australian Fleet on 21 May 1913. One month later, Patey's flagship, the battle cruiser HMAS *Australia,* was commissioned at Portsmouth. On 23 June Patey hoisted his flag aboard *Australia* and, on the same day, during a visit to Spithead to review the Australian fleet before its departure for Australia, King George V knighted Patey, appointing him a KCVO on the quarterdeck of the Australian flagship.

Three months later the RAN squadron entered Sydney Harbour to a tumultuous welcome, with thousands flocking to see the pride of the nation. *The Daily Telegraph* reported the arrival:

> It was a splendid spectacle to watch. Each ship equidistant and following in its predecessors wake. On the precise spot where the flagship veered in her course the others as they reached it, veered also. So precise were the movements that the ships might have been railway engines running on a railway track...

From every flagstaff, north, south, east and west flew the British-Australian colours. It was truly Australia's national day, a day that meant much to its history. And notable, too, was the pride which the younger generation, seen on almost every vessel afloat, took in this spectacular demonstration that signified the realisation of ambitious hopes.

Following in *Australia*'s wake were the light cruisers *Melbourne*, *Sydney* and *Encounter*, and destroyers *Parramatta*, *Yarra* and *Warrego*. The submarines *AE1* and *AE2* were slower to arrive, only entering Sydney on 28 February the following year although, in doing so, they completed the longest submarine journey ever undertaken.

HMAS *Australia* was one of Britain's newest Indefatigable class battle cruisers. In terms of firepower the flagship was the most heavily armed ship ever to serve in the Australian navy and the only capital ship commissioned in the RAN. The British-built warship was ordered in 1909, launched in 1911, and commissioned in 1913. *Australia* boasted a complement of 820 souls. With a displacement of between 18,800 and 22,490 tons (depending on load), mounting eight 12-inch (305-millimetre) and fourteen 4—inch (102-millimetre) guns and with a speed of 25 knots, *Australia* was fast and lethal. Although more than a match for any of Spee's ships, the battle cruiser class was something of an unproven experiment.

REAR ADMIRAL SIR GEORGE PATEY, KCVO, RN
COMMANDING HIS MAJESTY'S AUSTRALIAN FLEET

Vice Admiral Sir George Patey, KCVO, RN in Bermuda in November 1915 when he was commanding the North American and West Indies Cruiser Squadron, which included HMAS Melbourne and HMAS Sydney. In January

1916 Patey was appointed a Knight Commander of the Most Distinguished Order of Saint Michael and Saint George (KCMG) and in January 1918 he was promoted to the rank of admiral (SPC-A).

George Edwin Patey (1859—1935) was born near Plymouth, England, and followed in his father's footsteps, joining the Royal Navy as a cadet in 1872 aged 12. As a midshipman he first saw action serving aboard HMS *Shah* as part of the British Pacific Squadron during the Battle of Pacocha. This action, fought alongside HMS *Amethyst* on 29 May 1877, involved the Peruvian armoured monitor *Huascar*, which had been taken over by rebels opposed to the Peruvian government and, it was feared, could be employed against British shipping. This battle was the only ship-to-ship action fought by the Royal Navy between 1850 and 1914 in the era of the *Pax Britannica.*

As a sub-lieutenant Patey next saw action with the naval brigade ashore during the Anglo-Zulu War (1879). Promoted to lieutenant in 1881, he was then sent to gunnery school before being assigned to naval intelligence and promoted commander in 1894. He saw further sea duty in the Mediterranean, participating in operations around Crete during the Greco-Turkish War (1897). After being promoted captain in 1900 he served as Assistant Director of Naval Intelligence and then commanded in succession HMS *Venerable,* HMS *Implacable* and, on promotion to rear admiral in 1909, took command of the 2nd Battle Squadron. In 1913 Patey was given command of the Australian fleet and appointed a KCVO. On the same day that Patey arrived in Sydney, Admiral Sir George King-Hall hauled down his flag as the last British Commander-in-Chief of the Australia Station, leaving the RAN governed by the Australian Commonwealth Naval Board, headed by Rear Admiral Sir William Creswell, and the Australian fleet under Patey. In less than a year Patey would be called on to pit his newly created fleet against the experienced German East Asiatic Squadron.

HMAS Australia, flagship of the RAN and pride of the Commonwealth, circa 1914. Two of the ship's four twin 12-inch gun turrets can be seen forward and amidships. Below them, the long diagonal booms attached to the ship's hull were used to deploy anti-torpedo nets (SPC-A).

The battle cruiser concept was the brainchild of Admiral Sir John 'Jacky' Fisher, First Sea Lord and influential naval reformer. His new class of heavily armed, fast ships was designed, in his words, as 'super-scouting cruisers' allowing them to be employed on multiple missions. When operating with the main fleet they were designed to conduct armed reconnaissance of the enemy where their superior speed would allow them, to outmanoeuvre the larger and heavier ships of the line, while their 12-inch guns could pummel lighter cruisers normally employed for reconnaissance tasks. Once action was joined the battle cruisers could reinforce the van (rear) of the battle fleet. Acting independently, they were powerful and swift enough to hunt down and destroy any armed merchant cruisers employed as commerce raiders.

The first battle cruisers entered service in 1908 as the Invincible class and they were followed by three ships of the Indefatigable class. While undoubtedly formidable, the multi-mission design of the battle cruiser meant that compromises had to be made in their construction. To gain speed they were lightened and this could only be achieved by a reduction in their armoured protection. Hence they were built with a medium armour package similar to the Minotaur-class cruisers. This made them vulnerable in fleet actions with comparable battleships. On the other hand, their big-gun package was meant to offset their lack of protection, allowing them to stand off and fight at long range where their reduced armour might not be such a disadvantage. For these tactics to be successful however, the battle cruisers required high gunnery standards, enabling the ship to hold an enemy at bay. The risk was that if their opponents closed the range, either by superior seamanship or in poor visibility, the battle cruiser would be vulnerable to even a weaker armed foe.

While Admiral Spee was sensibly cautious about facing *Australia*, the RAN's flagship shared the strengths and deficiencies of the battle cruiser class. Of particular note is the fact that its armour was not thick enough to withstand the shells of equivalent German ships and, once a shell penetrated that armour, inadequate British anti-flash precautions coupled with dangerous work practices meant that an explosive flame could rip from the working chambers down into the magazine below with catastrophic consequences. No ship could survive such an explosion. During the Battle of

Jutland on 31 May 1916, HMS *Indefatigable,* the lead ship of the class and sister to *Australia,* was hit by two 28-centimetre shells fired by a German battle cruiser. One shell struck the battle cruiser's aft superstructure triggering a massive explosion which caused the ship to capsize and sink with the loss of all but two of the ship's 1017 officers and men. HMS *Invincible,* on which the Indefatigable class was based, was another Jutland casualty when German shells penetrated one of the ship's turrets, igniting propellant in the hoist and travelling down the turret trunk to the magazine, causing two turret magazines to explode. The whole central section of the ship was ripped apart and the stricken ship broke in half and sank. All but six of the ship's company of 1031 men were lost. Patey, who was well aware of his ship's characteristics, always planned to 'turn away' from Spee's ships, fighting instead at long range where his guns were at best advantage and the weakness of his armour negated as far as possible. But if Spee did chance his hand in an engagement with Patey and he could close the range, either in darkness or confined waters, his odds were better than he could have anticipated.

HMAS Sydney, the RAN's most famous Great War-era vessel. After service in New Guinea waters, Sydney was employed on convoy escort during which the ship demonstrated its technical superiority by destroying the German light cruiser Emden on 9 November 1914 off the Cocos (Keeling) Islands (SPC-A).

In addition to *Australia,* Patey's squadron included three light cruisers. *Encounter* was an older Challenger-class protected cruiser lent to the RAN in 1912 as a training ship until HMAS *Brisbane* was commissioned in Britain. The ship had a main armament of eleven 6-inch (15-centimetre) guns and a top speed of 21 knots. HMAS *Melbourne* and *Sydney* were constructed to the design of the newer Chatham group of Town-class light cruisers, each mounting a main armament of eight 6-inch (15-centimetre) guns and with top speeds of between 25 and 27 knots. *Encounter* was commanded by Captain Charles Lewin, RN; *Melbourne* by Captain Mortimer L'Estrange Silver, RN; and *Sydney* by Captain John Glossop, RN. The three Australian cruisers were all more powerfully armed than any of Spee's light cruisers.

Nominally, the fourth cruiser at Patey's disposal was the Pelorus-class HMAS *Pioneer*. This vessel had been commissioned in the RN in 1900 and had served on the Australia Station before being paid off and gifted to the RAN in 1912. Like most gift horses it didn't pay to look too closely at the aging vessel. With a speed of just 20 knots and a main armament of only eight 4-inch (10-centimetre) guns, the ship was not capable of challenging more modern ships. On 1 January 1914 *Pioneer* was commissioned as an independent command for service as a seagoing training ship for the Naval Reserve.

HMAS Yarra on operations in the Pacific, 1914—15. Yarra was one of three RAN torpedo boat destroyers which were designed to operate as a flotilla, hunting their targets at night or in low visibility. Note the black-painted hull and upper works, and the splinter mats fastened around the exposed bridge (SPC-A).

In addition to his larger ships, Patey had a small destroyer flotilla, two submarines, and a number of auxiliary vessels. The three destroyers—*Parramatta*, *Yarra* and *Warrego*—were all built in Britain and launched and commissioned between 1910 and 1912. Based on the British Acheron class, each carried a single breech-loading 4-inch (10-centimetre) Mark VIII naval gun, three 12-pounders and three 18-inch (46-centimetre) torpedoes. Fast and manoeuvrable, they had a top speed of around 26 knots. Unlike larger ships, the destroyers were designed for the new trend which saw oil replace coal as the primary fuel. Burning oil generated faster speeds, an important advantage for the destroyers which relied on swiftness and agility to close to within torpedo range of an enemy. The three ships operated as a flotilla under Commander Claude Cumberlege, RN, who was also Commanding Officer (CO) of *Warrego*. According to his biographer: 'By temperament and personality he was well suited to destroyer command ... he was handsome, unconventional, dashing and breezy, and his courage, initiative and lack of "frill" inspired respect and affection.'

AE2 in Simpson Harbour, 1914. AE2 was one of the RAN's two E-class submarines, neither of which was destined to survive the war (SPC-A).

The inclusion of submarines in the RAN's squadron, as with many other early Australian defence initiatives, demonstrates considerable foresight. In the early twentieth century submarines were regarded as a tactical adjunct to surface combatants and, while clearly useful in both offensive and defensive operations, the limitations of the early models meant that they were far from the potent weapon systems they would become. Even so, Patey declared: 'With submarines as fists and aeroplanes as eyes, the naval service appears to be at the commencement of a new era.' The two Australian E-class submarines had a range of 3225 nautical miles at

10 knots on the surface or 25 nautical miles at 5 knots submerged, with a maximum speed of 16 knots surfaced and 10 knots submerged. They were armed with four single torpedo tubes but carried only one spare torpedo for each tube. *AE1* was commanded by Lieutenant Commander Thomas Besant, RN; *AE2* by Lieutenant Commander Henry 'Harry' Stoker, a cousin of Bram Stoker, author of *Dracula*. The limited range and speed of the E class was particularly telling in the Pacific where long transits were the norm and so, unless the boats were confined to defensive tasks in coastal waters, they were usually accompanied by a parent ship to act as escort and stores vessel. For these tasks Patey's fleet included the aging gunboat HMAS *Protector* and the auxiliary ship SS *Upolu*.

Unbeknown to Patey, his arrival at Sydney in October 1913 left him with exactly 10 months in which to weld his squadron into a fighting force. He wasted not a moment. By the early New Year Patey was putting his ships through a series of exercises. In January a squadron battle practice was conducted off Hobart, Tasmania, involving gunnery and torpedo training. At its conclusion Patey reported the exercise a success and considered *Australia* to have performed very favourably in comparison with other ships of its class. In June the bulk of the squadron conducted a 'Preparation for War' exercise, including countering a simulated torpedo attack by HMAS *Warrego*. Later in the same month, as part of a squadron northern cruise off the coast of Queensland and Papua, the flagship practised live-fire gunnery off Pentecost Island in the Whitsunday Group. In July *Australia, Melbourne, Warrego* and *Yarra* again conducted gunnery practices by day and night off Palm Island north of Townsville and at Port Moresby in Papua.

Ashore, matters were developing equally rapidly for the army. Australia's colonial military forces had been limited to a gaggle of unpaid volunteer companies and small bodies of militia with matters changing little even after the withdrawal of the British garrison in the 1850s. Following Federation, efforts were made to standardise the scattered forces, but these remained small and mostly part time. The only regular troops, termed Permanent Military Forces, were small bodies of artillerymen and engineers who manned the fortifications that protected Australia's main ports and strategic waterways. In 1910 the Australian government invited Lord Kitchener to inspect Australia's defences and to make organisational recommendations. Kitchener's report highlighted the inadequacies of the present arrangements—exactly as the government had expected and as it wanted to hear, allowing a major program of reform to be initiated. A number of politicians, including Deakin, who favoured a Swiss Army model, had contemplated a compulsory service scheme for several years. With voluntary enlistments, numbers fluctuated with public interest and enlistment periods proved too short to achieve competence. Compulsory service would increase numbers and, starting with cadet training for schoolboys, trainees would build a range of basic military skills by the time they transferred to the ranks of the militia. In early 1911 the government introduced the Universal Training Scheme with mandatory cadet training commencing in July that year. The first intake of 18-year-old recruits into the newly reorganised military followed in July 1912.

Kitchener's proposals called for an 80,000-strong citizens' territorial army organised into 21 infantry brigades, 28 light horse regiments and 56 batteries of artillery, with field engineer, communication and departmental troops in proportion. All men aged from 18 to 25 were expected to register, although there were many exemptions. Those for whom exceptions were made included the medically unfit, police and prison officers, teachers who were officers of cadets, those who resided more than eight kilometres from a place of parade, non-British subjects and those who were not substantially of European descent. The annual training obligation for most enlistees in the infantry was 16 days, including eight days of continuous training in camp, while the more technical artillery and engineers were required to serve 25 days with a 17-day camp. Under the *Defence Act 1903* however, this new and growing army was prohibited from employment overseas and the Australian government refrained from providing a commitment to furnish military forces to Britain in the event of war, although it had agreed to hand over control of the RAN.

BRIGADIER GENERAL JAMES LEGGE, CMG
CHIEF OF THE GENERAL STAFF

Major General James Legge in 1915 on his way to Gallipoli. In 1914, Legge was a brigadier general and the Australian Chief of the General Staff. He was the man responsible for mobilising and despatching the ANMEF (AWM C01011).

James Gordon Legge (1863—1947) was a rising star in the Australian

Army in 1914. Born in London and educated in Britain and Australia, in 1891 he was admitted to the Bar in New South Wales. In his early working life he taught at a school, practised law and served in the militia. In 1894 he embarked on a career in the Permanent Military Forces of New South Wales and was commissioned as a captain. When war erupted in South Africa, Legge was appointed to command one of two New South Wales infantry companies offered for service on the veldt. Captain William Holmes, then a 37-year-old militia officer, served as one of Legge's subordinates. During their service together there was some tension between the two, arising from questions of Legge's tactical competence, although this does not appear to have damaged their long-term relationship.

On his return to Australia in 1902 Legge worked in the usual staff and instructional appointments assigned to regular officers, putting his legal training to use as secretary to the committee charged with drafting the Commonwealth's military regulations. When the *Defence Act 1903* was proclaimed in March 1904, Legge published a handbook on Australian military law and, in the same year, produced a booklet outlining rules for framing operational orders in the field. In 1907 he was assigned for duty at Army Headquarters, Melbourne, where he served under Colonel William Throsby Bridges, and later worked closely with George Pearce developing the universal military service scheme. Legge served in various staff positions on the Military Board and in 1909 was personally involved in assisting Field Marshal Lord Kitchener, Commander-in-Chief in India and the Empire's most prestigious soldier, in his review of Australia's defence. Kitchener in turn adopted much of Legge's work on the Universal Training Scheme as the basis for his recommendations. In 1912 Legge was nominated as Australian Representative to the Imperial General Staff in London. In 1914 he was due to return to Australia having been designated as the next Chief of the General Staff.

While Australia's navy was preparing for war, the army was left in something of a quandary over how to deal with the nearby German territories in the event of war. It was only in the last few years before the outbreak of war that Australia, after deliberations at successive Imperial Conferences, turned its attention to planning for raising an Australian expeditionary force in the event of war. It was no coincidence that, across the Tasman Sea, the New Zealand government and military authorities were involved in similar discussions. These separate considerations led to the first plans for the formation of a combined division between the two neighbours.

With the appointment of Major General Alexander Godley to command the New Zealand forces in 1912, the possibility of combined action took shape when he initiated discussions with James Allen, the New Zealand Minister for Defence. Godley, assuming a war with Germany to be the most probable threat to the British Empire, proposed a number of possible options for the employment of a New Zealand expeditionary force. Prophetically, Godley suggested that the New Zealanders might be sent to reinforce Egypt where it was likely that the Ottomans would join Germany and threaten the Suez Canal. Closer to home he also identified German Samoa as a possible target for the New Zealand forces. After discussing the matter with his Defence Minister, Godley was authorised to initiate planning and, shortly thereafter, while visiting Australia in November 1912 for army-to-army talks, he was able to discuss the matter in person with the Australian Chief of the General Staff, Brigadier General Joseph Gordon, a fellow British regular on secondment to Australia. Fortuitously, elements of the Australian government, especially Pearce, were thinking along similar lines. Pearce opened the talks and, during discussions, indicated that, in the event of war, Australia would consider raising an expeditionary force of around 10,000 and that New Zealand could contribute some 6000 troops to allow the formation of a combined Australasian infantry division. At the same time Pearce stressed that these discussions did not amount to a commitment to supply forces to Britain, but rather simply recognised the necessity of planning for such a possibility. The discussions also concluded that, on the matter of the neighbouring German territories, the Commonwealth should plan on seizing Germany's possessions in the Bismarck Archipelago and that New Zealand might deal with Samoa. There matters rested.

In Australia any public acknowledgement that the government was planning to raise an expeditionary force to support Britain was guaranteed to provoke political controversy. Hence the planning initiated in 1912 was only undertaken on a contingency basis even though the government and the opposition were well aware that there was likely to be widespread support for Britain in the event of a war with Germany. Despite this, the government would not countenance any concrete planning for an expeditionary force;

instead, planning remained indirect, revolving around mobilisation for the defence of Australia, from which it would be possible to draw volunteers. For these reasons there were no firm plans to seize German New Guinea and when war did break out the Commonwealth was caught well and truly off guard.

CHAPTER 3

A GREAT AND URGENT IMPERIAL SERVICE

On 28 June 1914 a disgruntled Serbian student, in an otherwise poorly planned operation, managed to assassinate Archduke Franz Ferdinand, the heir to the Austro-Hungarian throne, and the Duke's beloved wife Sofia. The murders provided a spark and, once the fuse was lit, matters rapidly deteriorated until Germany mobilised and, in accordance with long-standing plans, the northern wing of its army drove into neutral Belgium, aiming to outflank and quickly defeat France before turning back to deal with lumbering Russia. On 4 August Britain declared war on Germany, ostensibly due to the German violation of neutral Belgium, although pre-war British discussions with France had all but committed Britain to intervene in support of its ally in the event of German aggression. With the British declaration, the rest of the British Empire was automatically at war. Under the *Commonwealth Act 1901,* Australia, despite being a 'self-governing colonial federation', was still a part of the British Empire ruled by King George V. When the sovereign declared war on the advice of his ministers, Australia too was at war even though it had not been consulted.

With the declaration of war in Europe, Britain found itself with five strategic tasks in the Pacific. First, it had to eliminate Spee's East Asiatic Squadron. Second, it had to secure its own holdings in China. Third, it had to safeguard British and French possessions in south-east Asia and the Pacific. Fourth, it needed to ensure the safety of Allied shipping in the Indian and Pacific oceans, which would soon include substantial numbers of Australian, New Zealand and Indian troops bound for Europe. Finally, it had to secure German possessions in China and across the Pacific to deprive Germany of its logistics and communication facilities.

On the same day as war was declared the Secretary of State for the Colonies, Lewis (later First Viscount) Harcourt, sent a cable to the Australian Governor-General, Sir Ronald Munro Ferguson, requesting that Australia take action against several of Germany's wireless stations. His cable read in part: 'If your Ministers desire and feel themselves able to seize German wireless stations at Yap in Marshall Islands, Nauru on Pleasant Island, and New Guinea, we should feel this was a great and urgent Imperial service.' Although British geography was a little confused since Yap was actually in the Carolines group and Nauru was just another name for Pleasant Island, the Australian government eventually assented. A similar telegram was sent to New Zealand requesting seizure of German Samoa and this too was agreed.

Even before the outbreak of war, following offers of assistance from New Zealand and Canada, Australia had committed to sending an expeditionary force of 20,000 volunteers for service in Europe. This force—eventually titled the Australian Imperial Force (AIF)—was to comprise an infantry division and light horse brigade, with command given to the Commonwealth's senior soldier, Brigadier General William Throsby Bridges. James Legge, who was the Commonwealth's next most senior army officer, was still at sea on his way back to Australia from London, having spent the previous two years as Australia's representative on the Dominion Section of the Imperial General Staff. On arriving in Adelaide, Legge disembarked, immediately assumed his new post as Chief of the General Staff and took the overnight train to Melbourne where he met his deputy, Major Cyril Brudenell White. To allow Bridges to concentrate on the task of raising and organising the AIF, Legge assumed responsibility for the overall defence of the country and was soon embroiled in raising the second expeditionary force for service in the islands.

According to the Australian *Official History*, Legge 'made the organisation of the islands force one of his first objects, and pushed it forward with swift efficiency'. These are grand words but they hide the fact that Legge had little to work with since there was no standing contingency plan for such an operation. While there had been pre-war discussions with New Zealand on possible combined action in the Pacific, in Australia planning had progressed little further than a broad intent. There was certainly no executable plan. The most recent mobilisation plan, issued in 1913, provided for several 'probable forms of employment of the Commonwealth Military Forces' including: 'The dispatch of small expeditionary forces against foreign possessions which might be used as a base for operations against the Commonwealth in the Eastern Indian Archipelago and the Pacific.' The list of possible targets identified 19 different ports belonging to seven countries including Germany, Japan, Britain's allies France and Russia, as well as countries unlikely to take part in a European war such as China, the Netherlands and the United States. The best advice offered on the composition of the expeditionary force was that it 'will be drawn from the troops of the 1st Military District

(Queensland)'. In 1914 these loose guidelines provided Legge with little to go on and he was left to devise his own campaign plan to meet the British strategic objectives.

Within 72 hours Legge and his staff had produced a workable scheme. Their efforts included what today would be described as a concept of operations and a task organisation for the land force component of the expedition. His first question was where to raise the force since there was no standing body of regular troops to undertake this type of mission nor was there a permanent mobilisation centre where the force could be conveniently concentrated. Compounding these difficulties was the fact that the New Guinea force would be competing with Bridges' AIF for personnel, equipment, accommodation and training facilities. Ignoring the sketchy 1913 mobilisation plan option of a Queensland force, Legge instead chose Sydney as the mounting base. Sydney was the nation's largest urban centre in the most prosperous state and it possessed an excellent port. It also housed the headquarters of the 2nd

Military District and happened to be the fleet base of the RAN. Importantly, it was located well away from the frantic activity at Army Headquarters in Melbourne where the focus remained firmly on raising Bridges' division.

Legge's next task was to appoint a suitable commander. On the morning of 10 August he telephoned the military district headquarters at Victoria Barracks in Sydney and directed the Commandant, Colonel Ernest Wallack, to convey an offer of command to his old subordinate from South Africa—Colonel William Holmes. The slightly built, 51-year-old widower, Secretary of the New South Wales Water and Sewage Board and a decorated veteran, was an obvious choice. He was the most senior field commander in the state, one of the most experienced native-born soldiers in the country and rather conveniently had been overlooked for command of the New South Wales-raised 1st Infantry Brigade (AIF) in Bridges' division. That command had gone instead to 36-year-old Colonel Henry MacLaurin. MacLaurin was a surprising selection as he was a comparatively untried militia officer with no operational service and only a little over a year's experience as a unit commander. In contrast Holmes had been commanding the militia's 6th Infantry Brigade for more than 18 months and was a widely respected soldier with a strong practical bent, having reformed battlefield marksmanship in his old unit and pioneered a new practical and suitably Australian field uniform. Despite his surprising omission from an AIF command, Holmes was keen to serve in any capacity and he readily accepted Legge's offer. Although not told where his force would serve, he was directed to have it ready to sail in six days.

Holmes' appointment was a popular one judging by contemporary media reporting. The *Sydney Morning Herald* announced: 'There is no more popular officer in [the] whole of the military forces of this state than Colonel William Holmes, DSO, VD. Everybody likes him, from the State Commandant to the latest joined recruit. And such unanimous goodwill presupposes many excellent qualities, for the average

Australian does not lavish affection on an officer for nothing.' The *Official History* later articulated his qualities somewhat less demonstratively: 'He had a keen, practical brain, a quick grasp of essentials, a knowledge of men, and a capacity for organisation and administration.' He would need all these attributes for the challenges that awaited.

The formation of the ANMEF was announced the same day as Holmes accepted command. Repeating advice from the Department of Defence, the Melbourne *Argus* ambiguously described the body as 'a small mixed naval and military force for service within or without Australia'. The announcement created considerable excitement and commentary in the press and the Melbourne *Age* probably spoke for most Australians on 12 August when it commented on the opportunity the war offered for the Commonwealth to extend its political sovereignty into the Pacific, while removing the German threat.

Unlike its larger sibling the AIF, which was purely an army organisation, Holmes had the challenge of creating a joint 1500-strong naval and military organisation. Given the time constraints, his force had to be built simultaneously from top down and bottom up. Holmes lost no time and immediately set to work identifying his brigade staff and organising the army component, which would eventually include two infantry battalions, one raised locally in Sydney and the other formed from volunteers drawn from the Thursday Island garrison in far north Queensland. Aside from the battalion to be raised in Sydney, Holmes' army contingent included two machine-gun sections, a brigade signals section and a medical detachment based on a field ambulance section. The navy took responsibility for raising the smaller six-company battalion.

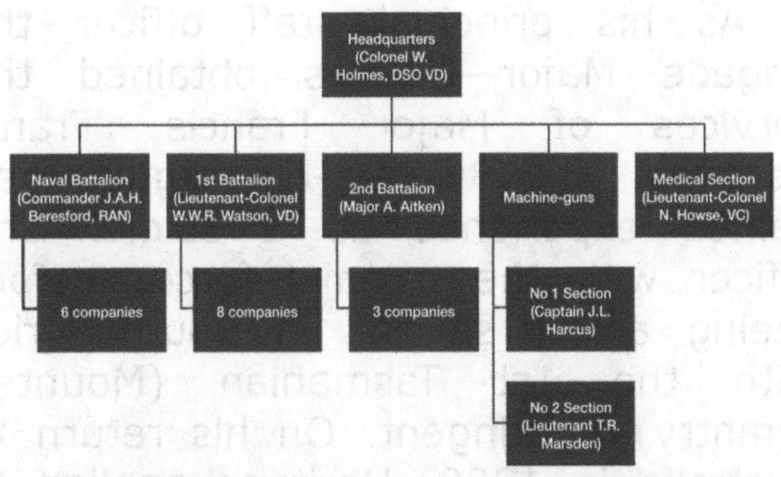

Chart 1. Australian Naval and Military Expeditionary Force, August 1914

Holmes' first task was to select his key subordinates. Since these men would have to turn his orders into actions, they had to be members of a strong team drawn from the best available talent. While he worked closely with Wallack who, as the full-time military district commandant was well informed on the capabilities of local regular and part-time personnel, Holmes gravitated to those he already knew, either through personal connections or from prior service in the militia or South Africa. With Wallack's assistance, Holmes quickly arranged for their appointment to the ANMEF.

As his principal staff officer—the Brigade Major—Holmes obtained the services of Major Francis 'Frank' Heritage. The 36-year-old regular had gained experience as a soldier and officer with the colonial forces before seeing active service in South Africa with the 1st Tasmanian (Mounted Infantry) Contingent. On his return to Australia in 1900, Heritage applied to join the Permanent Military Forces and was gazetted as a captain in the Administrative and Instructional Staff in 1901. Given his strong personal interest in small arms training, he was sent to Britain in 1908 for advanced instruction at the British Army's prestigious School of Musketry at Hythe in Kent. On his return he was promoted major and took up the appointments of Commandant and Chief Instructor of the Commonwealth School of Musketry at Randwick in Sydney's eastern suburbs. The only anomaly in his background was that he was a Catholic, an unusual religious affiliation at the time for a regular officer in a country that was still prone to sectarian prejudice.

COLONEL WILLIAM HOLMES, DSO, VD
COMMANDER ANMEF

Colonel William Holmes, DSO, VD (SPC-A).

William 'Billee' Holmes (1862-1917) is the man who looms large in the story of the ANMEF. He was born in Sydney, the son of Captain William Holmes, a former British regular and the Chief Clerk of the New South Wales Military Forces. Billee Holmes was educated at Paddington Public School and, after leaving school, worked at the Sydney Mint before joining the Department of Works as a clerk in 1878. In August 1887 he married Susan Ellen Green, whose father was also a regular soldier and whose family were neighbours in Victoria Barracks. The following year Holmes became Chief Clerk and

Paymaster of the Metropolitan Board of Water Supply and Sewerage. Under his leadership the department underwent a major expansion and the Cataract, Cordeaux and Avon dams were built. By 1914 he was Secretary of the Board.

Public service was in his blood and from an early age Holmes combined first school and later work with an active part-time military career. In 1872, at the age of 10, he joined the New South Wales militia as a bugler and served in every enlisted rank before being commissioned in 1886. His reputation as a soldier was made in South Africa where he initially served under Legge until he was given his own mounted infantry company. For his services he was Mentioned in Despatches (MID), awarded the Distinguished Service Order (DSO) and finished the war as a brevet lieutenant colonel.

Holmes returned home with some fixed views on the abilities of Australia's citizen-soldiers. He was reported in the press as criticising the

British regulars he encountered in South Africa, contrasting them with the Australian irregulars who, by their training and nature of employment, were more often able 'to use their own judgement at a critical time and so elude disaster'. Holmes was hardly alone in holding such views. Unfortunately the hubris of colonial superiority remained strong among Australia's soldiers and politicians despite rapid changes in warfare and British Army reform following its early humbling on the veldt. The exaggerated reporting of colonial prowess only reinforced dubious notions of discipline that, in South Africa, had often manifested in acts of drunkenness, looting and murder. By 1914 Holmes was commanding the 6th Infantry Brigade and, whatever his assumptions about the natural Australian fighter, he had the right pedigree and reputation to command the Commonwealth's first expeditionary force.

ANMEF senior headquarters staff, Rabaul, 1914. Standing foreground (left to right): Lieutenant Frank Cresswell, RAN (Fleet Wireless Telegraphy Officer); Captain Reginald Travers (Staff Captain, Paymaster and Intelligence Officer, ANMEF). Seated (left to right): Colonel William Holmes (Commander ANMEF); Major Frank Heritage (Brigade Major ANMEF) (AWM J03102).

Holmes' second most important staff vacancy was that of his Staff Captain, the officer charged with implementing the brigade's administrative arrangements. For this position Holmes selected 26-year-old Captain Reginald 'Jack' Travers, a draughtsman with the Department of Lands who was another militiaman well known to him. Travers had been commissioned in 1908 in the 1st Infantry Regiment before transferring to the Australian Intelligence Corps as an engineer survey officer. He later served as an area officer under the compulsory training scheme, while also completing military science courses at Sydney University. In addition to his many professional qualifications, Jack Travers was also about to marry the boss's daughter. His father-in-law clearly had considerable faith in him since Travers was eventually triple-tasked as the brigade's Staff Captain, Paymaster and Intelligence Officer.

Other key brigade appointments were those of Orderly Officer, Quartermaster and Brigade Sergeant Major. Keeping it in the family, 22-year-old Lieutenant Basil Holmes was appointed Orderly Officer and aide to his father. The 51-year-old Honorary Lieutenant Bede Goadby, who was a regular soldier with service in the British and Australian forces since 1886, was appointed Brigade Quartermaster. The brigade's senior soldier was Staff Sergeant Major William Wilkinson, a regular soldier of wide experience.

To command the army battalion Holmes chose Lieutenant Colonel William Watson, an Australian-born dentist and long-serving militia officer who was another South African veteran and well known to Holmes. 'Willy' Watson first joined the New South Wales Scottish Rifles and in 1896 was commissioned as a second lieutenant in the 4th Infantry Regiment. He served as a lieutenant in the 1st (New South Wales) Mounted Rifles under Holmes in South Africa. As a staff officer with the 2nd Imperial Mounted Infantry Corps, Watson was despatched to demand the surrender of Pretoria and finished his war service as a captain with an MID. Watson was promoted major in 1905 and lieutenant colonel in 1912. According to the Australian *Official History,* Watson's 'genial personality made him popular with officers and men, and he had the faculty of enforcing discipline and getting things done without appearing to assert his authority.'

In consultation with Holmes, Watson was given considerable latitude in selecting his key subordinates. Colonel

John Paton, a 47-year-old Australian-born merchant, was another long-serving militia soldier and one of the few ANMEF senior officers who had not seen active service. He joined the New South Wales Military Forces (Volunteers) in 1887 and was commissioned as a second lieutenant in December that year. By July 1914 he was a colonel commanding the 4th Infantry Brigade. So keen was he to serve, he took a drop of two ranks to become Watson's second-in-command.

1st Battalion staff off Rabaul, September 1914. Left to right: Colonel William Holmes; Lieutenant

Colonel William Watson (CO 1st Battalion); Lieutenant Colonel John Paton (Second-in-Command 1st Battalion); Captain Sydney Goodsell (Quartermaster 1st Battalion) (AWM H12840).

The senior soldier of the 1st Battalion was Warrant Officer Class One William Inglis, a 39-year-old former British regular who was the ANMEF's most experienced soldier. Inglis had amassed 24 years with the British Army, including service in South Africa, where he took part in seven engagements between 1899 and 1902 with the 2nd Battalion, Argyll and Sutherland Highlanders. In 1912 he was granted a royal warrant and appointed Regimental Sergeant Major of the battalion. Retiring from the British Army, he and his wife Mary migrated to Australia where he sought to extend his career by joining the Australian Permanent Forces in 1913. In August 1914 he was selected as Regimental Sergeant Major, 1st Battalion, ANMEF, and his primary job became policing discipline among the inexperienced soldiers. In New Guinea his duties would be expanded when he was appointed Assistant Provost Marshal.

While Holmes appears to have had his pick of officers, there were some inevitable clashes as the AIF was also trawling the same talent pool in New South Wales. For example, Holmes originally selected Major Charles Macnaghten as Watson's battalion Adjutant and he was an excellent choice. A well-known citizen-soldier with a commanding presence and proven track record, historian Charles Bean described how, under the compulsory training scheme, Macnaghten 'made a name for himself by his remarkable training of senior cadets in one of the half-slum areas of Sydney ... in which the bane of area-officers, the larrikin, was probably strongest.' Macnaghten personally taught drill to his officers on the flat roof of the University Club's premises in Castlereagh Street and his Woolloomooloo cadets became known as the finest in the city. In short he was the right man for the job and, although Macnaghten accepted Holmes' offer to join the ANMEF, within a week he had disappeared. Holmes learned that his Adjutant had been poached by MacLaurin. Acting on the advice of Military District Chief Clerk, William Sherbon, MacLaurin secured Macnaghten's services with a better offer by allowing him to keep his rank and, instead of an Adjutant's appointment as a captain, he became Second-in-Command of the 4th Battalion (AIF) as a major. Holmes was miffed and took MacLaurin to task, but it made no difference and he was forced to find a replacement. Similarly, Holmes had sought to have some of the recently commissioned graduates of the Royal Military College, Duntroon, posted to his brigade to provide a leavening of professional junior officers. His request was denied as Bridges' need was deemed greater.

Another notable ANMEF 'deserter' was 20-year-old Geoffrey Street. In 1914 Street was studying at the University of Sydney. With the outbreak of war the young student rushed to volunteer, joining the throng of hopefuls at Victoria Barracks keen to secure a place in the ANMEF's ranks. Although accepted, Street was soon persuaded that Europe was the place to serve and obtained a transfer out of the smaller force to join the 1st Battalion (AIF) with the added bonus of a commission. He was destined to become a decorated AIF officer and post-war politician.

At the same time as Holmes was building the army component, the navy was assembling its contribution. In fact the task facing the ANMEF was probably best suited to a force such as the Royal Navy's Corps of Royal Marines. In 1914 Britain's marines comprised two branches: the Royal Marine Artillery and the Royal Marine Light Infantry. These two bodies provided field artillery and infantry for naval landing operations, although their original purpose had been to fight afloat. The shift in role was a product of Britain's triumph in the Napoleonic Wars and its resultant status as the paramount maritime power. In the wars of empire which followed, the navy often found itself with a limited role since it was rarely challenged at sea. A lack of comparable threats did not mean that the navy was idle however, far from it; rather its service involved a great deal of patrolling and logistics support to Britain's land campaigns. So it was that in this same period the RN developed the concept of naval brigades. These ad hoc brigades comprised bodies of sailors trained as infantry and supported by artillery and machine-guns landed from its vessels, often fighting alongside the marines but just as often operating independent of them. Various British naval brigades saw service in the Indian Mutiny (1857-59), the Maori Wars (1860-64), Abyssinia (1867-68), the Second Ashanti War (1873-74), the Zulu War (1879), the Anglo-Egyptian War (1882), the Anglo-Sudanese War (1884-85), South Africa (1899-1902) and China (1900).

Although the Commonwealth did not have a permanent body of marines, it did have some experience with naval brigades. In 1900 the colonial navies of New South Wales, South Australia and Victoria all supplied small contingents to help suppress the revolt by Chinese nationalists led by the Society of Righteous and Harmonious Fists, otherwise known as the Boxers. The combined Australian contingents departed home waters in August 1900, but by the time they arrived in China in mid-September, the siege of the legations in Beijing (Peking) had been lifted and the fighting throughout northern China had become more sporadic. The Australians saw limited service and even less fighting and, after enduring a bleak northern winter, returned home in April 1901. Among the contingents' personnel was a smattering of officers and sailors who would join the ANMEF.

Despite the fact that a naval brigade was not a permanent formation in the post-Federation Australian navy, the Royal Australian Naval Reserve (RANR) was nonetheless formed in 1912. The RANR was established as the naval equivalent of the army's compulsory part-time militia and by 1914 comprised some 1646 officers and men. Its members were trained in basic seamanship and weapon handling, including field artillery pieces carried aboard most major naval combatants. While Holmes later claimed that many of the sailor-soldiers had never been to sea, the RANR was certainly the most appropriate organisation to furnish men for a mission likely to involve beach landings and the capture of naval communications installations. The navy agreed, promising to furnish the 14 officers and 489 ratings needed for its six-company battalion.

To command its battalion, the Naval Board chose Commander Joseph Beresford, RAN. Beresford was Welsh-born and had served 17 years in the RN before transferring to Queensland colonial service in 1897 as a gunnery officer. Though experienced and in appearance a good choice, the 53-year-old had health problems in the tropics and, while popular with some of his subordinates, others marked him as an early liability. Providentially, he was supported by a leavening of particularly good junior officers.

ANMEF naval officers and staff, Kokopo, October 1914. Back row standing (left to right):

Sub-Lieutenant Avenal Hext, RANR; Lieutenant Thomas Bond, RANR; Lieutenant Oscar Gillam, RANR; Warrant Officer Gunner Young, RAN; Petty Officer Hoffman, RANR; Chief Petty Officer George Palmer, RANR; Signal Boatswain William Hunter, RAN; Chief Petty Officer Beaton, RANR; Writer A.D. Adam, RANR; Lieutenant Stewart Cameron, RANR; Sub-Lieutenant Charles Webber, RANR; Petty Officer Instance, RN. Second row, seated on chairs: Lieutenant Leighton Bracegirdle, RAN; Commander Joseph Beresford, RAN; Lieutenant Rowland Bowen, RAN. Front row, seated on ground: Writer Ronald Fowler, RANR; Engineering Midshipman Henry Willian, RANR; Midshipman James Stirling, RANR; Midshipman Richard Veale, RANR; Midshipman Reginald Buller, RANR; Midshipman Charles Cock, RANR; Writer Leslie Trickey, RANR (SPC-A).

To fill out the ranks of the battalion, the naval authorities placed advertisements in the press calling for time-expired sailors or naval reservists. Almost immediately, 471 men from Brisbane, Newcastle, Sydney, Melbourne and Adelaide were identified and enrolled. Furthest away were the South Australians, but the call for 80 volunteers quickly brought forth a contingent of ex-seaman and serving reservists who were formed up at the Largs Bay Naval Depot. Although not all contingent members had uniforms, each man was issued a rifle, bayonet, kit bag and gaiters, and they left Adelaide by express train at 3.15pm on 15 August. The New South Wales contingent was kitted out in Sydney and the men were ready to sail two days later. By that time the South Australian and Victorian contingents had concentrated at Williamstown Naval Depot in Melbourne. They boarded a special overnight train and, aside from an unscheduled collision with a bullock outside Albury on the Victoria-New South Wales border, the train arrived safely at Central Station in Sydney at 10.40am on 18 August.

Beresford's battalion followed normal naval organisation of that time, being smaller than its army counterpart because it was designed for shipboard service. Tactically the Naval Battalion was divided into left and right wings, with each three-company wing commanded by a British officer: Lieutenant Commander George Browne, RN and Lieutenant Commander Charles

Elwell, RN. Each of the six companies comprised around 50 men commanded by a lieutenant. The companies were further subdivided into left and right halves under a junior officer. Companies 1, 2 and 3 were drawn from New South Wales, 4 and 5 from Victoria, and 6 from South Australia. The Queenslanders were billeted among the New South Welshmen. The Australian services, following British custom, deemed the navy the senior service and so the single Naval Battalion did not require a numerical designation.

Victorian and South Australian naval contingents of the ANMEF at the Williamstown Naval Depot, Melbourne, before their departure for Sydney. The officers in the foreground are (left to right): Lieutenant Rowland Bowen, RAN; Sub-Lieutenant Charles Webber, RANR;

Sub-Lieutenant Avenal Hext, RANR; Midshipman Charles Hicks, RANR; Midshipman Richard Veale, RANR and Engineer Midshipman Henry Willian, RANR (SPC-A).

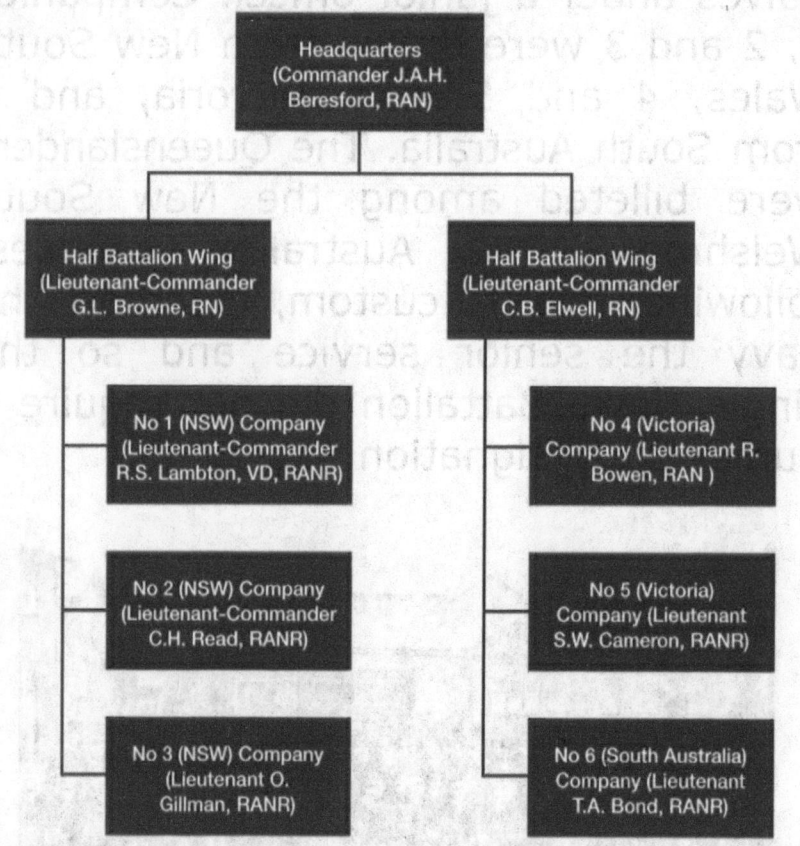

Chart 2. Naval Battalion ANMEF, August 1914

Lieutenant Commander Charles Elwell, RN. Elwell commanded the Right Wing of the Naval Battalion. At Bita Paka he would lead the first Australian bayonet charge of the Great War (SPC-A).

No.4 Company was a typical naval sub-unit. Lieutenant Roland Bowen, RAN, commanded the company and had two junior officers, each responsible for a half-company group: Sub-Lieutenant Charles Webber, RANR, and Sub-Lieutenant Avenal Hext, RANR. The company's senior NCO was Petty Officer George Palmer, RANR. This company was slightly larger than the average with a total strength of 75 all ranks—three officers, one petty officer and 71 ratings.

Lieutenant Leighton Bracegirdle, RAN, shown here in 1900 when he first saw active service in China with the New South Wales Naval Brigade (AWM P00417.036).

Experience among the naval officers varied widely. At one end of the spectrum was Lieutenant Leighton Bracegirdle, a 33-year-old who joined the New South Wales Naval Brigade as a cadet in 1898 and was commissioned as a midshipman two years later. By 1914 he had already seen service with the China Field Force during the Boxer Rebellion and in South Africa as a lieutenant with the South Africa Irregular Horse. During his service on the veldt he narrowly escaped death after being thrown from his horse and shot by a Boer rifleman.

At the other end of the experiential spectrum was Midshipman Richard 'Stan' Veale, RANR. Veale was a 20-year-old naval reserve officer who was only appointed a midshipman on 19 August to take up an appointment with the ANMEF. As a small boy he had witnessed the departure from Port Melbourne of troops destined to take part in the many military conflicts in which the Australian colonies became involved. He saw the Victorian Naval Brigade depart for the Boxer Rebellion in June 1900, and the departure of Victorian contingents for the South African War. An enthusiastic sailor, he had served in the naval cadets since he was 15. In civilian life he worked for the Metropolitan Gas Company in Melbourne. No matter what their actual experience however, the navy expected all its officers to maintain the high standards of personal conduct set by the senior service.

Army enlistments commenced the day after Holmes was appointed to command. Unlike the Naval Battalion, which mostly consisted of serving reservists or ex-permanent sailors, Holmes' troops were rather more varied. Given the time imperative and restrictions on the militia serving outside Australia, recruiting was restricted to volunteers from the 2nd Military District, which covered most of New South Wales. However, in reality, the timeframe meant that most were drawn from the Sydney metropolitan area. Given the lack of permanent facilities to house the force, arrangements were made with the Royal Agricultural Society for the local showgrounds to be made available and the staff moved into offices there.

There was no special machinery in place to assemble a force for overseas service. The management of recruiting, medically checking and inducting volunteers fell to the small regular staff of the military district headquarters. As word spread, volunteers began to assemble at Victoria Barracks, Paddington, where they were screened by Lieutenant Colonel John 'Bull' Antill, who was serving under Wallack on the local staff and would later achieve notoriety for his role in the disastrous attack at The Nek on Gallipoli on 7 August 1915. The formidable Antill, brusque in manner and speech, had few tools for filtering the gaggle of enthusiastic volunteers and, while serving, single soldiers or ex-servicemen were preferred, there was neither the time nor means to verify claims. This was an era before aptitude testing became standard for armies and so the basis for selecting personnel was necessarily crude. Worse, without police checks or psychological vetting, a minority of those selected proved mentally unsuitable, untrainable or criminal. Holmes would later write of 'a few men with rather unfavourable reputations; men who I am informed have gaol records.' Unfortunately by the time his 'problem soldiers' were discovered it was too late and the damage to the ANMEF's reputation was done.

To hide an unsavoury past was relatively easy in those days and there was little the authorities could do to uncover subterfuge in the available time. One Scottish-born volunteer, John

Freeborn, adopted the identity of a fellow Scot because that man had served as a soldier in the Seaforth Highlanders and so had a better chance of being accepted by the authorities. As 'Mr John Plimer', Freeborn's ruse was successful; he enlisted and was promoted sergeant. Only in New Guinea did he confess to the use of an alias and there he reverted to his rightful name. There is no indication why Freeborn adopted another man's identity, although his ability to pass himself off as a veteran and serve successfully as a sergeant indicates that he was probably a former soldier. Perhaps he had previously deserted or perhaps he was avoiding an unhappy marriage. What is certain is that, unlike many others who lied about their past, he served without blemish and was discharged honourably back in Australia on expiration of his term of enlistment. Meanwhile the real John Plimer enlisted in the AIF with the Army Medical Corps and finished the war as a staff sergeant.

The motivation of each volunteer was as unique as the individual himself.

Some joined out of loyalty to the 'old country' because this was an era when loyalty to King and Empire was strong. Others joined out of an embryonic sense of nationalism, a desire to prove Australia's worth on the world stage, and a determination to remove the German threat in the Pacific and Europe. Intermixed with lofty sentiments were less altruistic reasons such as the lure of adventure, a desire to see the world and even a subtle form of economic compulsion, since work was scarce in 1914 and ANMEF and AIF pay was among the best in the British forces.

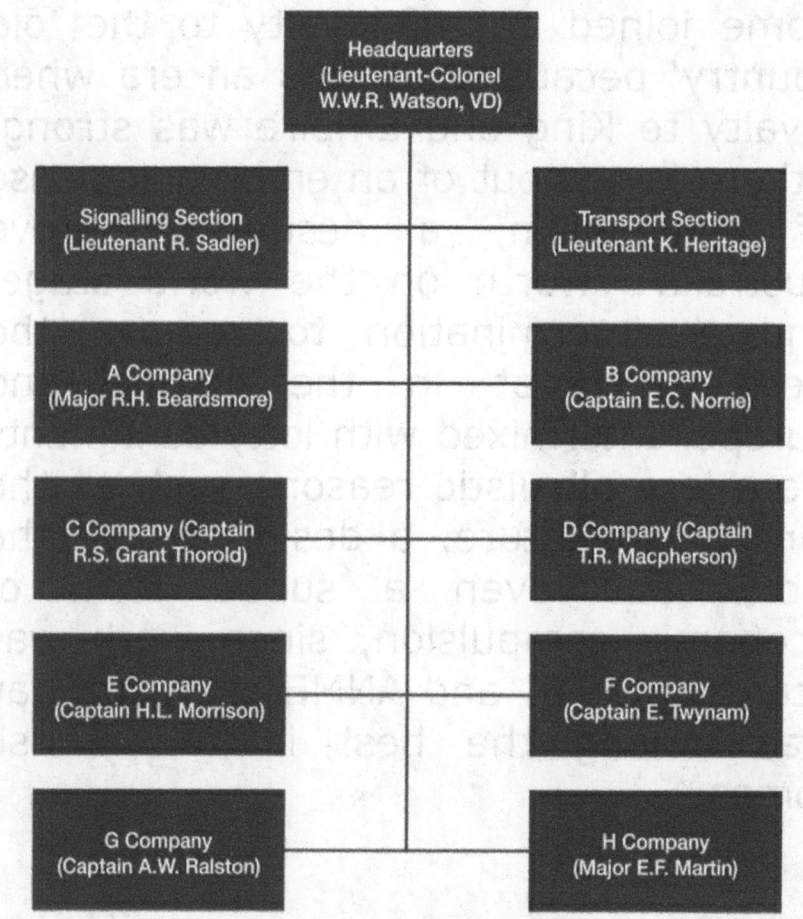

Chart 3. 1st Battalion ANMEF, August 1914

When it came to organising and equipping the force, Holmes followed extant practice. The army battalion was organised along the lines of the existing eight-company British battalion, an organisation that was obsolete and more suited to the Crimean War of the mid-nineteenth century than the early twentieth century. Even though the eight-company model had recently been superseded by a newer four-company structure and this had been adopted by the British Regular Army and the New Zealand Army, the older structure was still employed by the Commonwealth and British Territorials.

Watson's battalion was organised with a small headquarters and eight rifle companies, a total of 1073 all ranks. Battalion headquarters included the key appointments of CO (Watson), battalion Second-in-Command (Paton), Adjutant (Captain Cyril Lane), Quartermaster (Lieutenant Sydney Goodsell), Signalling Officer (Lieutenant Rupert Sadler) and Transport Officer (Lieutenant Keith Heritage). The eight rifle companies were both tactical and administrative sub-units of the battalion, with each containing around 120 men and commanded by a major or captain. The companies were subdivided into left and right half-companies, each under the command of a lieutenant or second lieutenant. The battalion was rounded out with a permanent machine-gun section, transport details and a signals section. Most of Watson's officers were drawn from the militia, and in all, three-quarters of the military officers were already commissioned. Only five appear not to have been currently serving. Most had only a few years' service and this was on a part-time basis of evening parades at the local drill hall and yearly camps. Watson's battalion was designated the 1st Battalion, although it stood behind the Naval Battalion in precedence.

Major General Neville Howse, VC, KCB, KCMG. Howse was the first Australian to be awarded the Victoria Cross, decorated for actions under fire in South Africa. In 1914 he was appointed Principal Medical Officer ANMEF. He later saw service on Gallipoli and the Western Front where he rose to become Director Medical Services AIF (AWM ART03351).

While the eager volunteers rushed the recruiting office, the force medical section was also being assembled at Victoria Barracks. As the Naval Board had limited resources and priority was to be given to staffing hospital ships, it was logical that the ANMEF medical staff be drawn from the Army Medical Corps. The detail, consisting of four officers, one warrant officer and 35 other ranks, was equipped as a field ambulance section, an organisation designed primarily to stabilise and evacuate casualties to hospital rather than treating and holding them. A quick search revealed a number of possible candidates to command the unit, with preference given to Major Neville Howse, a 50-year-old British-born and trained medical practitioner who earlier had become the first Australian serviceman to be awarded the Victoria Cross (VC). Howse, who was a militia medical officer and a personal friend of Holmes, had a practice in the western New South Wales country town of Orange. He was clearly a busy country surgeon as, when Wallack telephoned the doctor's residence on 10 August, he was advised by Howse's pregnant wife that the doctor was 50 kilometres away operating on a serious abdominal case. On his return his wife reluctantly handed him the message to contact Victoria Barracks. Eager to serve, he hastily rearranged his operating schedule, left his wife, and rushed off to Sydney, arriving at 9.30am the next day. Howse, who was hoping for an appointment with the AIF, was disappointed to find that Colonel Charles Ryan had already secured the position of Assistant Director of Medical Services to Bridges' 1st Division. Instead, Howse was offered the appointment of Principal Medical Officer (PMO) ANMEF. His disappointment was softened by the inducement of promotion to acting lieutenant colonel.

Howse quickly secured the services of three young doctors to round out his team. They were: Captain John Donaldson, a recently commissioned Sydney University graduate; Captain Frederick Maguire, who came from the recently mobilised 8th Citizen Force Field Ambulance; and Captain Brian Pockley, a Shore School old boy and former member of the Sydney University Scouts. Pockley, a champion athlete, also happened to be the nephew of 'Bull' Antill. While a talented group, the *Official History* notes that 'although a small school of tropical medicine existed at Townsville (Queensland), none of the officers chosen had received any special training in tropical medicine and hygiene.'

When Howse was advised that the force was destined for New Guinea he quickly sought out additional stocks and stores. First, he managed to secure some quantities of quinine and emetine and then requisitioned a microscope. Various other medical stores, including mosquito nets and dressings, were supplied by the Red Cross Society. Howse's senior soldier was Warrant Officer Henry Hazlett, who had 23 years' service as a citizen-soldier with the Medical Corps. The remainder of the staff were drawn from volunteers holding civilian qualifications in first aid or nursing. As no dental officer was authorised on the field ambulance establishment until early 1915, Howse secured the services of John Henderson, a fourth-year dentistry undergraduate from the University of Sydney, who enlisted as a private and brought his dental instruments with him.

Once assembled, Howse and his staff began to sift the fit from the unfit as the brief initial medical screening had not always detected pre-existing medical conditions. At least physical standards were set high, the same as those for enlistment in the pre-war Permanent Military Forces. Despite this however, a number of men managed to slip through with undeclared and undetected ailments. In fairness, the busy doctors were more accustomed to dealing with part-time compulsory inductees who were more likely to bring to a doctor's attention any abnormality that might excuse a man from service. They were less accustomed to volunteers attempting to conceal defects. Hence some men evaded detection even though they suffered from epilepsies and other chronic medical conditions, while others who attempted to conceal inguinal hernias, varicocele, and varicose veins were more easily weeded out. In the absence of an army dental service, oral examinations were conducted by volunteers from the Dental Association of New South Wales. Once enlisted, all men were inoculated against typhoid (then known as enteric fever) in accordance with government policy, even though it was a procedure that was far from standard in military forces at the time. The force was also vaccinated against smallpox.

VICKERS-MAXIM MACHINE-GUN

Machine-gun section, 8th Infantry Regiment (Oxley Battalion), a standard battalion machine-gun section containing two

Vickers-Maxim guns. The two ANMEF sections were organised identically to the section shown here (AWM P02141.001).

The ANMEF's firepower was bolstered by the inclusion of two army machine-gun sections. The Maxim machine-gun first entered British service in 1893 and the .303-inch Maxim Converted was approved for service in 1897. Based on Sir Hiram Maxim's first successful design of a self-powered machine-gun, the British company Vickers improved and manufactured the gun for the British Army. The Vickers-Maxim was introduced into the British Army in 1912 and adopted by Australia soon after. The weapon was water-cooled, fired a 0.303-inch (7.7-millimetre) round loaded in fabric belts, had a rate of fire of around 550 rounds per minute, and was sighted to 2500 yards (2286 metres). Under existing doctrine a two-gun section was allocated to each infantry battalion and employed as a section, ensuring that one gun was always capable of engaging a target.

Although different to its successor—the more famous and longer serving Vickers gun—the Vickers-Maxim was a formidable weapon with a reputation for reliability, durability and potency. Its main disadvantage in the jungles of New Guinea was its weight of 26 kilograms and the prevailing belief that machine-guns were primarily a defensive weapon. Each gun had a four-man crew: one to fire, one to feed the ammunition belts, the others to help carry the weapon, its ammunition and spare parts.

Members of the 1st Battalion at camp in the Agricultural Showgrounds. They are wearing the Universal Training Pattern uniform with British 1908 Pattern webbing equipment and are carrying the .303-inch Short Magazine Lee-Enfield rifle (AWM H19498).

The first 330 army volunteers selected by Antill and passed by the medical examiners arrived at the Sydney Agricultural Showgrounds on Tuesday 11 August. They were attested and enlisted for six months' 'foreign service' but, as no arrangements had been made for sleeping accommodation, they were sent home that evening with instructions to report back at 9.00am the next day. That day, Wednesday, a further 723 enlistees joined. Another 53 were attested on Thursday 13 August, bringing the total to 1106 all ranks. The final group of six recruits for the battalion and 20 for the medical section were attested on Friday 14 August. The first battalion parade was held on Saturday, while Sunday was devoted to the habitual church parade. On Monday 17 August training began with drill and rifle exercises and, on Tuesday, just seven days after recruiting commenced, the contingent was inspected by the State Governor. This must have been a frantic week for Holmes as his force swiftly assembled and, on top of everything else, he arranged the wedding of his daughter Dorothy to Jack Travers on Wednesday 12 August. Like Spee, Holmes was now taking two sons to war.

Uniforms and other personal equipment for the soldiers were drawn from local ordnance stores or, in the case of serving militiamen, they brought their issue uniforms with them. This uniform was not the more famous pea-green livery adopted by the AIF, but was the more easily sourced Universal Training Pattern uniform. This outfit consisted of a fur felt slouch hat or woollen forage cap, woollen shirt, cord breeches, puttees and brown leather ankle boots. While much praised for its utility, the uniform was designed for the temperate climate of Australia rather than the heat and humidity of the tropics. Personal equipment comprised British-manufactured 1908 Pattern webbing equipment consisting of a harness supporting a haversack, ammunition pouches, water bottle, bayonet and entrenching tool. Soldiers and sailors were both issued the .303-inch Short Magazine Lee-Enfield rifle.

Naval members of the ANMEF dressed in their improvised field uniform. The white cotton naval rig was dyed a more suitable brown colour by soaking the uniforms in a solution of Condy's crystals (SPC-A).

While the issue army uniforms proved less than ideal in the islands, the navy was able to improvise using existing uniforms more suited to the tropics. On the voyage to New Guinea the resourceful sailors adapted their conspicuous white cotton rig by dyeing it in a solution of potassium permanganate (commonly known as Condy's crystals) which turned it various shades of tan. A little experimentation soon achieved the desired result of an inconspicuous muddy brown.

RIFLE, SMLE .303-INCH NO.1 MARK III*

Rifles for the ANMEF were drawn from existing stocks of the British .303-inch Short Magazine Lee-Enfield (SMLE). The Mark I version of this rifle was introduced into the British Army in 1903 and the improved Mark III of 1907 was adopted by Australia and commenced production in 1912 at the newly established Small Arms Factory at Lithgow in New South Wales. However production at Lithgow lagged and in 1914 the bulk of the Australian forces were still armed with British-manufactured rifles, with most of the sailors and soldiers of the ANMEF carrying these rifles rather than the Australian version.

The Lee-Enfield had an effective range of 500 metres and a maximum range of over 2500 metres. British and Australian soldiers were supposed to be trained to fire at least 15 aimed shots per minute, although it is doubtful that many members of the ANMEF ever achieved that standard. The main advantages of the SMLE were its reliability and rate of fire. Ruggedly constructed and dependable under even the most testing conditions, the Lee-Enfield was a weapon trusted by the troops. The rifle also had a fast bolt action and 10-round magazine, giving it a high rate of fire compared with the German Mauser. In fact the record for aimed bolt-action fire was set in 1914 by a British musketry instructor armed with an SMLE who fired 38 rounds into a 300-millimetre-wide target at 270 metrepeaks including Tavurvurs in one minute. The Lee-Enfield's main disadvantages in New Guinea would prove to be its length and ammunition. At 113 centimetres long, the rifle could become tangled in vegetation and, if the firer was not careful when going to ground to take aim, the muzzle could become clogged with mud or dirt. The SMLE fired a rimmed cartridge and, to avoid jamming, the rounds had to be carefully loaded. Nonetheless the rifle proved a steadfast, durable, hard-hitting and accurate weapon in the hands of a well-trained soldier or sailor.

1907 SMLE Rifle No. 1 Mark III* (AAIM).

There was no artillery component included with the brigade, although the navy could be called on to provide such support if required. Naval bombardment of shore targets had a long history and the large-calibre guns mounted on naval vessels could prove devastating when turned inland. The problem with naval gunfire support however, was that the guns and shells carried by most naval combatants were designed primarily for ship-to-ship combat. For example, the 12 and 6-inch guns mounted on the RAN's various cruisers were designed to fire armour-piercing rounds that could penetrate the armoured sides of enemy ships. Such weapons fired on a very flat trajectory, making them less suitable to engage targets protected by physical barriers such as ridgelines or dug in below ground. Even so, a big gun salvo could have a devastating psychological impact on troops even if it failed to physically destroy the target.

Naval 12-pounder breech-loading gun (AWM P06162.001).

In addition to the shipboard guns, the larger combatant vessels of the RAN also carried one or two smaller field guns designed for use ashore. The Australian colonial navies and militias both purchased 12-pounder field pieces in the late nineteenth century and, while the army later converted its guns, the navy maintained the original guns for use by landing parties. The 12-pounder derived its name from the weight of the shell it fired, as per standard British practice, unlike the Germans who classified their guns by the diameter of the barrel. The 12-pounder had a calibre of 3 inches (76 millimetres) and, although it only fired a 5.7-kilogram shell, it could reach a maximum range of 6000 yards (5486 metres). The 12-pounders were mounted on a field carriage and, while each weighed 915 kilograms, it could easily be manhandled by its crew of nine.

By 14 August Holmes' force was assembled, the men completing a crash course in soldiering in the remaining time before embarkation. Although volunteers were plentiful and keen, it appears that few of those selected were currently serving in the military. The *Official History* notes that: 'Of the infantry enlisted, comparatively few belonged to the existing units of the Commonwealth Military Forces', while journalist Frederick Burnell, who accompanied the force as an embedded reporter for the *Sydney Morning Herald*, described how a 'heavy sprinkling of the force consisted of men who had served in South Africa or in China, but the majority were the rawest recruits.'

Among the sprinkling of veterans was 32-year-old George Finlayson. He was born in Berrima in the Southern Highlands of New South Wales, the son of a well-to-do pastoral family. Sent to England for his education, he attended Harrow and Trinity College, Cambridge, before returning home to work on the land as a station manager. During the Anglo-Boer War he served two stints in South Africa, the first for a year as a sergeant and quartermaster sergeant with the 2nd (New South Wales) Mounted Rifles, and a second 15-month tour as a lieutenant with the 3rd (New South Wales) Imperial Bushmen. Despite his experience, Finlayson was content to enlist as a private in the ANMEF, although his tertiary education and rural background made him an anomaly among his peers.

The bulk of the ANMEF's army personnel shared a profile similar to contemporaneous AIF volunteers. The majority were single and of prime military age, with most soldiers aged between 20 and 24 years. They had grown up during the great depression of the 1890s and had experienced its hardships. Overwhelmingly they hailed from Australia's major urban centres. Most ANMEF volunteers declared allegiance to one of the four main Christian churches (Anglican, Presbyterian, Methodist and Roman Catholic), while there was a small number of Baptists, Congregationalists and Wesleyans, and at least four Jews and two Greek Orthodox. Surprisingly for that time, there were a couple of declared agnostics, a 'freethinker', a few who listed no religion, and one avowed atheist.

Demographic information on Beresford's personnel is not complete, although they most likely maintained a similar profile to their military cousins. They were recruited from the coastal state capitals of Brisbane, Sydney, Melbourne and Adelaide and most had seafaring backgrounds or at least an interest in nautical matters. A typical reservist was Able Seaman William 'Billy' Williams. Billy Williams was born in the southern capital in 1885 and grew up in the working-class suburb of Northcote. He was still a boy when he first went to sea, working on the steamer *Westralia* and on the *Loongona* and *Paloona.* Returning to land he found a job with the Melbourne City Corporation and worked in the power plant's engine room in the city centre on Spencer Street. Typically he was single and lived at home with his mother and a married sister. He was a member of the Richmond Rifle Club and was reputedly an excellent marksman with pistol and rifle. He joined the naval reserves on leaving the merchant marine and had served five years by the time war broke out. At the time he was 28 years old and in the last week of his reserve service, but volunteered immediately.

Able Seaman William George 'Billy' Williams, a 28-year-old member of No.4 Company of the Naval Battalion ANMEF (SPC-A).

While Billy Williams and most of his peers were Australian-born, the ANMEF represented a cross-section of Australian society and, alongside the native-born, there was a significant minority from Britain and a sprinkling of others from around the British Empire, including Canadians, New Zealanders, Rhodesians, and South Africans. In all, around one-quarter of the 1st Battalion was British-born.

Educationally, the ANMEF covered the full range, from those with a minimal primary education to the tertiary educated. Compulsory education had been introduced in Australia across the separate colonies in the 1870s. The introduction of free public education was designed to lift literacy and numeracy and to inculcate discipline as a counter to the perception of widespread larrikinism among juvenile males and females. Schooling in this instance meant children aged between six and 13 and, although it was compulsory, it had yet to be treated as such by many parents. In 1914, of some 700,000 school-aged children, 500,000 were enrolled at state schools, 100,000 at private schools including in the Catholic system, 17,000 were home schooled and 64,000 were not attending school. Secondary and tertiary education were considered luxuries with just 6.5% of males aged between 15 and 19 remaining in full-time education.

While most volunteers came from blue-collar backgrounds, there was plenty of diversity in the ranks. One volunteer noted: 'We have, engineers, dentists; uni boys, government officials ... & every other conceivable trade and profession.' Indeed the cross-section of occupations represented working Australia at that time, with bakers and butchers, banister-markers and basket-makers, barmen and brewers, bookbinders and boot-repairers, boundary-riders and bus drivers, blacksmiths and builders. There were those who worked in emerging industries (cinema photographer, electrician, motor mechanic and wireless manufacturing engineer), and those with more traditional occupations (armourer, cooper, hatter and valet), as well as some whose occupations have disappeared (compositor, lift attendant, milk vendor and theatre usher). There were a number of self-professed gentlemen of independent means and one professional pugilist.

At least 15 Sydney University alumni or former students served with the ANMEF. By the outbreak of the war all Australian states had a university, with Sydney University, established in 1852, the oldest. Attendance at university at this time was a rare privilege and mostly reserved for the upper middle-class sons of Australia's 'Establishment'. The universities provided the elite of Australia's medical, legal and academic professions and were also rich breeding grounds for many of the nation's part-time and regular military officers. In Edwardian Australia, military service was seen as a natural obligation and it was assumed that all 'white' males would play a role in national defence.

Captain Brian Pockley. A Sydney University graduate and medical practitioner, Pockley was one of three young doctors recruited to serve with the ANMEF's medical detail (SPC-A).

Most of the ANMEF's university graduates were commissioned. These men included two of Howse's doctors (Captains Frederick Maguire and Brian Pockley) and two of Watson's company commanders (Major Robert Beardsmore and Captain Alexander Ralston), while four of those who enlisted in the ranks were subsequently commissioned (Brigadier Lionel Lehmaier, Captain Harold Henley, Squadron Leader Frederick Sandford and Captain John Henderson). One of the more interesting characters was Wilfred Dovey. Dovey was educated at Sydney Grammar School and was studying at Sydney University when war broke out. He decided to pause his education to volunteer for a martial 'gap year', also pausing long enough to marry Mary Duncan prior to embarking. Dovey initially joined G Company, but before the landing on New Britain he was transferred to Headquarters 1st Battalion. After serving in the islands he returned to Australia, completed a

Bachelor of Arts in 1916, and then moved to Queensland with his wife to teach at Brisbane Grammar School. During this time he studied law at the University of Queensland, was admitted to the New South Wales Bar in 1922 and appointed King's Council in 1935. After many highly publicised cases, Dovey was appointed as a judge of the Supreme Court of New South Wales in 1953. His daughter, Margaret, married the future Prime Minister (Edward) Gough Whitlam.

Among the ranks there was also a sprinkling of ex-regular soldiers. Many of these men were identified and promoted to NCO rank and played an important role in training and disciplining the force. Among this group was Sergeant Maurice Lawton who had previously served 12 years with the Munster Fusiliers, including service in India and the East Indies. Sergeant John Leadbeater served 14 years with the 'colours', rising to colour sergeant before taking his discharge from the British Army. Not all 'old soldiers', however, proved to be a positive influence on the force.

Henry Langtry was a former soldier of the Scots Guards and, on the strength of his military credentials, he was appointed Company Sergeant Major, H Company. Less than two weeks after the German surrender, Langtry faced a field general court martial on charges of opening dispatches and striking a native. He was found guilty and sentenced to be reduced to the ranks and discharged with ignominy. But this was not the end of his story. On his return to Australia he volunteered for the AIF and, notwithstanding his earlier termination, he was re-enlisted and promoted sergeant. In Egypt he was found to be suffering from venereal disease and was returned to Australia and despatched to Langwarrin Camp in Victoria for compulsory treatment. On his release he was shipped back overseas and, in early 1916, served briefly with the Australian Provost Corps before someone realised the error and he was transferred to the 46th Battalion (AIF). He served in France but, following another court martial, he was reduced in rank. He was also discovered to have a severe drinking problem as a result of his previous service, probably a symptom of what is known today as post-traumatic stress disorder. This would account for his hostile, suspicious behaviour, violent temper, insomnia and nightmares. He was finally discharged in 1917 for mental instability.

Sergeant William Watriama, a New Caledonian native who served his adopted country in South Africa, New Guinea and, as shown here, as a member of the AIF in 1915 (AWM DA14272).

Heterogeneous rather than homogenous, the ANMEF contained a

scattering of friendly aliens who gave the force colour, figuratively and in some cases literally. Among the ANMEF's originals were an American (mining engineer Lionel Lehmaier), a Frenchman (hairdresser Joseph Deroubaix), two Greeks (musician Arthur Kyriako and barman Nicholas Paidas) and a Russian (cook Julian Szabowski), while Herman Stiefvater, though Australian-born, was obviously of German heritage. Perhaps the most exotic individual was William Watriama. One of the few men of colour to attain acceptance in pre-war 'white Australia', Watriama was born on Mare, one of the Loyalty Islands of French New Caledonia. He migrated to Australia around 1890 where he became an outspoken critic of French rule in his homeland. He publicly urged British expansion in the Pacific and joined the National Association of New South Wales, a conservative nationalist organisation. Watriama backed his patriotism to his new country with action and he was a keen part-time soldier, serving with the very Anglo militia regiment, the St George's English Rifles. His pre-war service covered 12 years during which time he went to South Africa with the 2nd (New South Wales) Mounted Rifles. When war broke out in 1914 he volunteered again, joining the ANMEF on 12 August.

The three Wallace brothers from Erskineville in inner Sydney. All three served in the ANMEF although, unusually, Arthur, Ernest and Fred served in separate companies despite the fact that it was more common for brothers to serve together. In the AIF it became common practice to allow serving siblings to 'claim' other family members when they enlisted. The Wallace brothers subsequently joined the AIF artillery in France and all survived to return home (AWM P03078.006).

As in the AIF, the ANMEF boasted a number of strong family connections. Aside from Holmes and his son and son-in-law, Frank Heritage served as Brigade Major along with his younger brother, Lieutenant Keith Heritage, who was the 1st Battalion's Transport Officer. Lieutenant Charles Manning served with A Company, while his younger brother, Second Lieutenant Guy Manning, served with E Company. Most rifle companies also sported one or more sets of brothers. There were the English-born Fox twins (John and Thomas) and Hardy brothers (Alfred and William) in A Company; the Montefiore brothers (Charles and Leonard) in B Company; the Kearns brothers (Arthur and Edward) in C Company; the Bush brothers (Bernard and Eric) and Plane brothers (Alfred and Leslie) in E Company; the Buchanan brothers (Angus and Frank) and Merrett brothers (Charles and Frederick) in F Company; the Meek brothers (John and Leopold) in H Company; and the three Wallace boys (Ernest, Frederick and Arthur) spread between B, C and G companies.

As the force prepared for its embarkation, security was tight and its ultimate destination remained a secret. Only a handful of senior officers were aware that their task was to secure Germany's Pacific territories, though newspaper announcements meant that speculation was rife and informed readers had little difficulty surmising how the ANMEF might be employed. On 13 August the Melbourne *Punch* printed remarks by the Director of Military Art at Sydney University, Colonel Hubert Foster, who publicly advocated for Australia—with or without British urging—to send an expedition to take the German concession at Jiaozhou Bay and seize the Qingdao naval base. He cited the earlier precedent of the American colonists who captured the French fortress of Louisburg in the 1700s with the assistance of a few British warships.

A member of the 1st Battalion marching through the streets of Sydney. Although the military authorities attempted to keep the departure of the ANMEF a secret, news quickly spread and the column was accompanied by a throng of thousands as it marched to Fort Macquarie, producing an atmosphere analogous to a fair rather than a march to war. Many of the soldiers walked arm in arm with friends and family (AWM H11567).

At 10.20am on 18 August the army component of the ANMEF left its temporary home at Moore Park and marched to Fort Macquarie which had once been a defence works at Bennelong Point before the fort was demolished in 1901 to make way for new electric tramway sheds. Today the site is occupied by the Sydney Opera House. Although the departure and destination of the force were kept secret by the military authorities and newspapers were forbidden to publish any details of preparations, word filtered out and, with more than 1000 soldiers camped at the Sydney showgrounds, news quickly spread that something was afoot. When the troops marched to the Sydney docks that Tuesday morning, thousands of people lined the streets to cheer them on. Signaller Lyle Reeves wrote:

> The force passed along Oxford, College and Macquarie Streets on their way to Fort Macquarie. Along Oxford Street the girls from the ribbon stores brought out rolls of red, white and blue ribbon, which was cut up and fixed on bayonet points, in hats, on sleeves—anywhere it would show up. Flags were in evidence all along the line, practically every other man

having a flag or patriotic emblem of some kind waving from his rifle. Not a few friends and relatives marched side by side in the ranks all the way from the barracks to Fort Macquarie.

The Sydney ferry Kulgoa loaded with ANMEF soldiers. The army contingent was transported from Fort Macquarie to Cockatoo Island where its transport awaited. The naval component had already arrived and boarded without the same fanfare that accompanied the army's departure (AWM H19497).

From Fort Macquarie the troops were conveyed to the naval base at Cockatoo Island in two large harbour ferries. There they found their transport, HMAS *Berrima,* lying at Sutherland Dock and their naval comrades already aboard. As the troops stowed kit and stores, Holmes visited Customs House where he met the Minister for Defence, Senator Edward Millen. If Holmes expected a few words of encouragement or some last-minute instructions from his government, he was quickly disabused. Millen, who had been Defence Minister for little over a year, simply expressed his dissatisfaction at the time taken to recruit and organise the force. Clearly the Minister expected miracles, although it is hard to see how the military district staff and Holmes could have done better. On the other hand, perhaps the Minister was simply peeved that New Zealand had upstaged the Commonwealth with its Samoan Expeditionary Force, which embarked six days earlier, its only delay caused by the arrival of Admiralty Sailing Orders and an adequate escort.

CHAPTER 4

OPENING MOVES

While the ANMEF was forming, the RAN had not been idle. On 28 July, exactly one month after the assassination of the Archduke Franz Ferdinand and as the situation in Europe spiralled out of control, the British Admiralty issued a warning order to all stations to prepare for the possibility of war. Rear Admiral Patey received the order on 30 July while he and most of his ships were at sea on exercise. He immediately ordered the scattered squadron to return to port to fuel and take on mobilisation stores in anticipation of war. By common agreement the RAN was now under the operational control of the Admiralty and Patey prepared to execute his war orders. These orders directed the Admiral, with *Australia,* to sail for Western Australia and then join the British China Squadron, while his other RAN combatants were to be detached to protect merchant shipping. However, this action was only to occur once all enemy armoured ships in Australian waters had been destroyed. At the time, primitive signals intelligence from the Naval Board in Melbourne, which had been tracking wireless communications from Spee's flagship, placed the German 500 kilometres north of Australian Papua. Patey therefore planned an attack on the German capital on New Britain to deal with this immediate threat. The Admiralty concurred.

On the evening of 4 August, Patey left Sydney aboard *Australia*, sailing for a northern RAN fleet rendezvous. Once he had collected his squadron he was bound for Rabaul where he suspected Spee, with *Scharnhorst, Gneisenau* and *Nürnberg*, was sheltering. The following morning, as *Australia* steamed along the Australian coastline, the Admiral was advised of the outbreak of war. He pressed on, hoping for a showdown with his German foe.

New Britain lies to the north-east of New Guinea and is the largest island in the Bismarck Archipelago. It has a crescent-shaped body around 480 kilometres long, with an average breadth of 80 kilometres and an area of approximately 33,500 square kilometres. It is mountainous and volcanic with a backbone of ranges running east and west reaching an altitude of between 1200 and 1500 metres. The eastern end of the island, at a point between Open Bay on the north coast and Wide Bay on the south, narrows to an isthmus around 38 kilometres across, and then spreads out again to the north and east, resuming the average breadth of 80 kilometres. The area north of this isthmus is the Gazelle Peninsula. The northern tip of the peninsula contains the deep and spacious Blanche Bay, within whose inner basin lies Simpson Harbour and Rabaul township.

Blanche Bay is an enormous oval volcanic crater into which the sea has broken. On the north and east the bay is bounded by the Crater Peninsula. On the south and west of the bay the country is rugged and jungle clad. Southwards the view is bounded by the lofty Baining Mountains, whose highest peak is Mount Sinewit, reaching 2438 metres. Surrounding Blanche Bay and rising above Rabaul are a number of volcanic peaks including Tavurvur(Matupit Crater) and Vulcan on either side of the harbour mouth, and Kabiu ('Mother'), Tovanumbatir ('North Daughter') and Turagunan ('South Daughter') to the north-east of the town. At the northern tip of Blanche Bay is Simpson Harbour and the smaller Matupi Harbour, with Rabaul spread along the north-east corner of the former. In 1914 Rabaul was the seat of government of the German Protectorate. Just outside the entrance to Blanche Bay on its southern extremity is the village of Kokopo, formerly the capital and in 1914 still its commercial centre.

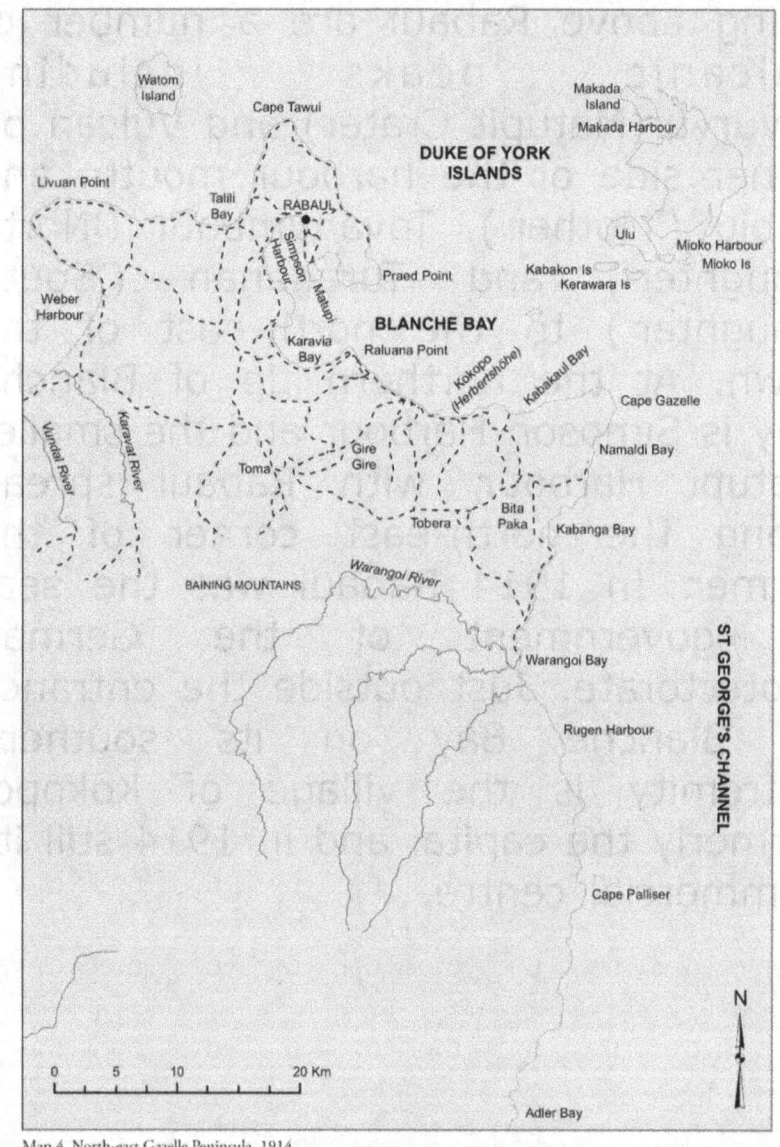

Map 4. North-east Gazelle Peninsula, 1914

On the afternoon of 11 August, in beautiful tropical weather, Patey's squadron ploughed north. Aboard *Australia*, Bandsman Arthur Bollard recorded:

[W]e are heading for Simpson Harbour New Britain: where the German ships *Scharnhorst* and *Gneisenau* are supposed to be in hiding ... Admiral Patey gave a speech to the ship's company in the forenoon, informing them, that he intended sending the *Sydney* and destroyers ahead to enter after dark *Simpsonhaven* and engage and draw the Germans out ... where *Australia* would be awaiting with her big guns. He said he had every confidence in the lads upholding the fighting honour of the ship.

In accordance with Patey's plan, *Australia* arrived off the Gazelle Peninsula that night but hung back, loitering in St George's Channel. *Sydney* took station guarding the entrance to the harbour, while the nimble, black-painted destroyers under Cumberlege slipped into the anchorage. Entering the wide bay, *Yarra* circled north while *Warrego* and *Parramatta* sailed west and then north along the coast. The crews expected battle and momentarily thought that the lights of Rabaul flashing between the trees were ship-to-shore signals and that the glow of a bushfire beyond the looming 'North Daughter' was a ship's searchlight hitting the land. For all the tension aboard the destroyers, the search failed to find any sign of the German squadron.

Their failure to locate Spee's squadron was in fact due to the inadequacy of contemporary intelligence gathering. The importance of information derived from intercepts of enemy radio communications was just beginning to be appreciated in 1914. As there was no specialised electronic warfare equipment, the leads derived from radio intercepts were often geographically inaccurate since they were calculated from positioning based on an estimate of the signal strength of the radio transmissions. Due to changes in atmospheric conditions and variations in signal power, these estimates could vary wildly. As Patey searched for Spee at Rabaul, the German squadron was actually 1400 kilometres further north at Pohnpei in the Carolines group.

The following day Patey's force was bolstered by the arrival of *Encounter* and *Melbourne.* Two small parties were landed from the destroyers and spent the day trying to locate the German wireless station. Offshore, *Encounter* captured the freighter *Zambezi,* a British vessel that had been commandeered by the German administrator on Nauru to carry dispatches and material for completing the undiscovered wireless station near Rabaul. *Zambezi* became the RAN's first wartime prize and, in forcing the freighter to heave-to by firing a round across the ship's bows, *Encounter* unleashed the first shot fired in anger by an RAN warship. Later that day *Australia* captured the enemy vessel *Sumatra.* In the meantime the landing parties searched Rabaul and Kokopo. Emerging empty handed, they had to be satisfied with destroying the local post office, telegraphic and telephone communications before re-embarking. Much later in the day Bandsman Bollard observed in his diary that 'we made a huge mistake by not destroying the town then and there, much further trouble would have been saved.' As the RAN dealt with Rabaul, Britain's other squadrons had not been idle. On the same day as Patey scoured Blanche Bay, Vice Admiral Sir Thomas Jerram's China Squadron put the German radio station at Yap out of action and severed the deep-sea cable to the island.

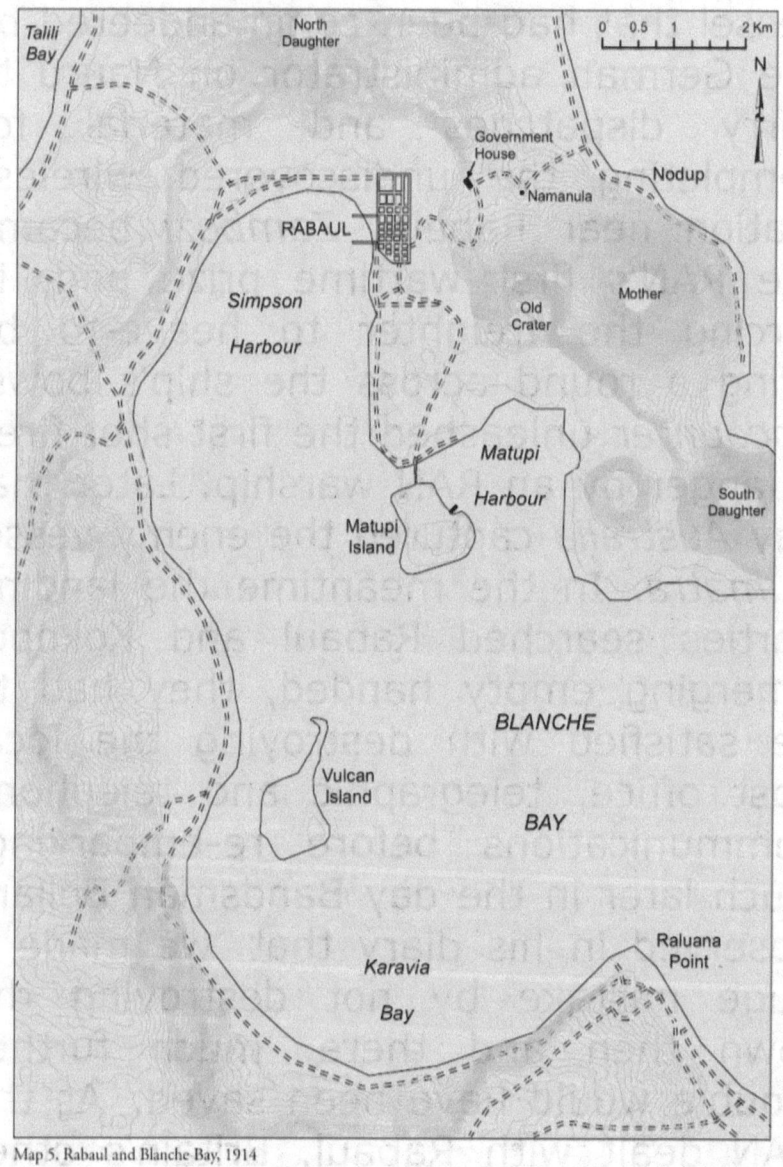

Map 5. Rabaul and Blanche Bay, 1914

Patey's lack of success was in part the result of the preparations completed by the Germans even before war was declared. On 1 August the Acting Governor issued a proclamation notifying the population of their liability to serve in case of war. Immediately following the declaration of war, the authorities mobilised in accordance with pre-war plans, despite the absence of Acting Governor Haber who was in Morobe on a tour of inspection of New Guinea. On 5 August an observation post was established on the summit of 'Mother' overlooking the seaward approaches to the capital. On 6 August an extra edition of the German New Guinea *Government Gazette* was published containing the announcement of war and mobilisation. The seat of government was transferred from Rabaul to the village of Toma, some 30 kilometres from Rabaul and around 12 kilometres inland from Kokopo. As part of the preparations the German treasury was transported inland and buried in several locations. Caches of supplies were also established at different places in the event of further withdrawals inland. On 7 August all British residents were arrested and their mail seized.

Having failed to find Spee or the German wireless station, Patey departed for Port Moresby on the afternoon of 12 August to coal *Australia* and *Encounter,* leaving the bulk of the squadron at Rossel Island in the Louisiades Archipelago off the south-east tip of New Guinea. Pondering his next move, he decided to take the squadron east towards Nauru. Before he could do this, however, on the afternoon of 16 August he received new instructions from the Admiralty directing him to Noumea where he was to rendezvous with and escort the New Zealand expedition bound for Samoa. Leaving Captain John Glossop of *Sydney* in command of the remainder of the squadron, Patey, with *Australia* and *Melbourne,* left on his new task.

HMAS Berrima, an 11,120-ton passenger liner requisitioned on the outbreak of war and re-commissioned as an RAN warship on 17 August. After delivering the ANMEF to New Guinea, Berrima joined the convoy carrying the first contingent of the AIF to Egypt and spent the rest of the war ferrying troops from and to Australia (AWM P09552.001).

Back in Sydney, just eight days after he was appointed to command of the ANMEF, Holmes' force was embarked. Following the outbreak of war, the P&O liner *Berrima* was chartered by the Commonwealth government for use as an auxiliary cruiser. Following the mounting of four 4.7-inch guns, the vessel was commissioned as an RAN warship and placed under the command of Captain John Stevenson, RN. With the formation of the ANMEF, *Berrima* was quickly reconfigured from an auxiliary cruiser to an armed transport.

One of the more remarkable achievements of the Naval Board in the opening months of the war was the rapid conversion of a large number of transports to carry Australian troops overseas. One of the first vessels to be converted was *Berrima*. As the ANMEF was assembling, workmen at the Cockatoo Island naval base worked feverishly to fit the vessel for its new role. The ship was well chosen for its task as the former liner was ideally suited for a troopship, with excellent speed and seagoing qualities, large holds providing fine troop decks, ample latrine and washing facilities and, though deck space was limited, it was sufficient for the exercise of troops. Significantly, a liberal supply of fresh water was available and this was an important factor in the excellent health record achieved on the voyage north. Although some of its uniformed passengers would complain about conditions, *Berrima* easily fell within the parameters set by the Admiralty for a troopship. The recently published *Manual of Combined Naval and Military Operations: 1913* stipulated that a troopship undertaking a voyage of more than seven days should have a size equivalent of four tons for every soldier embarked. As *Berrima* weighed over 11,000 tons, it was technically almost twice the minimum deemed acceptable for a force the size of the ANMEF.

By the afternoon of 18 August, amid a flurry of activity as troops boarded and stores were stowed, the ANMEF was ready to go to war. While Holmes had hoped to sail that evening, a series of delays stymied his plan. As stores were still being loaded and the last punt was not due to leave the wharf until 4.00pm, Stevenson decided to move the departure time to the next morning. Later that evening Holmes was informed that he was not to leave until after the next day's mail train arrived from Melbourne, as it was carrying dispatches from Legge. The train was not due until around 10.00am. With sealed orders, *Berrima* finally sailed at 12.15pm on 19 August. Although the ship's departure was meant to be a secret, the liner received a rousing farewell as it made its way down the harbour. A number of pleasure craft accompanied the ship, passing ferries tooted their whistles and, from windows facing the harbour, sheets and towels fluttered their goodbyes. The transport cleared Sydney Heads at 1.00pm and steamed north in fine weather. Preparations and training continued aboard while the four newly mounted guns were test-fired to prove their mountings.

Once at sea Holmes opened his orders from Legge. These came in the form of a secret two-and-half page letter penned by Legge and dated 15 August 1914. The letter quoted the cablegram from the Colonial Secretary requesting Australian action 'to seize German wireless stations at Yap..., Nauru..., and New Guinea'. It also made explicit the limits of Holmes' authority as 'any territory now occupied must be at the disposal of the Imperial Government for purposes of an ultimate settlement at [the] conclusion of the war.' Legge's letter included a list of the forces available, including all naval assets, Australian and British.

It also provided limited intelligence on the strength of the German naval squadron and land forces and a brief description of where the wireless stations were reported to be situated. As this was a joint operation, Legge directed Holmes to 'act under the instructions of the Rear Admiral Commanding HMA Fleet, on land in the event of receiving no orders, or in an emergency, ... carry out the objects set out.'

While Legge has been accused by some historians of not providing sufficient detail in his orders for Holmes to execute his mission, this was not actually the case. In the first instance, Legge was not in a position to provide any further particulars, even had he wished, since Holmes was conducting the operation on behalf of the British government—in essence he was being subcontracted by Australia to Britain to complete an imperial task. This is why Legge's orders quoted the original cable sent to the Governor-General on 5 August, but not the 18 August cable as this arrived after he had despatched his orders to Holmes. Even so, Legge's letter complemented the British orders but did not supersede them. Hence Legge's letter, read in conjunction with the 18 August cable, confirmed Holmes' mission ('find and destroy all German wireless stations'), qualified his directed tasks ('British flag should be hoisted in all territories occupied . and suitable arrangements made for temporary administration'), and it confirmed his limitations ('No formal proclamation of annexation should . be made'). Within these parameters, the execution of the mission was left to Holmes with Legge advising that he should act 'in such manner as may seem best'.

Shipboard life aboard Berrima was a rude shock for many of the soldiers. A lack of privacy and amenities were the main irritants for the enlisted men who were accommodated in the lower decks. Life for the commissioned officers was considerably better as they travelled in the upper deck cabins. Information on the mission was closely controlled and, where there was a lack of information, rumour filled the void (AWM H12831).

The directions given to Holmes may have been short and sharp, but they contained much the same information today's soldiers would expect and understand. Legge provided some background information on the general situation, including the main geographic issues and a tally of available friendly and enemy forces. The letter provided an unambiguous mission, his specified tasks and the restrictions on his freedom of action. It concluded with the command arrangements for the expedition and the extent of his authority. This type of 'mission command' was common at the time since British doctrine (and by default Australian doctrine) stressed the importance of allowing the man on the spot to decide how best to achieve the mission without the directing superior being overly prescriptive. This reflected the British Army's long experience with colonial warfare in which every situation was potentially different, since the army was scattered around the globe where it faced multiple threats in diverse operational theatres. Today this type of decentralised command philosophy is once again endorsed by Commonwealth armies, although habitually the pedigree for the concept is traced to German mission-type tactics (*auftragstaktik*) rather than the British tradition. Holmes' orders were sufficient and in accordance with contemporary practice and he would have recognised them as such.

As *Berrima* ploughed north, all hands adjusted to life afloat and, although accommodated aboard a former liner, the experience was no holiday cruise for those forced to live cheek by jowl. Perceptions of conditions aboard the transport varied widely depending on rank and service. For officers such as Brian Pockley, the view from his private cabin was of a 'Fine ship and very comfortable.' Below decks, life was less salubrious, as Private Conrad Eitel recorded in a letter published in the *Sydney Morning Herald*:

What a revelation life on a troopship provides for the kid-gloved youngster who in a wild burst of patriotism enlists ... First of all when he boarded the troopship he was ushered down into the 'tween decks, where there were rows upon rows of white pine tables. A seat at one of these long tables was allotted to him, also a small place in which to stow his marching kit, rifle, and kit-bag. He considers where on earth he is going to sleep. But after supper each man has a canvas hammock served out to him, and soon the low space of the 'tween decks is filled with hammocks swung so closely together that if a man fell out of his hammock he would fall into another ... Five hundred men cooped up in a confined space make it pretty murky, especially when the dining-room and the bedroom are one and the same.

Even members of the Naval Battalion observed the more obvious differences 'tween decks. Able Seaman Angus Worthington recorded in his diary:

The routine on the *Berrima* was easy but, at times, a trifle irksome—one of the disabilities of routine. A little stimulant on occasion would have proved acceptable, but the rank and file were debarred from this. It was different with the officers. They had but to press a button in bar or saloon, sign a slip, and their wants were supplied. This and other privileges enjoyed by them made the moral clear: be an officer.

Such close living and the inherent differences between the ranks and two services had the potential to cause problems.

Navies and armies are designed to operate in very different environments. Navies are shaped by the confines of shipboard life and the necessities of managing major warships afloat. Army culture is rooted in the complexities of land operations and the demands of officer-soldier relations under dispersed conditions. The vastly different circumstances each service faces give rise to peculiar service organisational cultures. These cultures are deeply rooted, often difficult to fathom for outsiders, and a potential source of friction in a joint organisation such as the ANMEF. While sailors traditionally go to war in ships and all members of a crew share a common fate under the direction of the ship's captain, soldiers serve in more abstract organisations that are not bound by the same physical restrictions. These extant environmental differences were further exacerbated in the ANMEF by the origins and development of the two indigenous services. The Australian Army was created following Federation, but had deep roots in the local soil and many of its militia units could trace their lineage back to the earliest days of European settlement with the first formation of local volunteer organisations. Later these organisations provided the bulk of the volunteers who served in the Sudan in 1885 and the much larger body that volunteered for South Africa. These soldiers were staunchly territorial citizen-soldiers. In 1914 the bulk of Australia's army, commissioned and enlisted, still comprised part-time militiamen who, for the most part, were native-born.

Although the CNF was also formed following Federation, the diverse collection of leftover colonial vessels hardly constituted a navy. In July 1911 the CNF was retitled the RAN, but it was not until 1913 that the Commonwealth acquired a fleet worthy of the name. This new force mostly served full-time—it could hardly be otherwise since running large and very expensive warships is not a job for amateurs. Hence the early RAN was moulded and led for the most part by professional RN officers, with 850 of the RAN's 3800 personnel boasting an RN background. Indeed the RAN in 1914 was little more than a splinter of the RN. Officers such as Patey and his captains insisted on establishing a disciplinary regime which echoed that of Britain's senior service. Even those British loan officers who joined the RAN adhered to British naval customs and procedures. No allowance was made for the natural differences between British and Australian practice, even though many of the RAN's newer officers were

Royal Naval Reserve (RNR) transferees or older CNF officers who began their careers in the merchant marine. Nor was there any concession to Australian patterns of behaviour which were rooted in different social conditions and a relatively egalitarian society. If the native-born who joined the fledgling service expected to be treated differently to long-serving British 'Jack Tars' beside whom they worked, they received a rude shock. As naval historian Robert Hyslop has described, the RAN in this era was United Kingdom-British rather than Australian-British.

Aboard *Berrima* conflict was even more likely to arise between the naval and military components. Once aboard the transport, naval brigade officers were thrust into an unfamiliar army chain of command and it was here that the service differences were most pronounced. Superficially, both organisations looked similar and replicated standard hierarchical military command structures. Both services divided their personnel into three categories: commissioned officers, warrant officers and the enlisted—ratings in the navy and other ranks (ORs) in the army. Navy and army commissioned officers both held a 'commission' from the King which empowered the holder to issue orders and granted him legal authority over subordinates. Both services also maintained gradations of officers without a commission including warrant and non-commissioned officers.

The most senior sailors and soldiers were appointed by 'warrant'. Army warrant officers were issued a royal warrant from the King while navy chief petty officers were issued a naval warrant by the Admiralty. This minor discrepancy made no difference to their authority over the lower ranks. The senior soldier in an army unit—the Regimental Sergeant Major—was an almost god-like figure who commanded respect and was held in awe by soldiers and even junior officers. Similarly, below decks, the chief petty officers were long-serving, highly experienced experts who ran ships' departments on behalf of the divisional officers. Discipline within a ship or an army unit was in large part managed by the warrants.

Answering to and acting on behalf of the senior sailors and soldiers were the various grades of NCO. Below them at the bottom of the chain of command were the non-ranked sailors and soldiers who comprised the bulk of both services. But if the power structures of both services approximated each other, their disciplinary codes certainly did not.

Superficially, discipline within the two services was analogous; in practice they were profoundly different. The RN and the British Army had both long been noted for their strictness and almost draconian discipline. These traits were transferred to their early Australian siblings. Under Section 36 of the Australian *Naval Defence Act 1910,* the provisions of the British Naval Discipline Act were applied to the RAN without caveat. The Australian Army, at least while on active service, was similarly subject to the British Army Act. The only exception was that Australia had modified the application of the Army Act for its forces to meet local requirements. Hence, under the *Defence Act 1903* (Section 98):

No member of the Defence Force shall be sentenced to death by any court-martial except for mutiny, desertion to the enemy, or traitorously delivering up to the enemy any garrison, fortress, post, guard, or ship, vessel, or boat, or traitorous correspondence with the enemy; and no sentence passed by any court-martial shall be carried into effect until confirmed by the Governor-General.

Similarities can be misleading however, and though both services maintained comparable structures and operated within comparable legislative frameworks, they operated in distinctly different ways because of their operating environments and the way their disciplinary models had been shaped by local conditions. The RAN inherited a particularly strong tradition of rank relations 'between decks' and this was only sharpened by the transfer of officers and petty officers from the RN to the RAN.

For its part, the army maintained similarly formal divisions between personnel, though in practice there was significant variation in the way the system was perpetuated. Most of Holmes' army officers were appointed from those who already held commissions in the part-time forces. In the pre-1912 volunteer and militia forces, officers were drawn from the professional classes much like their naval counterparts, although few army officers served full-time. High-ranking militia officers were most often businessmen, bank managers, public servants or pastoralists because they had the money, education and time to pursue their hobbies and philanthropic pursuits, which included part-time military service. Junior officers usually held relatively well paid sedentary jobs in the public service, insurance or law. With the introduction of universal service in 1912 matters changed little and officers continued to be drawn from the 'white collar' middle class while the soldiery were mostly 'blue collar' urban working class.

Lieutenants Arthur Cooper (left) and John Maughan (right). These two officers are typical of the ANMEF's regimental officers; both had prior commissioned service with the militia and, while 23-year-old Cooper was a clerk, Maughan was a 36-year-old solicitor with a bachelor's degree from Oxford University (AWM H12830).

In the old volunteer units, discipline, such as it was, was generally easy and consensual because it was shaped by an environment of self-restraint and dignity and underscored by the volunteer's status as a citizen-soldier. Officers earned respect for their good judgement, social standing and ability to command men without talking down to them or falling back on punishments which in any case were usually impossible to enforce. Trouble most often began when officers coupled autocratic airs with a lack of ability to command. The post-1912 compulsory militia maintained a similar regime since it too was based on weekly drills and yearly encampments with an officer corps that was part time and middle class. At their first camps at the end of 1912 and the beginning of 1913 the Melbourne *Argus* praised the high attendance by Victorian trainees but lamented that many new officers had been unable to teach or even control their men, concluding that 'there promises to be difficulties in the way of securing young men who fully appreciate the [officers'] responsibilities without arrogance.' Other, more worrying problems emerged in camps at Liverpool near Sydney where newly commissioned junior offices proved incapable of controlling their troops.

The two component battalions of the ANMEF inherited their character and culture from their respective services. The Naval Battalion's model was the

RN, while the army battalion's was the Australian militia. In Beresford's battalion there was a strict maintenance of rank formality, rigid discipline, leadership that demanded instant obedience and heavy punishment for transgressions. In Watson's battalion it was more earned respect over formality, discipline that was more carrot than stick, leadership that did not presume deference, and the use of formal punishment as the option of last resort.

However the primary difference between the two battalions was to be found between the naval wardroom and army officers' mess. Whereas few naval officers had served as ratings, most junior army officers had spent some time in the ranks before being commissioned. Although the brevity of the campaign would allow limited opportunities for advancement, a significant number of soldiers and NCOs who served in the islands were later commissioned in the AIF. This group included Sergeant (later Major) Alan Anderson and Colour Sergeant (later Major) Harold Johnson, who were among the handful of ANMEF soldiers commissioned while still serving in New Guinea; Private (later Lieutenant) John Axtens; and Sergeant (later Captain) John Leadbeater and Regimental Sergeant Major (later Major) Inglis who were both ex-British Army regulars. Such a situation would have been anathema to RN officers.

Despite its internal diversity, the ANMEF does not appear to have suffered any significant breakdown or fissures between its components. This stems from two considerations that militated against inter-service friction. First, the senior officers of both services appear to have behaved maturely and professionally. It began with Holmes and Stevenson. The army commander was fortunate to have such an experienced officer appointed as his naval adviser. The 38-year-old Stevenson entered the navy from the Royal Naval College, HMS *Britannia*, as a midshipman in 1892. After two decades of service he joined the RAN in July 1912, first as a commander, then as acting captain and, from January 1913, he was CO *Encounter*. In 1914 he was appointed to command *Berrima* with the additional responsibility of Naval Chief of Staff ANMEF. He was a fortuitous choice as his *Australian Dictionary of Biography* entry makes clear, describing him as 'well-spoken and of a retiring disposition ... he cloaked a sense of humour beneath a formal personality that earned him the nickname "Stiffy Steve".' His advice to Holmes was crucial in ensuring the brigade settled in smoothly to the unfamiliar routine of life aboard a warship. A similar relationship appears to have prevailed later between Patey and Holmes. Importantly, the senior officers of the task force set the tone, not the lower ranks. The smooth atmosphere within the ANMEF is all the more surprising given the need to mix groups in some of the task-oriented, ad hoc organisations that served ashore. Typically this occurred in the allocation of army machine-guns and medical support to the naval landing parties and the naval field guns to support army columns. Fortunately, professionalism at the senior levels and limited cross-attachments at the lower levels effectively minimised day-to-day opportunities for disruption. When criticism was levelled, it was more often based on personality than service.

The collier SS Koolonga, one of three such vessels that supported Patey's squadron during the New Guinea campaign (SLV H91.108/429).

An expedition of the size of the ANMEF required substantial logistics support and, given the distance from Australian territory, it all had to be carried afloat. It was fortunate that, at the time, the RAN was funded to maintain mobilisation stores that could be quickly loaded, bringing the warships of the fleet up to war standard soon after war precautions were advised. In addition to the individual ships' stores, Patey's squadron included five support vessels to keep the fleet fuelled and provisioned. These ships were all merchantmen taken up from trade and chartered by the Australian government. They included four colliers (SS *Kaituna, Koolonga, Waihora* and *Whangape*) catering for the larger coal-fired warships, two oil tankers (SS *Murex* and *Telena*) for the oil-burning destroyers and submarines and a fleet supply ship (SS *Aorangi*).

SS Aorangi, the fleet supply ship, a 4163-ton former Union Steamship Company cargo vessel chartered by the Commonwealth in August 1914. Unlike Berrima, Aorangi was not commissioned as an RAN ship; rather the vessel continued to be manned by a civilian crew although the men were subject to naval discipline (AWM 300181).

Aside from fuel to feed the ships, the Australian expedition required substantial supplies to sustain its personnel afloat and ashore. To cater for the other natures of supply, the expedition was supported by SS *Aorangi*. Quickly converted with the addition of magazines and shell rooms, the former cargo vessel became the fleet supply ship, carrying foodstuffs, ammunition and general stores. In *Aorangi*'s holds were provisions for 2400 men for 60 days. Other vessels also carried various quantities of supplies. For example, *Berrima* held provisions for 1700 men for 60 days' ship's service and an additional 90 days' shore service. *Berrima*'s supplies were further topped up at Palm Island where a consignment of 32,000 kilograms of frozen mutton was taken aboard.

SS Grantala following conversion to Hospital Ship No VIII. An Adelaide Steamship Company vessel, Grantala was converted in August 1914 to act as fleet hospital ship (AWM EN0406).

To cater for the inevitable casualties, the fleet was supported by a fully equipped hospital ship—SS *Grantala*. Built in Britain in 1903, *Grantala* was a passenger vessel employed in coastal trade between Sydney and Queensland ports, but its inclusion in Patey's squadron was no last-minute decision. Admiralty pre-war planning included a scheme under which merchant ships were to be commissioned and fitted out as hospital ships at various ports throughout the Empire in the event of mobilisation. Sydney was one of the identified ports and its hospital ship was earmarked to support British naval operations in the Pacific. Material for the ship was stored at Garden Island Naval Base in Sydney and transferred to the RAN in July 1913. This material included iron swing cots, blankets, sheets, hospital crockery, drugs, dressings and a complete hospital laundry. In accordance with these plans, *Grantala* was requisitioned on 7 August and fitted out in just three weeks. After conversion, Hospital Ship VIII could accommodate 180 patients, with capacity to boost this number to 300 casualties in an emergency. The ship boasted a modern operating ward, a bacteriological laboratory, x-ray studio, a laundry with a steam disinfector and steriliser, and even a small mortuary. The PMO was Acting Fleet Surgeon William Horsfall, RN. Horsfall's staff included six surgeons, an anaesthetist, a pathologist and a radiographer. The nursing staff included seven female nurses—one matron and six sisters—who were recruited from the Royal Prince Alfred Hospital in Sydney. Given the absence of a full-time military nursing service, the sisters were required to purchase their uniforms, a procedure made more difficult since they were given no indication as to their likely destination. Half an hour after leaving Sydney they were advised that the first port of call was to be Townsville. In accordance with the 1907 Hague Convention, *Grantala* was repainted white with a green horizontal band along the length of the hull and large crosses displayed on both sides. The extensive refurbishment meant that the hospital ship was not ready to accompany *Berrima* when the ANMEF departed Sydney. Eventually *Grantala* departed Townsville on 8 September, arriving off Rabaul five days later.

Medical staff aboard Hospital Ship VIII. Back row: none identified. Middle row (left to right): Dr A.J. Trinca, unidentified, Chief Petty Officer J. Gregg, unidentified, unidentified, Matron Sarah De Mestre, unidentified, Chief Petty Officer A. Wilson, unidentified, unidentified, Chaplain Charles Henderson. Front row: unidentified, Sister Stella Lillian Colless, Sister Florence McMillan, Sister Constance Neale, Surgeon William Horsfall, RN, Sister Rachel Clouston, Sister Rosa Kirkcaldie, Sister Bertha Burtinshaw, unidentified (AWM 302802).

After *Berrima* left Sydney there was a certain amount of rearranging of the mass of stores hastily stowed before departure. This task was supervised by quartermasters Bede Goadby and Sydney Goodsell who checked all stores against requisitions. During this process it was discovered that mess tins for the troops had not been loaded, so when the *Berrima* reached Moreton Bay off Brisbane on 21 August, Holmes sent a message to the Commandant of the 1st Military District via the Navy Office in Brisbane requesting 1043 mess tins. After an exchange of signals through naval and military channels, Holmes was eventually provided with pannikins and plates as the requisite army mess tins were unavailable. Another potentially more serious deficiency was signalling equipment. Requested on 21 August, the stores were sent from Melbourne to Sydney by express train five days later and were supposed to have been loaded on *Aorangi*. But when *Aorangi* arrived at Palm Island on 30 August the equipment was not on board, as it had been mistakenly placed in the ordnance store in Brisbane instead of being loaded aboard the supply vessel. Arrangements were then made for the equipment to follow on the next available ship. Even more serious was a missing box of machine-gun spare parts. Initial suspicions pointed to sabotage and guards were quickly placed on the ANMEF's stores. Further checks revealed a less sinister cause when the box was located and it was discovered that it had simply been misplaced during the frenzied loading and cross-checking.

ANMEF personnel wading through the waters of Palm Island. The force had less than two weeks' training in the tropics before it was committed to its first battle (AWM P03078.003).

From Moreton Bay, *Berrima* proceeded along the Queensland coast to Palm Island near Townsville. Soon after leaving, the transport was joined by *Sydney* and, waiting at Palm Island, was *Encounter.* Patey ordered a pause while he completed the Samoan mission. Although unwelcome, the enforced delay provided the opportunity for some further training and a landing rehearsal was conducted on 24 August with B and C companies, three companies of the Naval Battalion, the two machine-gun sections and a medical detachment. The landing force was taken ashore and launched a mock attack in the thick, tropical bush country. Afterwards the men re-embarked and were back on *Berrima* by 6.00pm. Further practice landings were conducted on five of the next seven days.

Patey's fleet had no specialised landing craft or amphibious equipment and the ANMEF's troops were ferried to shore in ships' boats in a manner similar to that later employed at the Gallipoli landing at Anzac Cove on 25 April 1915. This photograph is of elements of Watson's battalion landing at Kokopo (SPC-A).

As occurred with the later Gallipoli landings, no specialised amphibious landing equipment was available so the sailors improvised. Tows were employed with 14 open lifeboats divided into two strings of seven, one pulled by a steam cutter from *Encounter* and the other by a launch from *Berrima*. Importantly for the landlubbers of the army battalion, the daily trips to and from the island provided an opportunity to practise getting into and out of the oared lifeboats that were to take them across a possibly hostile shore. To assist during the early exercises the boats carrying the army companies were manned by a bowman and coxswain from the Naval Battalion.

It was on Palm Island that Holmes was particularly struck by just how differently his Naval Battalion managed affairs. During the training ashore the naval officers habitually remained apart from the ratings, delegating most of the training tasks to the petty officers who took charge of the work. Such conduct appeared alien to Holmes who observed that his junior army officers were more closely involved in the men's training. Despite this, it was noted by observers that, other than some good-tempered, if keen, rivalry, service differences appear to have caused little friction.

Once ashore on the tropical island both naval and military officers had to adjust to the unfamiliar conditions by adapting the doctrine on which they had been trained. Australian doctrine and training at this time was derived wholly from British sources and practice since the dominions had by agreement adopted British doctrine, equipment and weapons to ensure that diverse imperial contingents could operate together in the event of war. Although the Australian defence forces had adapted some practices to meet local conditions, especially in light of the South African War experience, for the most part Australian troops trained in much the same way as part-time British Territorials.

The relevant British doctrine for the ANMEF was enshrined in the 1911 manual *Infantry Training*. This manual provided a handy reference for company and battalion drill and general guidance on conducting tactical operations in the field. In terms of tactics it stressed fire and manoeuvre to close with the enemy, followed by a decisive final shock delivered at bayonet point. This was seen as the key to solving the problem of infantry attacking into the face of the lethal fire generated by magazine-fed rifles and machineguns. The problem for the Australian Army was that these tactics were tailored to long-serving regulars and the one thing Holmes lacked more than anything else was time. Furthermore, there was only limited advice on fighting in 'close country' or jungle, other than noting the obvious problem of restricted visibility and movement which demanded more initiative from subordinates. Perceptively, the manuals' authors observed that: 'Troops fighting in close country are usually very sensitive as to their flanks, as they are unable to see what is going on. This fact affects the defence more than the attack, for there is danger that a defended line penetrated at one point may give way everywhere.' In an attack it was recognised that: 'Close country enables the attacker to approach his enemy with less loss than is usually experienced in more open ground ... [but] special care is ... necessary if the direction of the attack is to be preserved.'

Machine-gun crews conducting live-fire training on Palm Island. While the machine-gunners and the riflemen of the two battalions all received much-needed additional instruction and field firing during the pause, firing practice was limited to just five rounds per rifle to conduct a grouping practice and 200 rounds per machine-gun (AWM H12841).

In addition to practising manoeuvre in close country, Holmes put his Brigade Major to work improving marksmanship. After the short sojourn at Palm Island, Holmes wrote to Legge on 9 September explaining that his troops:

...received most valuable individual instruction in musketry under the personal direction of Major Heritage and Lieutenant Marsden, who is on the Staff of the School of Musketry ... I established a short range on shore which answered all purposes admirably ... The men have got quite handy and expert with the rifle, including both soldiers and sailors, the latter were very green at first but are now splendid.

Frederick Burnell, the expedition's embedded journalist, later claimed that the brief stopover allowed the force to attain 'a degree of competency and training [of] which any army in the world might feel proud.' Less effusive, the Adjutant 1st Battalion, Captain Cyril Lane, observed of the musketry training on Palm Island: 'Have been carrying out desultory rifle firing. Result rotten, lots of us have never handled a rifle before.' On the other hand, the *Official History* noted that the force was 'taken ashore nearly every day, across a shingle beach to rocky ground and bush—a terrain ill-suited to manoeuvres: but it taught them how to maintain touch in thickly-wooded country, and the lesson afterwards proved invaluable in the dense jungles of New Britain.'

The shift to the tropics also exposed Holmes' force to a more debilitating climate as his men had mostly come from a southern, temperate spring into the build-up to a northern 'wet season'. It was here that Holmes began to fully appreciate the worth of his medical staff. Writing to Legge he confessed, 'L[ieutenan]t-Colonel Howse and the three other doctors, particularly Captain McGuire [sic], have amply justified their selection ... The whole of the men were inoculated against typhoid and on board ship they have been done a second time, also the whole of the Naval portion of the Contingent.' The health of the force would remain remarkably good, at least until the onset of the wet season, and much of the credit for this state of affairs belongs to Howse.

On 30 August, the day Samoa was occupied by the New Zealanders without a shot being fired, Patey sent instructions to Glossop ordering him to bring the convoy to Rossel Island on 9

September. Accordingly, *Sydney, Encounter, Berrima, Aorangi,* the submarine tenders *Protector* and *Upolu,* along with *AE1* and *AE2,* sailed for Port Moresby on 2 September, arriving three days later. There Holmes found SS *Kanowna* with four companies of volunteers from north Queensland who Legge had previously advised him were to form the second army battalion for his brigade.

On 4 August, in a precautionary act in case war broke out, the Commonwealth government issued a proclamation initiating a partial mobilisation of various militia units across Australia. On the evening of 6 August, militiamen around Australia received telegrams ordering them to report for duty at 9.00am the following day. In accordance with prearranged plans in far north Queensland, part-time members of the Australian Garrison Artillery and the 2nd Infantry (Kennedy Regiment) were called out. The artillerymen were to supplement the small permanent garrisons manning the fixed fortifications and batteries that protected strategic points around the

Australian coast. The infantrymen of the 2nd Infantry were to guard against landing parties from Germany's prowling warships.

SS Kanowna. The troubled transport departed Townsville on 8 August 1914 bound for Thursday Island and later carried the 2nd Battalion ANMEF to Port Moresby (NAA J2879 QTH544).

The regimental title of the 'Kennedy Regiment' derived from the unit's recruiting area which was explored by Edmund Kennedy in the nineteenth century. This area covered the Townsville and Atherton districts stretching from Cairns in the north to Mackay in the south. In 1912, with the introduction of the Universal Training Scheme, the previous local militia unit (1st Battalion, Kennedy Regiment) was expanded and redesignated the 2nd Infantry (Kennedy Regiment).

In addition to the active militia, members of various rifle clubs were also called up. Rifle clubs had a long history in Australia and were linked to the early volunteer movement of the nineteenth century. In 1914, although they consisted of non-uniformed and unpaid personnel, their members were provided with ammunition by the military authorities so they could conduct small arms training. They were considered part of the army's reserve, although technically they were not soldiers. Answering the call, men from Mackay, Bowen, Ravenswood, Charters Towers and Townsville concentrated at Townsville, while those from further north gathered at Cairns. Advised that they were to provide the wartime garrison at the Green Hill Fort and Milman Hill on Thursday Island in the Torres Strait, the soldiers and rifle club members had little time to prepare before they embarked.

The Kennedy men march through the streets of Cairns. This photograph, probably taken on 9 August 1914, shows mobilised militiamen of the 2nd Infantry (Kennedy Regiment) on their way to board SS Kanowna. They are dressed in the Universal Training Pattern uniform and are led by the unit band (NAA J2879 QTH534).

Their transport was equally unprepared for the task ahead. SS *Kanowna* was a 6942-ton coastal steamer belonging to the Australian United Steamship Navigation Company and commanded by Captain J. Ward. Chartered by the government, *Kanowna* was to transport the troops to Thursday Island. The ship departed Townsville on 8 August to a rousing farewell and collected the Cairns contingent on the way. At Thursday Island the regiment, now swelled to more than 1000 strong, settled in before, just a few days later, volunteers were called to make up a second ANMEF army battalion. More than 400 men signed on.

The formation of the 2nd Battalion was even more haphazard and ad hoc than the 1st Battalion. One of the volunteers, Driver Bernard Cripps, recorded in his diary how he came to be part of the force:

> Troops mobilised at Townsville 4 Aug. 1914. Members of rifle clubs and those who volunteered came in at all times.
>
> 7 August: Received orders to leave by the SS *Kanowna* for Thursday Island.
>
> 8 August: Busy all morning loading troop ship with stores. Had a few minutes talk with Jan [female friend]. Ship left wharf about 12 o'clock midst the most enthusiastic farewell that Townsville had ever seen.
>
> 14 August: The troops issued with ball cartridges last night ready for an attack which was expected from the Germans.

15 August: About 11 o'clock tonight the Captain came and told us that 4 volunteers were wanted to join the expeditionary force to go on the Pacific Ocean. Company Serg[eant] Major Collum, Drivers Johnstone, Graham [and Cripps] volunteered at 2 minutes to 12 o'clock. We signed an oath of allegiance, as we were to be under the Imperial authorities. We then went and had a light supper and toasted good wishes to the Force.

Of the Queensland volunteers, around one third were militia trainees with the remainder drawn from various rifle clubs. The force was told off into four improvised companies as *Kanowna* sailed to Port Moresby where one company was landed to provide protection for the local wireless station.

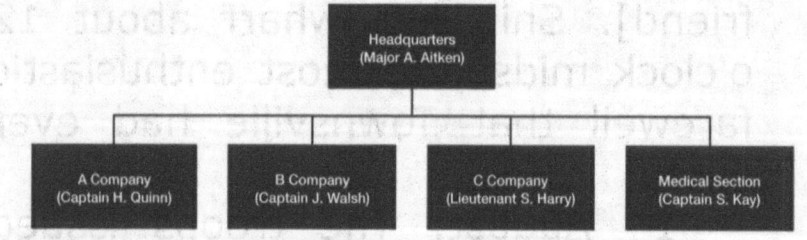

Chart 4. 2nd Battalion ANMEF, September 1914

Although the reinforcement should have been a welcome boost, Holmes had already formed a negative opinion of the Queenslanders even before laying eyes on them. The battalion was commanded by Major Arthur Aitken who Holmes considered had little military training or experience and was, apparently, not sufficiently self-reliant, although he seems to have done a reasonable job organising his volunteers and getting them to Papua. Furthermore, according to Holmes, there were just two captains who had eight and six years' part-time service while the other 10 junior officers were all young and inexperienced. To make matters worse there were no battalion staff, with Captain Hugh Quinn acting as Adjutant in addition to his responsibilities as a company commander. To relieve Quinn, Second Lieutenant Walter Fry from Watson's battalion was appointed Adjutant with the acting rank of captain. There was one regular staff sergeant major, George King, a British-born regular soldier who had served 21 years with the British Army before joining the

Australian Permanent Forces and, by the end of the war, would be a major in the AIF. Although Holmes claimed that no other NCOs had been appointed, this does not appear to be true and there seems to have been a rank structure and company organisation in place. While the battalion had its own Regimental Medical Officer, Captain Stuart Kay, Howse was sent aboard to inspect and report on the men's condition. He advised that the men were in good health and there had been no serious cases of sickness since leaving Thursday Island. However he noted that some of the men had ailments that rendered them unfit for active service while others were aged under 18, despite instructions that no 'boy soldiers' were to be embarked. A naval officer recalled that they 'were to say the least a somewhat raw crowd'.

The rag-tag battalion was equally unprepared for campaigning, although that was hardly the men's fault given the speed with which they had been mobilised. The troops had been issued with only one uniform, which they had been wearing for five weeks. Some 400 suits of dungarees were subsequently procured for them in Port Moresby. Some of the men had new or ill-fitting boots, while others were wearing non-issue boots, often in a poor state of repair. They had no tents or mosquito nets, but they had been issued 500 rounds of ammunition per man. They also had some signalling equipment—two lamps, two heliographs, two telescopes and three message bags—which Holmes promptly grabbed to offset his shortfall. *Kanowna* also carried provisions for 10 days' ship's service and an additional 30 days' shore service.

While there is no doubt that most of the Kennedy men were not seasoned soldiers and had been inadequately prepared, in fairness they were probably not much worse than Holmes' 1st Battalion. For all Holmes' claims about his force and Burnell's journalistic hyperbole, most of Watson's soldiers and their officers were just as inexperienced.

Captain (later Major) Hugh Quinn. The young militia officer is shown here dressed in the uniform of the 2nd Infantry (Kennedy Regiment). Quinn was a 26-year-old public accountant and auditor prior to being appointed a captain in the 2nd Battalion ANMEF. While his participation in the New Guinea campaign was short-lived, he returned to Australia and volunteered for the AIF, joining the 15th Battalion of Colonel John Monash's 4th Infantry Brigade. He landed on Gallipoli late on the afternoon of 25 April 1915 and in subsequent weeks defended the Australian beachhead. He established the post that was subsequently named in his honour before he was killed in action on 29 May (AWM H17225).

It appears that the New South Welshman Holmes was very quick to form an overwhelmingly negative opinion of the Queenslanders. In his 'Appreciation of the Situation' (see Appendix 5) completed on 1 September, Holmes made it clear that he had little interest in this unwanted reinforcement. The two captains Holmes dismissed happened to be Hugh Quinn and John Walsh. Quinn, a north Queensland boxing champion, had six years' commissioned service in the militia and would later serve with distinction on Gallipoli where he gave his name to the famous post he commanded before his death. John Walsh was another officer with considerable potential; he too would be serving as a major when he was killed within days of the Gallipoli landings. Among the other junior officers was Second Lieutenant Hutton Armstrong who, at 23, was young, but already had four years' service with the Australian Garrison Artillery where he rose to company sergeant major before he was commissioned with the 2nd Infantry. He had also been a member of the Townsville Rifle Club for more than two years and was a member of the Bisley Rifle Team in 1913.

Based on these examples it would appear that some of the Kennedy officers were at least as capable as their 1st Battalion counterparts, which calls into question Holmes' pessimistic judgement. Perhaps he felt he had no need of reinforcement or perhaps he simply did not trust the mixed force of militiamen and rifle club members. Perhaps he was reluctant to share any glory with a group of officers he had not selected or perhaps it was simply old-fashioned parochialism.

On 6 September Aitken's extemporised unit formally joined Holmes as the 2nd Battalion ANMEF. Holmes now had to decide what to do with his unwelcome reinforcements. At first he considered leaving the protection company at Port Moresby where it had already landed—until the Lieutenant Governor of Papua, Judge Hubert Murray, advised him that he had already organised his own body of local troops for the purpose. Holmes' next thought was to send the men home, but that decision was not his to make since

Patey was in overall command of the expedition and the admiral was reluctant to lose the additional contingent. For the time being, the Kennedy men would stay.

With the ANMEF now swelled to more than 2000 all ranks, the joint task force sailed from Port Moresby on 7 September. Glossop remained in temporary command with *Sydney*, *Encounter*, the destroyers *Warrego* and *Yarra*, the two submarines, *Berrima*, *Kanowna*, and *Aorangi*. The destroyer *Parramatta* was to follow, escorting the slower oiler *Murex* and collier *Koolonga*. The convoy steamed east towards its rendezvous for several hours until *Kanowna* suddenly slowed and hoisted a signal indicating that the vessel was out of control. It transpired that the 'firemen' or stokers aboard the ship, who were all merchant seamen, had not been consulted about their new mission and had refused to stoke the ship. The *Official History* labels the action a 'mutiny' and, although technically it was, like other similar incidents early in the war, it was, in reality, a workers' strike. *Kanowna* was a coastal steamer which had been conducting its normal coastal work when war broke out. Requisitioned by the government, the ship had only just changed crews at Townsville when it was commandeered to transport the Kennedy men to Thursday Island. With the formation of the 2nd Battalion, the ship was then despatched to Port Moresby. All this occurred at short notice and with little information passed to the crew. Ships of *Kanowna*'s class were designed for short-hop, coastal tasks and their crews were engaged for this type of work. The civilian seamen were certainly not naval men who signed on for long service with the expectation of extended absences from their home port and families. No matter how the incident is labelled, *Kanowna* was now a handicap rather than an asset.

As the ship lay dead in the water, volunteers among the troops took the place of the strikers. Hurried consultation between Glossop and Holmes saw quick agreement that *Kanowna* should be sent home. The circumstances and their recommendation were relayed to Patey by wireless and he concurred. The ship returned to Townsville, stoked by the troops, and the force was disbanded. *Kanowna* too was returned to her owners before being resumed in June 1915. Thereafter she remained in military service as a hospital ship and troop transport for the rest of the war.

The rendezvous of the Australian Squadron off Rossel Island on 9 September 1914. The conference aboard Australia was the first opportunity for Patey and Holmes to discuss their task face-to-face. This photograph, taken from Encounter, shows (left to right): Sydney (partially obscured), Berrima, Aorangi and Australia (partially obscured) (AWM H12595).

Patey, with *Australia* and the colliers *Waihora* and *Whangape,* rendezvoused as planned with Glossop on 9 September. Patey's command now represented almost the entire fighting strength of the RAN. If it possessed one significant deficiency, it was the lack of dedicated mine warfare vessels. If the Germans deployed mines in the sheltered waters of Simpson Harbour these would have to be swept as best they could by picket boats from *Australia,* a risky undertaking for any unarmoured vessel. The difficulties of such a task could not be dismissed as the Allies would soon discover when the British and French fleets attempted to force the Dardanelles in March 1915. Only in 1917, in response to the sinking of three merchant ships by German-laid mines in home waters, did the RAN form a minesweeping squadron.

After leaving Samoa, Patey had temporarily detached *Melbourne* on a preliminary operation to destroy the German radio station at Nauru. The RAN warship reported on 9 September that the station had been disabled by its staff and the island surrendered without opposition. As *Melbourne* completed its task, the fleet and ANMEF commanders had their first opportunity to discuss the task ahead face-to-face.

At Rossel Island Patey convened a meeting aboard *Australia* with Holmes, Glossop and Stevenson in what was Australia's first high-level joint conference on active service. The Admiral explained to the assembled officers that his orders provided for the occupation and garrisoning of Kokopo and Rabaul, which he aimed to effect on 11 September. He also made it clear that he expected the landings to be a repeat of his August affair and he did not anticipate any resistance ashore.

Holmes then briefed the Admiral and others on his plan of occupation, which was likewise based on a belief that there would be no German resistance. His intention was to employ Watson's battalion to garrison Rabaul, leaving Kokopo to Beresford and the Naval Battalion. As a preliminary operation to the main landings, two small naval parties were to be put ashore to search for the two suspected radio stations, one six kilometres inland from Kokopo and the other eight kilometres inland from Kabakaul, a small village seven kilometres east of Kokopo. Neither commander really knew what the men might face ashore because there was little hard intelligence on their objective, aside from recent information collected at Port Moresby on the disposition of the suspected radio sites. As the Australian *Official History* suggests, part of German New Guinea's defence in 1914 was its 'unknownness'.

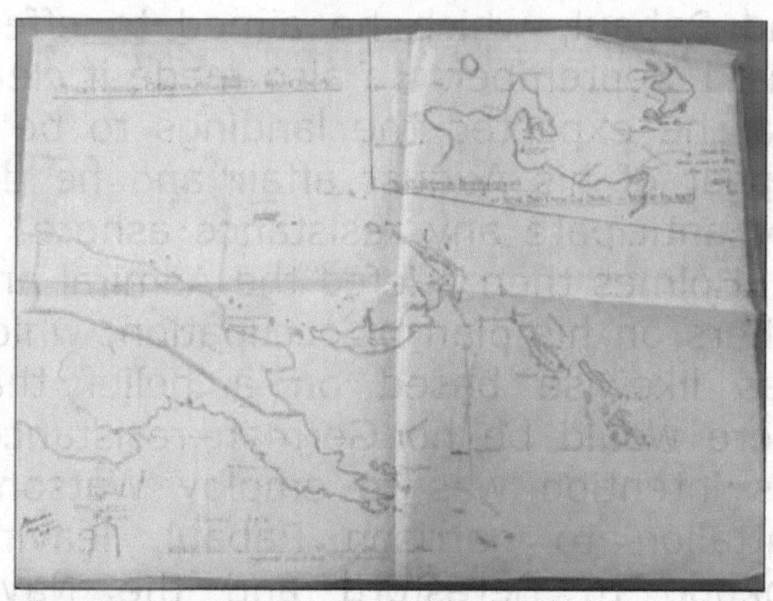

Lieutenant Rowland Bowen's map of New Britain. This map, dated 6 September 1914, was provided by the ANMEF's Intelligence Officer and shows all the topographical information Bowen possessed when he landed with his party on the shores of New Britain. It is now in the collection of the AWM (author image, from AWM 3DRL/7734).

This brings us to the issue of what intelligence Holmes and Travers had at their disposal while planning their mission. For commanders to defeat an enemy, they must be able to find and fix their opponent before it is possible to bring the enemy to battle. This requires intelligence on both the enemy force and the terrain over which the operations are to be conducted. Holmes' resources in this department were paltry. Although there was an Australian Intelligence Corps responsible for collecting and distributing maps and other information on Australia and neighbouring countries, this was a part-time body and there was little pre-war emphasis on Germany's Pacific colonies. In Legge's instructions, which were only received on the day of Holmes' departure from Sydney, there is a brief description of the German forces likely to be encountered in the islands, but this intelligence provided nothing more than the overall number. As for the topography, the available Admiralty charts gave a reasonably accurate picture of the littoral waters of German New Guinea, but provided scant detail beyond the coastline. Among the papers of Lieutenant Rowland Bowen, RAN, is a hand-drawn linen map prepared by Travers, which Bowen used during operations ashore. There is no detail on this map and it appears to have been copied from a commercial atlas. This meant that while the operational-level intelligence was adequate for the senior commander's planning needs, the tactical-level commanders would be landing virtually blind.

Having listened to Holmes' briefing, Admiral Patey approved his plan. That afternoon all ANMEF officers mustered in *Berrima*'s wardroom to be briefed by Holmes. The next day Holmes confirmed his verbal orders with a one-page summary issued under Heritage's signature (see Appendix 6). The issue of orders by Patey and Holmes allowed their subordinates to make plans for the morrow.

It is not clear what specific orders were given to the sailors and soldiers charged with the landings other than Holmes' pithy directive. What we do know is that Howse issued his own

'Corps Order No 15' early on 11 September detailing the deployment of his medical personnel that day. According to that order a party of 11 medicos, including Captain Maguire, was to land at Rabaul to support the 1st Battalion. A second group of 10 was to join Pockley who was ultimately destined for Kokopo to support the Naval Battalion. This left Donaldson aboard *Berrima* in charge of the remainder until *Grantala* arrived. In the short term, Pockley and a single army medical orderly were to land at Kabakaul in the early morning to provide immediate support to the landing party that was to search for the wireless station.

It appears that little concrete information was passed to the men lower down the chain of command. Able Seaman Worthington, serving in Beresford's battalion, recorded in his diary:

> September 9. Great excitement reigned during the early hours of this morning ... After an interview with the Admiral our officers returned, and it was not long before we steamed out to sea. Meanwhile

all manner of rumours and conjectures were in circulation as to what was about to happen, but it was a case of wait and see.

September 10. Excitement still reigned. There is land on our port bow, and the conclusion arrived at was that manoeuvring would soon cease and that we would speedily make the acquaintance of our enemies there.

September 11. The *Berrima* had been dodging about all night, but most of us knew nothing of this.

It is not clear if Worthington's ignorance was accidental or it reflects a difference between navy and army chains of command and the emphasis placed on giving orders to those involved in the forthcoming operation. In any competent army unit, considerable importance was (and is) placed on formally briefing all ranks on the plan of operation down to the lowliest private. This is because small groups or even individuals may become separated during the confusion of battle and even privates are expected to be able to act on their own initiative in accordance with the commander's intent. In contrast, while naval commanders usually briefed the ships' company before an operation, as Patey did in August, less emphasis was placed on detailed lower-deck briefings because professional sailors knew their duties while the officers made the major decisions concerning the manoeuvring and fighting of the ship. Again the two approaches reflect the primary operating environment of each service.

On the same day as the commanders finalised their plans, Howse began to issue quinine to the troops as a prophylactic against malaria. In the absence of any medical intelligence he tried to fill gaps in his knowledge and, according to a letter written by Brian Pockley to his father, himself a noted doctor and president of the New South Wales branch of the British Medical Association, Howse requested any references on the use of alcohol in the tropics. Howse's diligence not only impressed his superiors, he was widely respected by his subordinates, with Pockley observing that Howse was 'awfully decent to work with and is universally liked'.

As the squadron sailed towards its objective, morale aboard *Berrima* was high and, despite the lack of preparation, the force was keen to fight. Holmes wrote, rather optimistically as it turned out, that his work 'will, as far as I can see, be carried out without a shot being fired, which will be a deep disappointment to many with me, who, like young foxhounds, will be all the better as soldiers if they are blooded. They are like Irishmen just spoiling for a fight.' Holmes' mis-appreciation of his opponent filtered down to his troops. On the night before the landings Pockley wrote to his parents: 'We make a night attack at 3.00am tonight. Probably there will be no opposition at all as on [the] previous occasion when the two destroyers and the *Sydney* entered *Simpsonhaven* and steamed peacefully out again after a landing party destroyed their office post ... Personally I think it will be a very pleasant little picnic.' Despite the widespread belief that the occupation would be implemented without a shot being fired, arrayed against the Australian force was a substantial opposition and the Germans were not prepared to simply surrender.

CHAPTER 5
DAY OF BATTLE

Preceding the main convoy, HMAS *Sydney* and the three destroyers, with No.4 Company of the Naval Battalion aboard, arrived off Cape Gazelle somewhere around 3.00am on 11 September. *Sydney* took station at the entrance to Blanche Bay while once again the destroyers combed the harbour and—once again—found it devoid of German vessels. Towards 6.00am *Australia, Encounter* and *Berrima* arrived and entered Blanche Bay. With the situation quiet, *Australia* deployed picket boats to sweep Simpson Harbour for mines, while *Parramatta* examined the long pier at Rabaul.

Meanwhile *Sydney, Warrego* and *Yarra* set off to deliver the two landing parties. The party from *Sydney* landed first, coming ashore at Kokopo. This group, under the overall command of Lieutenant Commander John Finlayson, RN, from *Sydney,* raised the British flag at 7.30am. Finlayson carried with him a letter from Patey calling on Haber to surrender. As the Acting Governor was inland at Toma, Finlayson directed a German civilian resident to take the letter to him. At the same time Sub-Lieutenant Charles Webber, with the left half of No.4 Company comprising some 25 all ranks, set off in the same direction in search of one of the suspected radio sites known as the Beretawl station. During the day his party advanced around six kilometres inland and glimpsed one enemy party, but encountered no opposition and found no evidence of a wireless station. Webber decided that it was unsafe to advance any further into the unknown with so small a force and began to retrace his steps.

The Kabakaul pier, the site of the landing by Bowen's force on the morning of 11 September 1914 (AWM H17182).

Five kilometres along the coast to the east at Kabakaul, *Warrego* and *Yarra* landed their party from ships' boats on a rubble pier and breakwater at around 7.00am. This group was commanded by Lieutenant Rowland Bowen, RAN, Officer Commanding (OC) No.4 Company. Bowen was a 35-year-old permanent naval officer. The seventh child of Welsh parents, he was born at Taggerty in north-eastern Victoria but grew up in Queensland. His father died when he was seven years old and the family moved to Petrie, north of Brisbane, where Bowen attended the local state school. After finishing school, he worked as a clerk for the Queensland Railway Department and was an early aviation enthusiast. A member of the Queensland Naval Reserve, Bowen was appointed to the permanent naval staff in 1911 and posted to Thursday Island as Sub-District Naval Officer. He was transferred to Sydney early in 1914 and posted to Melbourne just before war broke out. On 14 August, three days before the Victorian naval contingent left Melbourne, Bowen married Agnes Grace Bell, the daughter of the Engineer-in-Chief of the Commonwealth Railways. Leaving his young bride behind, he joined the expedition and, on the steamy morning of 11 September, landed with a party of 40 men with orders to find and secure the German wireless station. Bowen was described as: 'Tall and distinguished in appearance, brisk in manner and speech, conscientious and inflexibly high-principled ... [a man who] ... probably commanded respect more readily than he inspired affection.'

Australian troops at Kabakaul. This photograph was taken in the afternoon as the troops were waiting to re-embark. The vessel in the background is the destroyer Yarra (AWM J03324).

Opposing the Australian landing parties was Klewitz who split his command into four groups covering the main German assets. Initially, he planned to hold his German reservists as a single body to form a strong reserve; however, having assessed the quality of his Melanesian troops he decided to divide most of his 50 Germans among the task groups to provide a stiffening of European leadership. The principal group was a reinforced company of 10 Germans and 140 police commanded by Mayer and codenamed 'Lüttich'. Mayer's contingent covered Kokopo and, in accordance with Klewitz's plan, Mayer was to offer no resistance to any significant landing and instead withdraw inland to Takubar, a village midway between Kokopo and Kabakaul. This would ideally place his group in a position to launch a counter-attack against any Australian advance inland from Kokopo towards Toma or from Kabakaul towards Bita Paka.

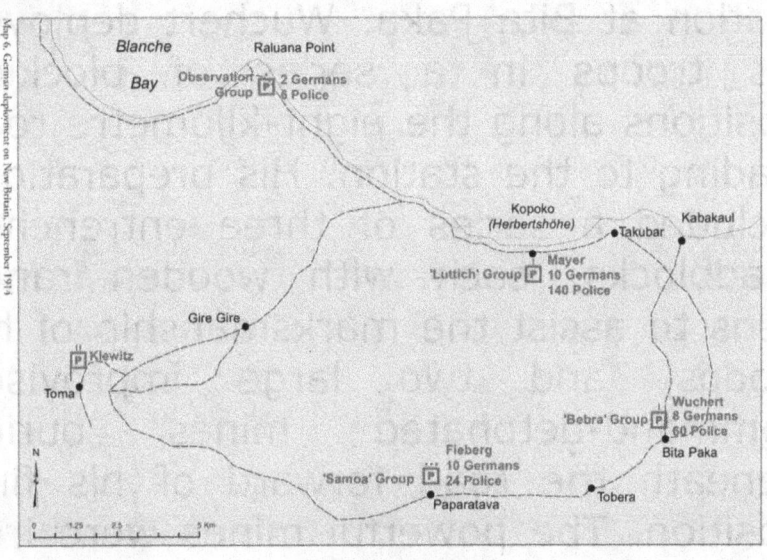

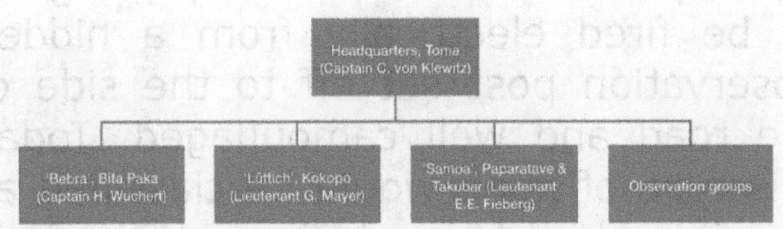

Chart 5. German military organisation, New Britain, September 1914

Directly opposing Bowen's landing party was a second group codenamed 'Bebra'. This smaller company was commanded by Captain (*Hauptmann*) Hans Wuchert, a plantation owner in the Pondo region of New Britain and the senior Imperial German Army Reservist. His command comprised eight Germans and 60 police and their task was to directly cover the wireless station at Bita Paka. Wuchert deployed his troops in a series of blocking positions along the eight-kilometre road leading to the station. His preparations included a series of three entrenched roadblocks, each with wooden range pegs to assist the marksmanship of his troops, and two large improvised command-detonated mines buried beneath the road forward of his first position. The powerful mines were iron pipes packed with dynamite, designed to be fired electrically from a hidden observation post set off to the side of the road and well camouflaged. Today this type of mine would be classified as an improvised explosive device. If detonated at the right time, this device had the potential to obliterate any force moving along the road.

German reservists mobilised for the defence of Rabaul, 1914. Initially, Klewitz planned to hold his German reservists as a body to act as a central reserve. However, the weakness of the Melanesian constabulary led him to divide most of his German troops among his four groups, thereby providing a leavening of experience and leadership (AWM A02543).

Klewitz's third group was designated 'Samoa' and commanded by reserve Lieutenant (*Oberleutnant*) E.E. Fieberg. This half-company or platoon-size group comprised 10 Germans and 24 Melanesian police. Initially Fieberg held the village of Paparatava, which was centrally located on a lateral track running between Bita Paka through Tobera to Toma.

Klewitz's fourth group comprised a number of small observation parties watching the maritime approaches to Rabaul and other possible landing sites. Telephone communications, which had been quickly re-established after Patey's shore parties departed in August, linked the groups with Klewitz's headquarters at Toma. All in all, the *Württemberger* had a well-considered plan, although he was dependent on his dispersed subordinates for its successful execution.

Bowen's knowledge of the German dispositions and preparations at this stage was virtually non-existent and he was advancing almost blind. While Legge had provided Holmes with a broadly accurate assessment of the total German forces available in the island territories, Patey and Holmes both chose to dismiss the threat of armed opposition. Furthermore, Bowen did not even have an accurate topographical map of the German settlement, nor was he certain that there was a radio transmitter inland from Kabakaul.

Landing at Kabakaul, Bowen's party crept ashore along the pier and went to ground. His party of 40 men comprised just 25 naval reservists from No.4 Company, supported by 15 other naval and army personnel providing medical support and communications back to the ship. The army supplement included two of Howse's medicos: Captain Brian Pockley and Private N.R. Gooch. As they landed in the stillness of the tropical morning, there was a collective sigh of relief when no enemy fire erupted from the shoreline, raising hopes of an uncontested advance. On shore, near the pier, Bowen's men found a bungalow surrounded by tended gardens and a few other outbuildings. They searched these and, in the course of their investigations, found four local Melanesians. Threatening the terrified natives, Bowen learned that the few Germans who lived in the Kabakaul area had fled earlier that morning when they saw the Australian ships arrive offshore. Evidence of their hasty departure was apparent with three pairs of high-quality Zeiss field glasses found on a veranda table of the bungalow along with two Browning automatic pistols. Two horses grazing nearby were seized and press-ganged into service, one as a pack animal for communications equipment, the other for courier duty.

Unlike Bowen, the Germans were well apprised of Australian movements. At around 4.00am Mayer received the unwelcome news that three warships had entered Blanche Bay. Soon after, at around 7.00am, he learnt that two of the vessels had arrived off Kabakaul and landed a party of some 30 men who were now moving inland along the Bita Paka road. Based on these timely reports Mayer withdrew 'Lüttich' to Takubar to act as a central strike force. Responding to Bowen's landing, Mayer split his force, taking Sergeant Major of Artillery (*Vizewachtmeister*) Maurice Mauderer (also spelled Maurder) and a half-company party of some 50 police down a rough bush track that ran south-east and intersected the Bita Paka road. If he timed his movement correctly he would arrive in time to ambush Bowen's outnumbered party as it advanced towards the first German position.

The Bita Paka road, 1914. This photograph indicates the density of the vegetation on either side of the road which the Australian flanking parties had to negotiate. It also shows the excellent field of fire the Germans enjoyed from their hidden entrenchments which were sited across the road and along the jungle fringe (AWM A03146).

Bowen pushed inland following a track fringed with coconut palms that took him to an intersection where the track crossed the main coastal road running east towards Cape Gazelle and west towards Kokopo. At the crossroads stood a small trading store with a Chinese shopkeeper in residence and there Bowen received his first piece of useful information. Threatening the man and several Melanesians who were apprehended nearby, Bowen learned that the road heading inland did indeed lead to a new wireless station, which was around eight kilometres away. Leaving a small group behind to act as 'connecting files' to maintain communications with the beach, Bowen set off with his half-company, taking the reluctant Chinese as a guide.

Bowen's advance began along the line of the dusty, jungle-edged road with two small scouting parties pushed ahead and out on his flanks. Writing six months after the event in a report to the Naval Secretary, Bowen recalled that he fully 'expected trouble and immediately increased the distance between the scouts, reinforced the firing line, and cut the telephone communications as it led along the wireless station road.' The scouts found it difficult to move through the bush and were constantly forced to return to theroad and find a way to bypass the thicker patches of undergrowth. To the sailors it was an alien world in which tall trees and creepers intertwined overhead creating a shaded green twilight beneath the primary canopy, while at ground level the tangled secondary vegetation slowed movement and reduced visibility to mere metres. By 9.00am Bowen's party had advanced some 1800 metres when his right flank group, led by Petty Officer George Palmer, struck a particularly thick patch of low growth forcing him to move deeper into the jungle. In doing so he lost sight of the road. Realising this, some of Palmer's scouts veered left to regain contact, while Palmer and Able Seaman Leslie Eastman ploughed on. Suddenly they spied a body of Europeans and Melanesians hiding in the jungle fringe some 30 metres away.

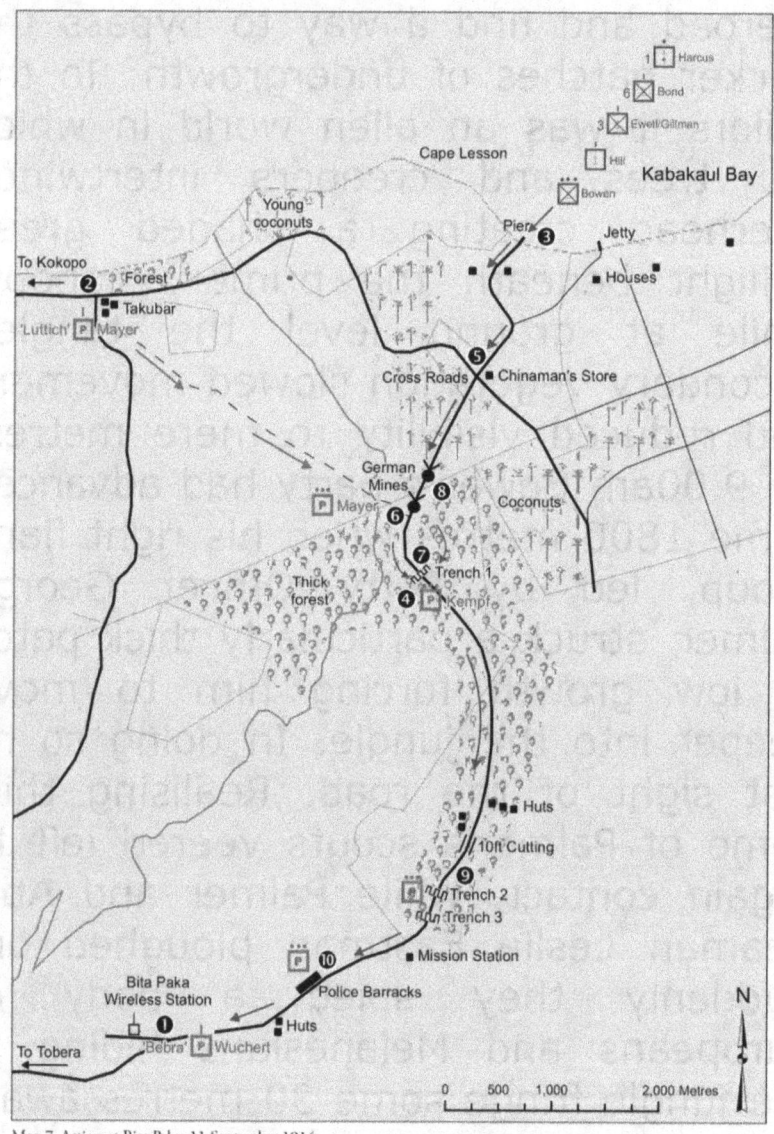

Map 7. Action at Bita Paka, 11 September 1914

Timeline
11 September 1914

Key	Time	Event
1	6.00am	Captain Wuchert (OC 'Bebra') despatches patrol north from Bita Paka.

2	6.30am	Lieutenant Mayer (OC 'Lüttich') withdraws from Kokopo to Takubar and then sets off for the Kabakaul—Bita Paka road.
	7.00am	Sub-Lieutenant Webber, with half No 4 Naval Company, lands at Kokopo from Sydney and advances inland towards Toma.
3	7.00am	Lieutenant Bowen, with half No 4 Naval Company and Captain Pockley, lands at Kabakaul pier from Warrego and Yarra and advances inland.
4	7.30am	Wuchert orders Lieutenant Kempf with 25 troops from Bita Paka Wireless Station to occupy the first German trench on the Bita Paka road.
5	8.00am	Bowen arrives at the crossroads and questions the Chinese storekeeper.
6	9.00am	Petty Officer Palmer wounds and captures Sergeant Major Mauderer.
6		Bowen forces Mauderer along the Bita Paka road calling for a German surrender. Mayer and Wuchert are captured in the confusion.
6		Bowen orders Midshipman Buller to escort prisoners back to Kabakaul and requests reinforcement.
	9.30am	Able Seaman Williams is mortally wounded, followed soon after by Pockley.
3		CO Warrego receives Bowen's message from Buller, signals Australia and lands 59 seamen under Lieutenant Hill to reinforce Bowen.
6		Buller rejoins Bowen and they continue the advance inland.

	10.00am	Hill joins Bowen and they agree on a plan to attack the first German trench.
3	11.30am	Lieutenant Commander Elwell and No 3 Naval Company land from Berrima.
3	12.00pm	Commander Beresford, Captain Travers, No 6 Naval Company (Lieutenant Bond) and a machine-gun section (Captain Harcus) land from Berrima.
7	12.00pm	Bowen is wounded and Hill assumes command of the advance.
		During the advance, Able Seaman Courtney and Signalman Moffatt are killed and Able Seaman Skillen is wounded.
8		First German command-detonated mine discovered by Elwell's troops.
7	1.00pm	Elwell joins Hill and assumes command of all naval troops.
7	1.30pm	Elwell attacks the first trench but is killed leading the assault. Lieutenant Kempf capitulates and is escorted by Hill back to Beresford.
		Kempf is escorted back to the first trench by Bond (with half No 6 Naval Company), Harcus's machine-gun section and Travers to take the surrender of the remaining German troops.
7		At Kempf's direction, the German troops at the first trench surrender.
	2.00pm–3.00pm	2.00pm–3.00pm Lieutenant Colonel Watson lands at Kokopo with four army companies, a machine-gun section and a 12-pounder naval gun.

9		At Kempf's direction, the German troops at the second trench surrender.
9		In a prisoner breakout at the second trench, 13 German troops are killed; Able Seaman Street is killed and Able Seamen Tonks and Sullivan wounded.
9		Bond consolidates at the second trench. Bond, Travers, Private Eitel and Kempf proceed on alone.
	6.00pm	Webber returns to Kokopo having made no contact.
10		Bond disarms eight Germans at the Police Barracks.
1	6.30pm	Bond's party arrives at Bita Paka, later joined by Buller with reinforcements.
1	7.00pm	Bond and Travers occupy the wireless station site for the night.

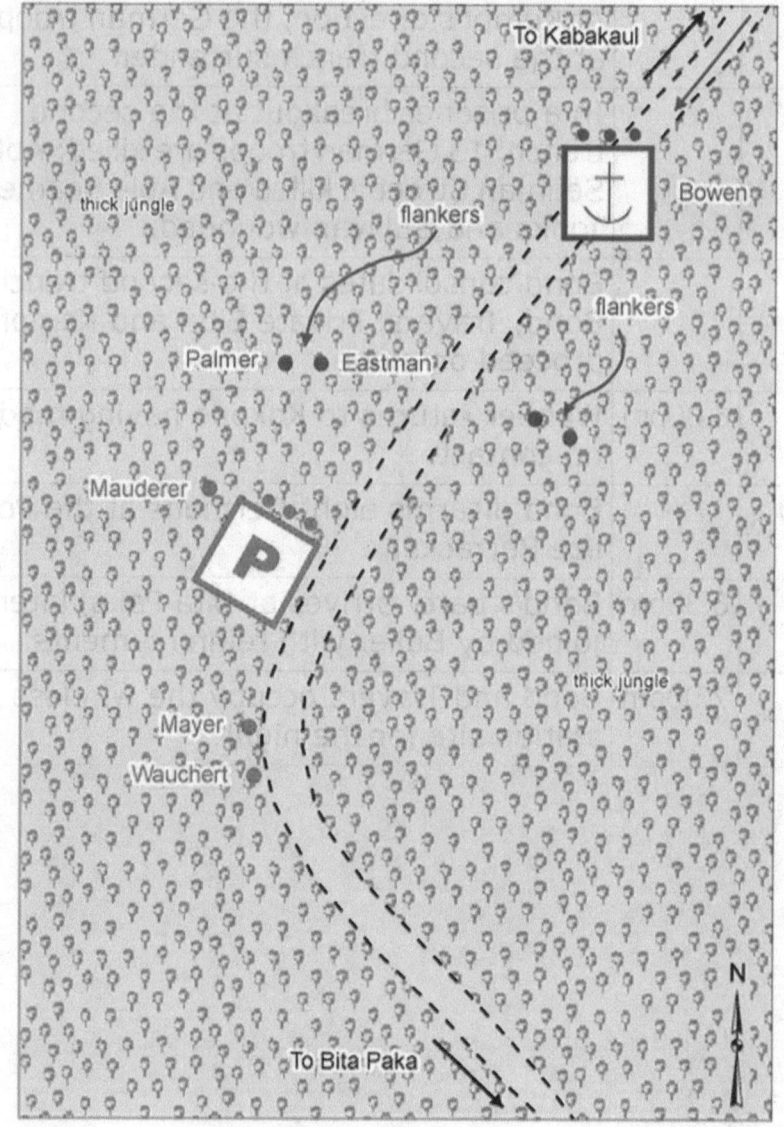

Map 8. First clash. At around 9.00am Petty Officer George Palmer initiated contact with a German ambush party which included Sergeant Major Maurice Mauderer. The German was wounded and taken prisoner.

At first sight the pair saw three Caucasians, correctly assuming they were Germans, along with around 20 Melanesians. They were split into two groups. The smaller party of two Germans and a single Melanesian lay hidden, observing the road along which Bowen's main body was advancing. The larger group comprised the remaining German and Melanesians and was sited deeper in the jungle. This German was using hand signals, motioning the men to keep quiet and remain still. Palmer reacted quickly and fired first, hitting the lone German in the hand and scattering the two parties.

The German, Sergeant Major Mauderer, dropped his rifle and attempted to reach for a revolver but saw that he was covered and so raised his shattered hand, indicting he was *hors de combat*. A few return shots came from the scattered Germans and Melanesians. The fire alerted the rest of Bowen's men to the threat and they joined in the brief, intense, close-range firefight. 'This is where the fighting began, shots being exchanged as fast as we could put them in our barrels,' recalled Able Seaman Sidney Staines. 'Bullets were buzzing all around us ... I was expecting to drop anytime at this stage, so we got together and started firing volleys.' In the exchange of fire, several Melanesian police were killed while Mauderer, under the steady gaze of Palmer, was forced to call on his men to cease fire before the German surrendered. Mauderer's fractured hand was bound up and the sailors took him to Bowen.

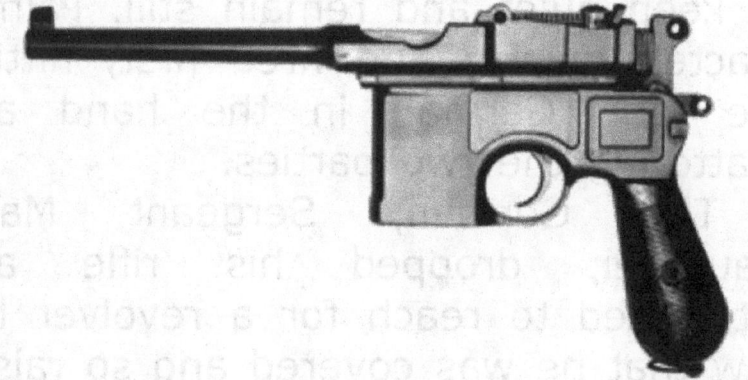

A 7.62-millimetre 1911 C96 Mauser pistol with detachable wooden stock. The Mauser C96 (nicknamed the 'broom handle') was a semi-automatic firearm. It was a popular choice of pistol as a private purchase option for officers in the Imperial German Army. Winston Churchill carried a C96 at the Battle of Omdurman during the Sudan campaign of 1898. This particular weapon belonged to Captain Hans Wuchert and was captured on the morning of 11 September when Wuchert was taken prisoner. It is now in the collection of the Australian War Memorial (author image).

Bowen realised that he had very nearly been ambushed and that there were more German troops ahead. Using his initiative, albeit in contravention of the rules of war, the naval officer pointed his pistol at Mauderer and threatened to shoot the wounded man if he didn't walk up the road calling on his comrades to surrender. Bowen plied the German with the false assertion that his party was closely supported by 800 other troops. The subterfuge worked and in the ensuing confusion both Wuchert (OC 'Bebra') and Mayer (OC 'Lüttich') were captured. Not only were the defenders deprived of two of their most important commanders, several of their marked maps also fell into Australian hands, providing a significant intelligence windfall. At the same time it appears that Bowen's false claim was widely reported, even making its way back to Klewitz at Toma. Although Bowen's unconventional action may be credited with ending the action sooner and thereby saving lives, he was later criticised for violating the Hague Conventions.

The position of the first German trench on the Bita Paka road. The 'x' beside the Melanesian man marks where the trench cut the road (AWM H19000).

Realising that his advance was going to be contested, Bowen contemplated his next move. Having gained a haul of prisoners, he needed to remove these men from the scene and so sent a small guard back to the beach led by Midshipman Reginald Buller. Before leaving, Pockley conducted an emergency field amputation without anaesthetic removing the unfortunate Mauderer's shattered hand. In addition to clearing the prisoners, Bowen had

Buller relay a message to Patey that he had been engaged and needed urgent reinforcement. On the way back, Buller met the connecting files at the crossroads and handed the prisoners to them, relaying Bowen's call for reinforcements. He then headed back to the scene of the fighting.

Without waiting for reinforcements Bowen pushed forward, his scouts working through the jungle fringe while his main body trailed along the edge of the road. His men soon came under fire from unseen enemy troops in the jungle, while others sniped from the towering treetops. For the most part the fire was ineffective, but at around 9.30am matters took a turn for the worse when one sailor was hit. Able Seaman Billy Williams, the crack shot from Northcote, was one of the group designated as connecting files. Williams was struck by a high velocity bullet at close range causing massive internal trauma. Stoker First Class William Kember, who was nearby, picked up the wounded man and carried him some 800 metres back down the road. There he met Pockley who was making his way south having operated on Mauderer. After treating Williams, Pockley removed his Red Cross armband and tied it to Kember's hat, before sending Kember and another sailor to carry Williams back to Kabakaul. Williams was evacuated to *Berrima* but died that afternoon.

Pockley, accompanied by Able Seaman A. Annear, started back for the front. Annear later recorded that the pair 'had gone about 50 y[ar]ds when a volley was fired at us from a bend in the road in front.' They took cover and waited around 20 minutes before Pockley decided that they must return to the fighting. Telling Annear to remain under cover, Pockley 'got up to have a look around, he had proceeded about 10 y[ar]ds along the road when a volley was fired at him, from the same direction as before & he was hit badly.' Severely wounded in the stomach, the doctor was picked up by an improvised ambulance cart and carried to Kabakaul and evacuated to *Berrima*. However, like Williams, he died that afternoon.

Meanwhile Buller had rejoined Bowen and the two discussed their options based on the intelligence gained from the captured maps. While they were engaged in planning, another hapless German was captured and he too was forced to march along the road calling on his companions to surrender. This time the ploy failed. By now Bowen's scouts had discovered the first German trench which was around 450 metres in advance of Bowen's main body. The German trench was dug across a bend in the road and extended for some distance into the jungle. The main trench was supported by further rifle pits dug on either side and concealed in the undergrowth. Unbeknown to Bowen the position was manned by nine Germans and 20 police under the command of reserve Lieutenant (*Oberleutnant*) E.E. Kempf.

When Bowen's message reached the destroyers, the information was signalled to the flagship. Without waiting for orders, Cumberlege immediately landed all available men from the destroyers. The volunteers, comprising 59 sailors from *Warrego* and *Yarra,* were placed under command of Lieutenant Gerald Hill, RNR, from *Yarra.* Hill was an

Australian-born master mariner and British naval reserve officer on loan to the RAN. He left a vivid account of his role in the day's fighting: 'About 8.30am when most of us were quietly enjoying our breakfast pipes and lazily watching the movements of a few natives on shore ... the two destroyers were ordered to land every available man, and reinforce the party already landed, whom we were informed were hard pressed.' Given little time to prepare, Hill's sailors were off the ships in less than five minutes. 'No time was allowed to don field service kits, men just tumbled into the boats in the clothes they happened to be wearing at the time (i.e. flannels and duck trousers), arms and ammunition passed in at the same time and away they all went for the shore.' The scratch force was poorly armed with no more than 14 rifles among them, others were armed with Webley revolvers and cutlasses, while a few had nothing more than timber clubs procured on shore. Meanwhile Bowen's message reached Patey who ordered *Berrima* to Kabakaul to land further reinforcements.

At around 10.00am Hill reached the front with his men. With the arrival of the welcome reinforcements, Bowen and Hill agreed on a plan in which a fire support group would remain astride the road to engage the German trench while two parties worked through the jungle to enfilade the trench from its vulnerable flanks. The main party was to move along the right (western) flank, while a smaller party manoeuvred on the left. The advance resumed with the unfortunate prisoner forced to march in front. Almost immediately Bowen was wounded by fire from the jungle. The bullet pierced his sun helmet striking him high above the temple and tearing a furrow through the scalp right to the back of his head. Command fell to Hill and he sent Buller back to hurry the reinforcements expected from *Berrima*.

In response to the call for reinforcements, *Berrima* arrived off Kabakaul and another two naval companies, reinforced with an army machine-gun section under Captain James Harcus, began landing. Holmes ordered Commander Beresford ashore to coordinate the operations of the three naval companies now advancing on Bita Paka. As well as providing him with a machine-gun section he also sent his Intelligence Officer, Captain Travers, to accompany the naval CO. Lieutenant Commander Charles Elwell, RN, who was commander of the Right Wing of the Naval Battalion, pleaded with Beresford to be allowed to join the lead company as it set off. No.3 Company was commanded by Lieutenant Oscar Gillman, RANR, but Elwell's intercession subordinated him under the senior officer. Elwell set off leading the right half-company, with Gillman following with the left half-company.

Some 1500 metres from the shore Elwell's party was fired on. The identity of the defenders is unclear, even in German accounts, but it was most likely either a patrol sent out by Wuchert earlier in the morning or a detachment of Mayer's company from Takubar. Without a firm grasp of the situation, Elwell took the wise precaution of deploying scouts ahead while the main body marched in fours along the road. As New Britain was in the grip of a long drought, the tropical jungle was paradoxically dry and the road dusty. The column was quickly enveloped in a cloud of fine dust that choked the nostrils and filled the eyes of the marchers. Even so, the sweating column easily outpaced the slower moving scouts and so Elwell deployed new parties of scouts, leapfrogging those parties that fell behind the advancing column. Those bypassed joined the rearguard under Signal Boatswain William Hunter. The column had advanced for around 40 minutes when it again came under fire from the right front, although the firers could not be clearly identified. The Australians now suffered a further casualty. Able Seaman John Walker, RANR, a stoker from Townsville serving under the alias 'John Courtney', suffered gunshot wounds to the chest and base of the skull and died before he could be evacuated. The fatal wounding of Walker prompted Elwell to deploy his half-company in extended order into the jungle to the left of the road, with Gillman following in support. Still under fire from unseen shooters, two of Gillman's men were hit in quick succession.

Signalman Robert Moffatt, another fatal casualty of the Bita Paka fighting. He was badly wounded on the afternoon of 11 September and evacuated to HMAS Australia but died the following day. He was buried at sea with full naval honours, the only Australian fatality to be interred in this manner (SPC-A).

Signalman Robert Moffatt, RANR, and Able Seaman Daniel Skillen were shot within metres of each other. Moffatt was struck in the spine, apparently by the same bullet that struck the elbow of Skillen. Moffatt's wounds were mortal, Skillen would survive. Soon after the shootings, one of Moffatt's mates crawled to Gillman and reported that he believed Moffatt had been shot by a Melanesian policeman from a treetop position. Gillman ordered the man to find and shoot the sniper. When the sailor reached the tree he found an unarmed Melanesian hiding in the undergrowth who attempted to grab his rifle. After a brief struggle, the native ran away, the sailor firing at him as he fled. At around the same time another sailor reported that he had come across wires laid through the jungle to the base of a tree some 110 metres from the road. Suspecting that it might be wires leading to a mine, Signal Boatswain Hunter was sent to investigate. At the base of the tree, at the end of the wires, he found an electric battery and firing key, while the tree had large spikes driven into the trunk and a rope fastened to an upper branch. The tree was obviously a lookout position for the firer of the mine. Elwell ordered the wires cut and the firing key removed.

Although the Australians did not realise it at the time, the mine was an iron pipe around 100 millimetres in diameter and six and a half metres long, packed with sticks of dynamite and buried lengthwise along the middle of the road in a trench one to one and a half metres deep. Its shrapnel effect was enhanced with nuts, bolts and stones liberally piled over the pipes before the trench was filled in and its location disguised so that it remained undisclosed even after Bowen's, Hill's and Elwell's parties had walked over it. Only later, on 4 January 1915, when a party was removing the first mine, was a second mine uncovered 20 metres from the first.

The German mine discovered during Elwell's advance. When the mine was eventually detonated after the battle, it left a crater eight metres long, four and a half metres wide and two metres deep. Only then did the Australians discover a second mine. If either of the mines been successfully fired while Bowen's, Hill's or Elwell's parties were moving along the road, the effect would have been devastating (SPC-A).

After disarming the mine Elwell continued to push forward, soon encountering Bowen's and Hill's parties. At this stage the two naval officers were still manoeuvring towards Kempf's trench. After discussing matters with Hill, Elwell took command as the senior officer. Having ascertained that the weight of the attack was on the left, Elwell took his half-company across the road to the right. It was a confusing situation as the three naval parties were intermingled and visibility was very limited due to the density of the vegetation. To forestall chances of a friendly fire incident Gillman ordered his men to cease fire until he could push his half-company forward to make contact with Hill and align his group with Elwell.

At around 1.00pm Elwell ordered the continuation of the double envelopment to attack both flanks of the German position. Elwell's group closed to within 70 metres of the trench using fire and movement. Having closed the range Elwell ordered his men to fix bayonets and follow him. As he rose, with sword in hand, to lead the charge he was shot in the chest. Although the attack stalled, and the trench was not stormed, Kempf realised that his position was collapsing as both flanks were threatened and his Melanesian police-troops werecringing in the bottom of the trench and refused to fire. Kempf decided to surrender and, at around 1.30pm, he raised a white flag. Hill, who was now in command again as Elwell died soon after being hit, ordered his men to cease fire. Kempf came forward, although he refused to surrender to Hill as the naval officer had removed his badges of rank and appeared so dishevelled that Kempf found it impossible to believe that he was actually an officer. Hill and Gillman decided to take the German and two others back to Beresford.

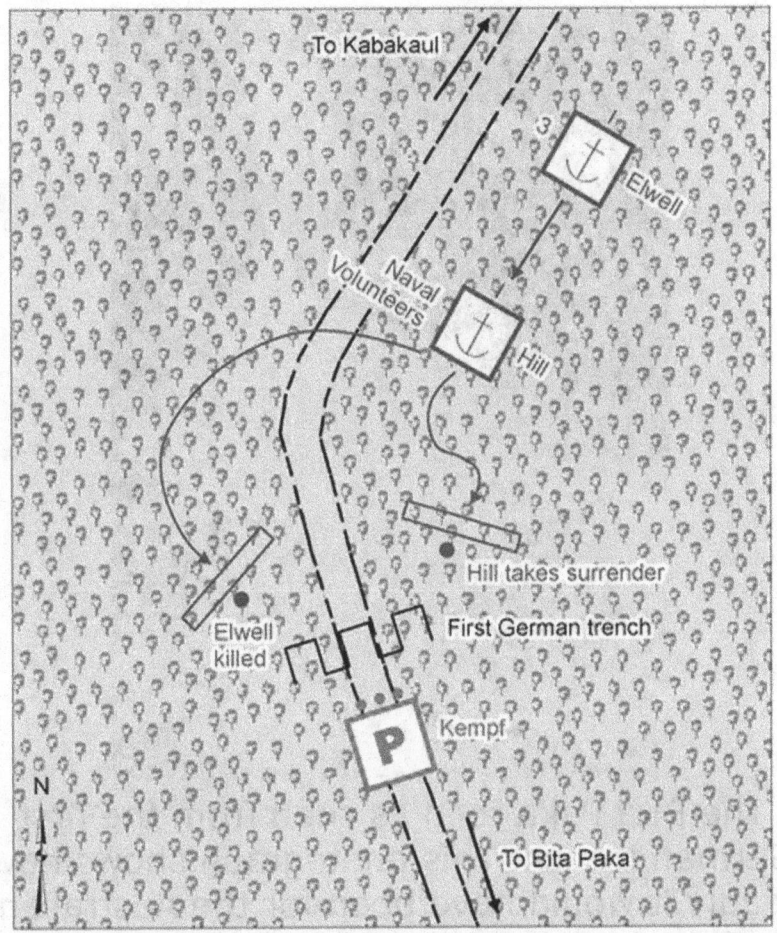

Map 9. Elwell's double envelopment of the first German trench. The German positions were well sited and possessed an excellent field of fire along the road, although they were vulnerable to any approach through the jungle. It was only the use of flanking movements that kept Australian casualties low.

The Bita Paka road as seen from the first German trench. This photograph shows how deadly it would have been for the Australians to advance along the centre of the road rather than deploying flanking parties to manoeuvre through the jungle (AWM H03286).

As the fighting ceased at the first trench, Beresford was moving up with the remaining reinforcements. Hill's command had pulled back around 1600 metres with the prisoners when the men encountered the Naval Battalion CO. Beresford immediately demanded that

Kempf surrender the wireless station and his remaining troops. With reluctance the German agreed, signing a quickly prepared surrender document drafted by Travers who had accompanied Beresford from Kabakaul. Lieutenant Thomas Bond, RANR, commanding the remaining naval company (No.6) with Beresford, was ordered to take Kempf, as interlocutor, and Sergeant Franz Ritter, as an interpreter, back to the trench to take the surrender of Kempf's remaining defenders and then move on to secure the wireless station.

Bond set out accompanied by a half-company of 30 sailors, Harcus's machine-gun section, Travers, Kempf and Ritter. While heading back south along the gently rising road, Bond ordered Kempf to stand over the disarmed mine to discourage any attempts at detonation. Bond who, like Bowen, believed he was using his initiative, clearly failed to realise that his actions contravened the Hague Conventions, both in forcing Kempf to walk down the road to parley the surrender and through his use of the

German as a human shield against the mine.

Approaching the first trench, Bond sent Kempf and Ritter forward to enforce the surrender. Although the remnants of Kempf's group were initially defiant and refused to obey, the sight of Bond's preparations for an attack forced the issue and they eventually surrendered. The six German and 20 police prisoners were sent back under guard. Bond's party then advanced almost three kilometres towards the second German trench. Although they were fired on from the jungle, the party suffered no casualties before arriving at the trench manned by another three Germans and 20 police. They too surrendered and, while Travers and Kempf walked on towards the wireless station, Bond supervised the disarming of the prisoners and made arrangements for their removal.

There are a number of versions of what happened next. According to Private Jack Axtens, who arrived on the scene last with the machine-gun section at about 5.00pm:

We had hardly been there 10 minutes when the blacks stampeded. They were supposed to have received a signal from one of the Germans. As soon as they started to bolt nearly everyone with a rifle banged away & about 12 niggers were killed & one of the Germans who attempted to get away was shot as well.

While Axtens is vague on what triggered the incident, Able Seaman Worthington, who was part of the prisoner escort, described it clearly in his diary:

Our prisoners ... were promptly disarmed and ordered to fall in, two deep. Four, myself included, were appointed a guard; and, with an escort, we set out with our dusky captives and their German friends for the base. My position was at the rear, between the natives and the bush. We had not gone far when a native stepped out of the ranks and pointed to the bush. At the same time he said something I could not understand. I looked in the direction indicated and saw a gleam similar to what would be caused by the sun's rays on a rifle barrel. Not being sure of the nature of what I saw I ordered the native back to his place and looked again. This time the gleam moved downwards, and before I could give warning firing started in the bush to my left and behind me. I, however, fired at the gleam and must have scored, for it suddenly disappeared and there was no answering shot. I then turned to the prisoners. They were dropping like rabbits in endeavours to escape, none got away. The incident took us quite by surprise, as we were not expecting trouble, but we nevertheless gave a good account of ourselves.

Although the German prisoners had given their parole, two of them, on a given signal, made a dash for liberty. One was shot through the heart before he had taken three steps, and the other was afterwards found in the bush wounded.

The key variation between Axtens' and Worthington's accounts lies in whether the breakout was instigated by one of the Germans or triggered by firing from the jungle or from a third trench further along the road. Whatever initiated the tragedy, once the Australians began shooting, the prisoners quite naturally attempted to take cover or flee to avoid being shot in the crossfire. Once the first shot rang out, the Australians were likely to shoot first and ask questions later. The natural action and reaction of both sides only fuelled each other's behaviour in the confusion.

With the passage of a century it is not possible to determine the exact sequence of events. The testimony of Axtens and Worthington should be given greater credence since they were eyewitnesses, although this has not stopped other stories circulating of a mass execution. In 2015 the Australian Broadcasting Commission reported the discovery of a tape recording reputedly made by an Australian planter in the 1960s. In the recorded interview a Kabakaul elder named Bob claimed that the Australians had lined up their prisoners, executed them and then buried the bodies in the trench. The veracity of this claim is difficult to substantiate. Bob claimed to have witnessed the event although he may have been repeating a story he heard as a child. While those wedded to conspiracies might claim an Australian cover-up, the weight of evidence is against such a flagrant atrocity. In the first instance, Bond and Travers, two officers who were unlikely to countenance (much less order) the murder of prisoners, were both present. Second, there is the matter of the surviving Germans, including Kempf, who made no such accusations even after their safe passage back to Germany. Ultimately, Bob's claims appear dubious.

Sergeant Major Maurice Mauderer (left) and Able Seaman Timothy Sullivan (right). Both men were wounded during the fighting on 11 September. Mauderer's life was saved by Brian Pockley who conducted an emergency battlefield amputation to remove the German soldier's shattered right hand. Sullivan sustained multiple gunshot wounds during the prisoner breakout incident (SPC-A).

Whatever the cause of the incident, it led to a bloodbath. In the mêlée one German and at least a dozen police were killed and three Australians were wounded, one fatally. The single German fatality was Ritter, the interpreter, who was shot by Bond as he attempted to rally the police prisoners. The Australian casualties were Able Seamen Henry 'Harry' Street, Timothy Sullivan and James Tonks. Street would die at the scene. The wounds sustained by Sullivan provide some indication of the proximity and intensity of the engagement. He received a total of nine wounds from direct bullet hits or fragments of bullets. His left hand was scorched by a rifle shot at close range, shattering several fingers; two bullets struck his left arm; one found the point of his chin; a piece of lead from a bullet lodged under the left side of his jaw; two of his teeth were knocked out; his chest was hit, leaving pellets under the skin so that they could be rolled about at a touch; while another bullet ripped away his belt and bandolier, exploding half of his ammunition.

Having cleaned up the mess and treated the casualties, Bond decided it would be prudent to consolidate his position. After posting his men at the second trench he decided to advance with a smaller group to take the German surrender. Setting off down the road accompanied only by Travers, Kempf and Private Conrad Eitel, a

German-speaking member of the machine-gun section, the party apprehended two German messengers carrying dispatches from Haber and Klewitz. At a police barracks 900 metres short of the wireless station, Bond encountered another group of eight Germans and 20 police. The Germans were armed with Mauser pistols and the police with rifles. There was a tense moment when the Germans defied Kempf's order and appeared on the brink of offering resistance until Bond, covered by the pistol-wielding Travers, rushed the Germans and snatched their pistols from their holsters. The disarmed Germans were taken by surprise, while the police could not fire for fear of hitting their officers, so the whole group admitted defeat. Adding them to his haul, Bond marched the group to Bita Paka.

Arriving at the site at around 7.00pm, Bond found the wireless station deserted and, while its masts were wrecked, the plant equipment was largely intact. The hilltop position where the station was sited was naturally strong, surrounded on three sides by wide, steep gullies, while the fourth side facing the road was a grassy slope devoid of cover. If the Germans had held this position strongly, the Australians would have been forced to storm it across difficult ground and undoubtedly would have suffered additional casualties.

As the dark, tropical night quickly descended, Bond, Travers and Eitel settled in for the night guarding their prisoners. Wisely, they kept them separated, with 10 Germans confined in one room and 20 Melanesians in another, forestalling any attempt at another breakout. At around 7.30pm Buller arrived with reinforcements.

Back aboard the fleet, Patey and Holmes were physically and metaphorically plunged into the dark. Throughout the day they had received little information on the whereabouts and fate of the Kokopo and Kabakaul landing parties other than Bowen's call for reinforcements. In response to the unexpected opposition, Beresford was landed at Kabakaul while Holmes directed Lieutenant Colonel William Watson to land at Kokopo with four companies of his infantry, the other machine-gun section and a 12-pounder naval field gun. Watson's task was to take the half-battalion group and find Webber's party and then cooperate with Beresford in attacking the wireless station. This force was not landed until 3.00pm. Holmes then conferred with Patey aboard *Australia* and recommended that the remainder of the troops still on *Berrima* be landed at Kabakaul to reinforce Beresford directly. He suggested that, if the wireless station could not be secured before last light at around 6.00pm, both Beresford's and Watson's groups should withdraw to the coast. The following morning the two battalions, supported by naval gunfire from the fleet, should carry both positions at Bita Paka and Toma.

As matters transpired, Watson had difficulty attempting to move cross-country between Kokopo and Bita Paka. By late afternoon it was clear that he could not effect a link-up with Beresford before dark and so wisely retired to Kokopo. By that time Webber's party had also returned, having advanced six kilometres to the village of Gire Gire, about halfway to Toma, without finding any trace of the reported wireless station. Although he made no contact with German forces, his movements were reported to Klewitz at Toma by his observation group.

At around 6.00pm Patey received a reply from Haber to the letter he had despatched early that morning from Kokopo. In the letter the duplicitous Acting Governor denied having the authority to surrender the colony, implied that it was Patey's fault that fighting had broken out, and asserted that, as a consequence, he could not cease wireless communications. By this time Patey and Holmes were aware of the orders Klewitz had given to his forces and Patey believed Haber's letter misrepresented the actual position while evading the real issues. As a result he wrote again to Haber pointing out the inconsistencies in Haber's letter and placing responsibility for the fighting that day squarely on his shoulders. He expected the German to arrange a more effective means of communication between the two parties and finished by advising: 'Communications as to transferring control of the Administration should now be addressed to Colonel Holmes, Brigadier of the Occupying Force, who will administer the Government.' To everyone's relief, at 1.00am on 12 September, news was received on the flagship that Bond was in possession of the wireless station.

Although most of Wuchert's 'Bebra' and around a third of Mayer's 'Lüttich' surrendered or deserted on 11 September, some opposition remained. Early the next morning Bond rounded up several more police while a party was sent from Kabakaul under Midshipman Stan Veale, reaching the station at around 10.00am. Veale's party encountered a good deal of sniping on the way, although it suffered no casualties. After consultation with Holmes, who was marking his 52nd birthday, Patey decided that the transmitter site was too isolated to be permanently occupied. Bond was ordered to put it out of action and bring back the equipment. That task was completed by the afternoon and the landing parties, returning at intervals to Kabakaul, were re-embarked and landed at Kokopo that evening. By the close of 12 September the initiative had swung to the Australians.

Casualties in the day's fighting on both sides were relatively light, especially in comparison with would soon follow on Gallipoli. Throughout the day some 200 Australians had been involved in the battle and had eventually achieved the ANMEF's primary task of securing the wireless station, losing in the process six dead (two killed in action and four who died of their wounds) and four wounded. They had faced a force of at least 140 Germans and Melanesians from Mayer's and Wuchert's groups who suffered one European NCO and some 30 Melanesian police killed; one German officer and 10 police wounded; and another 19 Germans and 56 police captured. Although the casualties are low in overall numbers, the distribution is unusual and requires some consideration.

Dealing with the ANMEF first, all bar one of the Australian casualties were sailors, reflecting the fact that the naval landing party and naval reinforcements bore the brunt of the short, sharp fight. Officer casualties were disproportionately high with Pockley and Elwell making up a third of the fatalities and Bowen a quarter of the wounded, indicating that the officers were at the forefront of the fighting. It is also likely, although the evidence is inconclusive, that a number of the Australian casualties were caused by friendly fire during the prisoner breakout. Compared to the Germans however, the ANMEF suffered just one casualty to every four of their opponents, excluding prisoners, or one to 20, if the prisoners are included.

In an engagement such as at Bita Paka, where the Germans were prepared and concealed and the Australians exposed as they advanced, the attackers would normally be expected to suffer the higher rate of loss. That this is not the case requires an explanation, although there appears to be no single, simple answer. Rather the disparity reflects multiple causes. First, the low German casualties (other than prisoners) suggests a lack of commitment by the German reservists to a task probably viewed as pointless. The single German fatality was Ritter and he was shot during the prisoner breakout at the second trench when he could not escape the fusillade. Bluffed by Bowen and Bond, most of the other Germans surrendered as they perceived their situation to be hopeless. Second, whatever complaints the Germans expressed later about being betrayed by their Melanesian troops, it is obvious the latter did most of the fighting and dying. The high casualties among the constabulary, which Seaforth Mackenzie in the Australian *Official History* admits 'could not be ascertained accurately', stem from a number of factors. As most of the *polizeisoldaten* were not highly trained, and all accounts indicate that they were reluctant participants, their high death rate is most likely due to inexperience and fear. This is highlighted in the prisoner breakout incident in which almost half their counted fatalities were sustained. While many of the *polizeisoldaten* sensibly chose to desert when the chance arose, others were reluctantly forced to die for the Kaiser.

Finally, there is the issue of the disproportionate ratio of dead to wounded. In modern military engagements the number of non-fatal casualties typically outnumbers fatalities by around three or four to one. At Bita Paka the ratio is atypical, with the Australians suffering two wounded for every three deaths while for the Germans the traditional ratio is reversed to one wounded for every three killed. The answer to this anomaly is complex. Certainly one factor was the terrain. The fighting occurred in dense bush with Hill recording that the jungle bordering the road was so dense 'that half a dozen men could be within a dozen paces of each other and remain quite invisible one from the other.' So while the fighting lasted it was at close range and deadly. Under such conditions quarter is less likely to be asked for or given.

Compounding the viciousness of the close-quarter battle was the attitude of the ANMEF. By and large the Australians adhered to the prevailing racial prejudices of their day, believing in the inherent superiority of white people, especially Britons. Quasi-social Darwinist beliefs predisposed the Australians to look down on Melanesians and such feelings turned violently antagonistic when they unexpectedly encountered the *polizeitruppen*. Matters were not helped by the German decision to arbitrarily divide their forces into 'military' and 'non-military' sections with uniform distinctions that were not readily apparent to the Australians. As noted previously, the military force consisting of the German reservists and *polizeisoldaten* of the expeditionary force were supposed to wear green armbands (green was the official colony colour for German New Guinea) or military headdress with an imperial cockade. Standard *polizeitruppen* were to wear white armbands and white cap covers. The ANMEF troops were not aware of the division when they landed.

Existing racial antagonism easily turned to rage when the Germans were suspected of using illegal ammunition. Throughout the ANMEF it was widely believed that the *polizeisoldaten* used so-called 'dum-dum' rounds during the battle. Lead-core dum-dum bullets, patented in 1897 and initially manufactured by the British at Dum Dum outside Calcutta, 'exploded' or technically mushroomed on contact, inflicting horrific and frequently fatal wounds. Europeans found them effective when hunting because they were capable of felling large, dangerous big game. In colonial wars they proved equally effective in dropping charging warriors in their tracks. While bagging rhinoceros and African tribesmen was considered legitimate, concerns over the use of this type of ammunition between European opponents led to their prohibition. In 1899 dum-dum ammunition was specifically banned from use by military forces under the Hague Convention 'On the Use of Bullets Which Expand or Flatten Easily in the Human Body'. It is possible that the constabulary may have had some soft-point or hollow-point ammunition, although this is unlikely. If such ammunition was used it almost certainly was not issued by the military authorities. The other option is more nefarious. Despite the outlawing of the dum-dum ammunition, some soldiers still illegally defaced the nose of their copper-jacketed bullets, exposing the lead core and creating an improvised dum-dum bullet. Those individuals who did this were generally quick to dispose of any evidence as, had they been captured, its discovery would almost certainly have led to their summary execution.

Despite the absence of evidence to support such a contention, it was widely rumoured that the Germans used such ammunition at Bita Paka. Midshipman Veale wrote at the time that the Germans used 'soft-nosed, split-nosed and dum-dum bullets'. Sergeant William Sheppard claimed that Pockley 'was shot with a soft-nosed bullet from a sniper rifle'. Private John 'Jack' Martin claimed that Pockley 'fell with a gaping wound in the side made by a Pom-Pom bullet'. Similar claims were made over Elwell's death. Convinced that some or all of the enemy behaved illegally, Sheppard recorded the prevailing mood: 'Our men are bursting to get revenge & God help any black snipers whom we get hold of, for they won't get quarter I can tell you.' Such revelations buttress claims that some Melanesians were murdered during the battle on 11 September and later.

Combat is a highly charged and visceral experience and the desire for retaliation against prisoners following the death of a comrade is an ever-present danger. In disciplined organisations such passions are controlled by leaders, either the officers or influential soldiers. However the veteran rankers in the ANMEF were unlikely to provide the sort of restraining influence expected from older heads because their experience was, for the most part, gained in South Africa where irregularities and atrocities were not uncommon. In New Guinea it is not hard to imagine how South African veterans, schooled in the precedents of 'Breaker' Morant's infamous 'Rule 303', could have influenced younger members of the force in a negative way, especially when passions were fuelled by speculation.

In the ANMEF on 11 September ill-informed gossip was running rampant and the deaths of Pockley and the others were blanketed in a fog of tall tales and baseless stories. The further these stories spread from the scene of fighting, the greater the chance of error. Lieutenant Rupert Garsia, RN, aboard HMAS *Sydney,* recorded one version of the action that was circulating on the day. 'Within 100 y[ar]ds of the landing Elwell was killed and Dr Pockley while attending to a wounded German was shot from a tree probably by an ignorant nigger.' Garsia was wrong but he was only recording a distorted version of the story that had passed from the scene of the fighting to the ships offshore in a form of military 'Chinese whispers'. An even more inaccurate rendering of circumstances surrounding Pockley's death was recorded aboard the flagship where Bandsman Bollard related an allegation in circulation on the day of the action that was a clear mix of fact and fantasy: 'we lost Dr Pockley, who was binding a German Officers arm, when with the other hand the German drew a revolver and shot Dr Pockley in the back and killed him, needless to say the "Hun" didn't live long after although he did throw up his hands.' Speculation derived in part from a semi-accurate recounting of Pockley's ministrations to the wounded Mauderer were embellished with wish-fulfilling tales of German perfidy. In the absence of reliable information, idle speculation abounded as uninformed opinion and half-truths passed by word of mouth became embellished with every telling.

Australian testimony on the prevalence of dum-dum rounds was accorded similar treatment, with most of it ultimately hearsay and clearly contradictory. While participants such as Martin, Sheppard and Veale claim to have seen these rounds or the wounds they inflicted, none had been in combat before and it is not clear exactly what they witnessed. Inexperienced troops commonly mistake the extensive tissue damage wrought by high-velocity, full-metal-jacket bullets for the devastating effects of dum-dum rounds. Australian troops were soon to make similar claims against the Ottomans in the early days on Gallipoli and, in most cases, these claims too were unsubstantiated and probably incorrect.

In the case of Pockley's death, Captain Maguire, who attended Pockley aboard *Berrima*, provided direct refutation of the rumours. The doctor rejected the stories of illegal ammunition, writing in a letter to Pockley's father:

> The bullet entered the abdomen in the midline ... & emerged in the lower part of the back, shattering the last lumbar vertebrae. I state here most emphatically that it was not a dumdum bullet. We have seen no dumdum wounds & and have given an official denial of the statement that our men were shot by dumdum bullets.

Journalist Frederick Burnell wrote that the bullet that struck Pockley was 'one of the new needle-pointed Mauser pattern [which] ... entered the stomach and turned, the soft butt spreading out mushroom-wise, tearing away part of the spine, and leaving a wound in his back as large as a man's clenched fist.' In other words, it was a standard 7.92-millimetre pointed, full-metal-jacket, military-issue round. Whatever the reality, the perception among Australians was that the German forces had employed illegal ammunition and they regarded this as a violation of the rules of war.

Compounding the problem of life-threatening wounds and casual atrocity was the added difficulty of removing the wounded from the battlefield. Today in emergency medicine the 'golden hour' is defined as a time period lasting from a few minutes to several hours following traumatic injury during which there is a likelihood that prompt medical treatment will prevent a casualty's death. The concept, while still contested, had its roots in research from the Great War which traced a causal link between the time taken to evacuate a casualty and a sharp increase in mortality. The evacuation of Australian and German casualties was hindered on New Britain by the lack of organisation. While Holmes was given a free hand to manage operations ashore, the orders governing the medical arrangements for the landing came from Patey. This is probably why no army stretcher-bearers accompanied the landing parties and the dressing station that was established ashore remained at the Kabakaul pier where first aid could be rendered before transportation offshore. Hence, during their evacuation along the Bita Paka road, the casualties were carried by naval medical orderlies with limited medical training since their primary employments were as cooks, stewards or stokers. More consideration of this aspect of the plan may have speeded evacuation, although there is no way of determining whether it could have saved lives.

At Bita Paka the odds were stacked against the wounded on both sides. For the Australians the early wounding of Pockley removed their only doctor from the battlefield, reducing the chances of stabilising the wounded before their evacuation to the dressing station at the pier and thence to *Berrima*. As the AIF would learn on Gallipoli, there is a fine balance between pushing medical support forward to save lives, while minimising the danger to medical staff who are of no use if they too became casualties. Pockley's bravery in giving away his Red Cross armband is commendable, his loss tragic and unnecessary, and it probably cost lives that might otherwise have been saved. Such an assessment is supported by the fact that Pockley saved the life of Mauderer with an emergency field amputation and only two of the Australian fatalities (Elwell and Street) were reported killed in action—they died on the battlefield—while the remaining four (Pockley, Moffatt, Walker and Williams) died of their wounds—they were evacuated and died later. Evacuation of the casualties was undoubtedly slowed by the absence of trained army stretcher-bearers. Treatment offshore was not helped by the late appearance of the hospital ship *Grantala*, which only arrived at Simpson Harbour on the morning of 13 September, by which time the fighting was over. As it transpired, a problem with decoding messages in the naval cipher delayed the ship's arrival.

The mortally wounded Captain Brian Pockley (face covered by a sun helmet) being brought aboard Berrima. Pockley was wounded earlier in the day after treating Able Seaman Billy Williams. Pockley died at around 2.00pm, Williams following soon after. Williams was the first Australian battle casualty of the Great War, Pockley was the first officer of the Australian forces to die (AWM P03078.004).

The Germans also appear to have made few plans for battlefield casualty treatment. In comparison with the efforts made to evacuate ANMEF casualties, the Melanesians are said to have been left in the bush for days before they were collected and evacuated to hospital. This is in spite of the fact that the Germans had two government native hospitals, one at Rabaul and the other at Kokopo. Given the prevalent hostility of the Australians, it is unlikely that they would have placed a high priority on clearing police casualties from the battlefield. Racist attitudes on both sides only drove up the Melanesian fatality rate.

Police prisoners aboard HMAS Sydney, 12 September. In all, 66 police were taken prisoner on 11 September. Most policemen were reluctant participants and took the opportunity to surrender when it presented, although the majority of German casualties were suffered by the constabulary (AWM P00316.002).

On 12 September Holmes consolidated his position, ordering Beresford to concentrate his battalion at Kokopo in accordance with the original plan. This battalion group comprised four naval companies, two army companies, a 12-pounder from *Sydney*, a machine-gun section and medical details. Watson's force, which had landed at Kokopo the previous day, was re-embarked and, by late afternoon, *Berrima* was alongside the long wharf at Rabaul. Watson's garrison comprised a single naval company, four army companies, the other machine-gun section and a medical corps detachment. They landed under Paton and, during the night, there was some desultory firing between the security piquet and German troops in the hills to the north and east of the town. There were no casualties and otherwise no opposition was offered. German reservists who were not government officials were rounded up and confined on *Berrima* while guards were placed on the residences of German officials.

Commander Beresford leads the naval contingent through the streets of Rabaul, 13 September. Holmes' formal announcement proclaiming the cessation of German rule was accompanied by the hoisting of the British flag at Proclamation Square, a 21-gun salute and the singing of 'God Save the King' (NLA PIC BOX PIC/15807 #PIC/15807/6).

Although the initiative had passed to the Australians with the wireless out of commission and the main settlements occupied, Haber still refused to capitulate. On 12 September Holmes sent a letter via motorcycle to the Acting Governor demanding his surrender. Haber replied that he would provide a response by 4.30pm the next day. Without waiting for Haber, Holmes formalised his position on Sunday 13 September, landing at Rabaul where he issued a proclamation announcing his formal occupation of the territory and the cessation of German rule. A substantial portion of the ANMEF paraded through the streets with the force forming up at Proclamation Square. In the presence of a large audience, including Patey, his senior naval officers, the ANMEF garrison and curious German inhabitants, the British Union Jack was hoisted, the ships of the fleet fired a 21-gun salute, the national anthem ('God Save the King') was sung and the troops gave three cheers for the King. Holmes was now established ashore with the bulk of his command and, while he would continue to consult with Patey on joint matters, dealing with the German capitulation was now his responsibility.

Haber did not respond satisfactorily to Holmes' letter and, by the night of 13 September, the Australian was convinced his opponent was just playing for time. Concerned that the Germans might withdraw inland to mount a guerrilla campaign such as that encountered in South Africa, with all its attendant violence against civilians and atrocities, Holmes decided to pre-empt matters. He prepared to send a force to Toma to arrest the Acting Governor. Watson was given the task and, taking two of his companies, a 12-pounder and a machine-gun aboard *Encounter,* he was landed back at Kokopo.

Holmes decided to employ some shock tactics to persuade Haber to finally surrender. Captured maps provided details of the German defences and, at daylight on 14 September, with Patey's approval, HMAS *Encounter* fired a 46-round fire mission at the Toma ridge. While the 6-inch bombardment apparently did little material damage to the German defences, Holmes' aim was not physical, but rather psychological. The show of naval firepower had the desired effect, promoting further police desertions while German morale plummeted. Following the demonstration, Watson and his four-company battle group began their advance. As they approached the village Watson ordered the 12-pounder to fire six rounds at the village defences and the Germans, finally acknowledging the futility of further resistance, sent a negotiator forward under a white flag offering to surrender. Toma was occupied at 3.00pm.

The only blight on the operation at this point was the sudden loss of *AE1*. On the afternoon of 14 September, as Watson was occupying Toma, the submarine was patrolling with HMAS *Parramatta* off Gazelle Point when the boat disappeared without trace, along with its entire crew of 35—14 RAN and 21 RN. It is suspected that the vessel struck an uncharted reef or suffered a catastrophic accident while submerged. The remains of the *AE1* were only discovered in December 2017 and the cause of its loss is yet to be confirmed.

Naval troops at Sydney in 1912 practising with a 12-pounder field gun and limber. Webber's party consisted of a similar grouping to that shown in this pre-war photograph (AWM 301564).

NAVAL GUNFIRE SUPPORT

HMAS Encounter. Throughout its long service with the RAN, Encounter was affectionately known as the 'Old Bus' by those who served aboard the ship (SPC-A).

On the morning of 14 September 1914, HMAS *Encounter* became the first RAN vessel to fire a naval gunfire support mission for the Australian Army. The forty-six 6-inch rounds were fired in salvos at German defences guarding the temporary seat of German government at Toma. The broadsides provided an awesome spectacle, sending sheets of flame and smoke from the guns and creating the most shattering noise that many of the soldiers and locals had ever heard. Lieutenant Colonel Watson reported the accuracy of the shelling as 'astonishing' and, while the German commander Klewitz claimed there was no physical damage, Acting Governor Haber admitted that it terrified the remaining police and killed a number of Melanesian civilians, although he provided no figures.

In 1914 many British commanders overestimated the effectiveness of fire from naval vessels. As the British and French were to find on Gallipoli, it took the right doctrine, considerable practice and suitable ammunition for shipboard guns to be effective against entrenched or covered shore targets. While Patey had trained the RAN well in the year before the war, his ships were no better prepared for supporting troops ashore than those of the RN. On the other hand, whatever the limitations of the RAN's first shore bombardment, it certainly had the desired effect of intimidating the Germans.

Holmes followed up the shock of the naval bombardment with an advance supported by a manhandled field gun from HMAS *Sydney*. The 12-pounder had been landed at Kokopo on 11 September under Sub-Lieutenant Charles Webber, while another was landed from *Encounter* under the command of Midshipman Stan Veale. On 14 September Webber's detachment supported Watson's advance on Toma. On approaching the village Watson ordered Webber to engage a group of defenders. Webber's crew fired six 12-pound shrapnel rounds, dispersing the enemy. Awed by the show of firepower, Haber finally agreed to surrender.

Haber agreed to meet Holmes at Kokopo on 15 September to open negotiations. No.6 Naval Company from South Australia provided a guard of honour. Haber arrived shortly after 11.00am to be met by Holmes and the pair retired to discuss terms. While disclaiming any authority to surrender in the absence of Governor Hahl, Haber gave assurances that there would be no further resistance. The first meeting lasted from 11.30am to 3.00pm, during which the French armoured cruiser *Montcalm* arrived and made a dramatic entrance, sailing past the post office to take up anchorage in Blanche Bay. The French flagship fired a salute which was returned by *Encounter.* An adjournment in negotiations was called until noon on 17 September.

On the designated day, Haber returned and the negotiations were finalised. Although some minor alterations were discussed and agreed on the second day, the meeting concluded with Haber and Holmes signing the Terms of Capitulation (see Appendix 7). Holmes was justifiably pleased with the outcome, since Haber agreed to the immediate cessation of all military resistance and the transfer of administration of the whole of German New Guinea.

After signing the terms, the Acting Governor returned to Toma to arrange for the surrender of his remaining troops and the handover of authority. This included the surrender of the colonial treasury. Holmes returned to Rabaul and, on the way, called on

Encounter and arranged for a wireless message to be sent to Legge briefly outlining the Terms of Capitulation. However the inevitable lag in wireless communications meant that the Chief of the General Staff did not receive the news until 20 September. Legge passed the message to Pearce who was once again Minister for Defence, the Labor Party having been returned to government following the 5 September election.

The German negotiating team arrives at Kokopo on 17 September. Acting Governor Dr Eduard Haber (mounted leading) and Captain Karl von Klewitz (mounted following) arrive at the Kokopo post office to finalise their negotiations with Holmes over the Terms of Capitulation (AWM H12842).

The Kokopo post office. Negotiations over the German capitulation between Haber and Holmes took place at the post office on 15 and 17 September. After signing the Terms of Capitulation, Haber, Klewitz and their remaining troops marched to Kokopo on 21 September to formally surrender (AWM H15077).

On the same day as the surrender terms were signed, Holmes despatched an army party on a mission to recover the German treasury, which had been buried for safe keeping in the rugged jungle country beyond Toma. Hoping to forestall any looting of the colonial treasury, Lieutenants Victor Sampson and Ivan Sherbon were despatched from Kokopo with 70 men on what turned out to be an arduous nine-day mission. Advised by Haber that the booty was buried in three separate locations, the pair set out, reaching Toma on the morning of 18 September. Plunging into the steep country beyond, they first encountered a party of 26 uniformed Germans and 79 police who had been advised of the surrender and offered no resistance. At the first site, the initial portion of the treasure was handed over by a guard of 50 police. After an hour's rest the young officers pushed on for another eight kilometres along a narrow track to the second site where the Germans had also established a field wireless station. The following morning Sampson and Sherbon, accompanied by seven men, marched to the final site where they found Haber and a number of officials with 10 cases of gold, silver and notes. The Germans handed over the treasure, which Sherbon sealed. Haber then informed them that a number of other cases were buried at the second site beneath the tent in which some of the party had slept the night before. Retracing their steps they dug up the treasure and this too was sealed. Having completed two journeys, the expedition successfully recovered the treasury and wireless plant. For Holmes, the first part of his mission was now accomplished.

CHAPTER 6

NO MORE 'UM KAISER

The New Guinea campaign was effectively concluded on 17 September when Haber signed the Terms of Capitulation. What remained was to secure the surrender of the remaining German forces on New Britain and the occupation of the outer territories. The first task was accomplished on 21 September when Haber, Klewitz and their residual troops (five officers, 35 NCOs and 110 *polizeitruppen*) marched from Toma to parade at Kokopo. Holmes had granted his opponents military honours, allowing them to march in under their flag to formally lay down their arms. Burnell wrote of the event:

Down the road the head of a marching column swung into sight, rifle on shoulder, the red lava-lavas of the black troops gleaming through the white dust clouds in picturesque contrast to the khaki of the thirty-five Germans who came first.... And the perfection of the drill displayed, not only by the whites, but by the black soldiery, one hundred and twenty strong, was a thing to make seasoned soldiers open their eyes with admiration and amazement. "Never seen anything to surpass it," murmured one officer to me, "and I've seen the Hausa troops, and the Somalilanders, and even native regiments in India."

While Holmes was later criticised for granting the Germans military honours, this was a compromise of form rather than substance. More importantly, he was convinced that, had he not made this concession, the negotiations would not have been concluded as quickly and there was a chance the Germans might resume hostilities and withdraw inland to mount a guerrilla campaign. Such an outcome could only have cost more Australian lives and consumed further resources.

Arrival of the remaining German troops who surrendered to Holmes at Kokopo on 17 September. Although Holmes granted the Germans military honours and their arrival created a favourable impression on Australian witnesses, the impressive drill belied the poor combat performance of the Germans and their Melanesian troops (SPC-A).

Word was passed of the surrender over Patey's naval communications and published in the press in Australia. The general air of celebration at the nation's first victory was muted in the homes of those who lost loved ones. For Francis and Helen Pockley, who lost a beloved and talented son, whatever their individual anguish, it was masked in the public language of duty, heroism and sacrifice for God, King and country. Of those killed in the fighting, Elwell, Moffatt, Pockley, Street and Williams were single; only Walker was married with a child.

With the German surrender on New Britain, Holmes' mission was now to occupy the rest of the Protectorate. Patey and Holmes departed Rabaul on the day after the surrender with *Australia, Montcalm, Encounter* and *Berrima,* bound for Madang on the northern coast of New Guinea and the centre of German authority on the island. The show of naval force was sufficient to ensure German acquiescence and Holmes landed unopposed. Unknown to Patey, the only hint of trouble came from the German auxiliary cruisers *Cormoran* and *Prinz Eitel Friedrich* which, like the *Emden,* had been detached from Spee's squadron to attack British shipping. While *Emden* was hunting in the Indian Ocean, the auxiliary cruisers planned to rendezvous in New Guinea waters before descending on the Australian trade routes. When Patey arrived at Madang, *Cormoran* was lying concealed at Alexishafen just 20 kilometres to the north. The raider had a narrow escape on 26 September when the ship's lookout reported the approach of four ships—the Australian force. *Cormoran* was anchored in one of the small bays behind a coral reef and alongside thick overhanging jungle. While the German crew held their collective breath, *Encounter* and *Berrima* entered Alexishafen, while *Australia* and *Montcalm* remained out to sea. Slowly the Australian ships circled the harbour as the German captain kept turning his ship so that all his guns came to bear on the Australians. Unaccountably, the crew aboard *Encounter* detected nothing untoward, even though they passed close by the Germans. When the Australian ships left the harbour, the Germans could hardly believe their good fortune and decided not to press matters. *Cormoran* eventually made its way to Apra Harbour in the United States Territory of Guam where it sought to replenish its dwindling stock of coal. The American Governor refused to supply the ship with more than a token amount of fuel and, in accordance with the Hague Conventions, ordered the ship to leave within 24 hours or face detention. The ensuing stand-off effectively interned the raider until it was scuttled by its crew in 1917 following the United States' entry into the war.

Prinz Eitel Friedrich missed the planned rendezvous with *Cormoran* and linked up with *Komet* instead. Short of fuel, *Prinz Eitel Friedrich*'s captain decided not to hunt off the Western Australian coast as directed but instead followed Spee east. For seven months the raider enjoyed some success, sinking 11 small Allied merchant vessels in the Pacific and South Atlantic. Eventually, its engines worn out and its bunkers almost empty, *Prinz Eitel Friedrich* sailed into Newport News, Virginia, on the east coast of the United States to be interned.

Even though Spee remained at large, it was pretty clear that he was no longer a threat to the Australian occupation. Patey had already examined the options open to his German opponent and correctly concluded that Spee was most likely bound for South America. To his frustration, however, the Admiralty refused to unleash him, and his squadron was not sent in fast pursuit, but rather ordered to patrol off Fiji in the unlikely event that Spee doubled back.

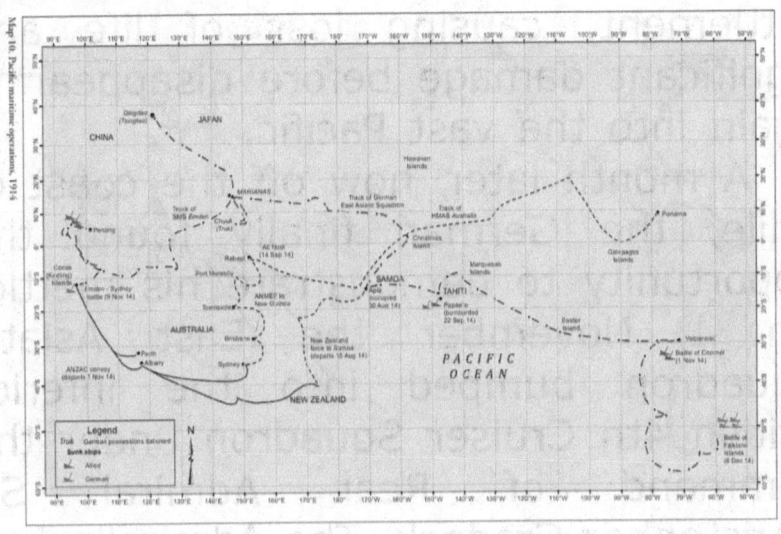

As Patey had calculated, Spee did indeed sail east. After the fall of Samoa to the New Zealanders on 30 August, the German hastened to the island, arriving there on 14 September in the hope of finding some British shipping still at anchor. Instead he found the harbour bare and some 1600 New Zealand troops ensconced on the island. Realising that any landing could only be of transient value and might entail significant destruction of German property, Spee departed without firing a shot. On 22 September he arrived off Papeete on Tahiti, the capital of French Polynesia, where he shelled the settlement, causing loss of life and significant damage before disappearing again into the vast Pacific.

A month later, now off the coast of Chile, the German finally found the opportunity to demonstrate his mettle. On 1 November the East Asiatic Squadron bumped into the inferior British 4th Cruiser Squadron under the command of Rear Admiral Sir Christopher Cradock. The Admiralty had sent Cradock to hunt for the German in the eastern Pacific, but when they encountered each other off the port of Coronel, the result was a lopsided engagement, resulting in the loss of two antiquated British armoured cruisers—HMS *Good Hope* and *Monmouth*. Cradock and his squadron were outclassed in both gunnery and seamanship. The Admiral went down with his ship, along with more than 1500 British servicemen. Although the victory lifted German morale, it did little to alter Spee's position and, at a reception with the German community in the Chilean port of Valparaiso following the battle, Spee was presented a bouquet of flowers. In response he prophetically observed that it would do nicely for his grave.

As Spee contemplated his next move, *Emden*'s short though successful raiding career was about to come to an end. To counter the German threat in the Indian Ocean, the cruisers HMS *Minotaur,* HMAS *Melbourne* and HMAS *Sydney,* along with the Japanese battle cruiser *Ibuki,* gathered at Albany on the south-west corner of Australia where the combined Australian and New Zealand contingents had assembled prior to commencing their voyage to Europe. On the same day as Cradock was defeated at Coronel, the Australian and New Zealand convoy departed Albany. The slow-moving procession was more than a week out of port on the morning of 9 November when *Emden* approached the Cocos (Keeling) Islands intending to destroy the British wireless station and sever the telegraph cable that made land at Direction Island. Before the station was closed down it broadcast an alarm: 'Strange warship approaching', then repeated the message with the prefix 'SOS'. The convoy was only 80 kilometres east and, just the previous day, *Minotaur* had been detached to head for South Africa where, following Spee's victory at Coronel, there was concern that the African trade route might be the German's next target. With *Melbourne* and *Ibuki* remaining to shepherd the transports, *Sydney* was detached to investigate. As Glossop approached, *Emden* opened fire first and hit *Sydney* at the extreme range of 9600 metres. Quickly recovering from this disconcerting surprise, Glossop manoeuvred to make the most of *Sydney*'s speed and its superior firepower. *Emden* was pummelled into submission and Glossop despatched his famous signal, '*Emden* beached and done for'.

On 1 December, with his ammunition depleted and his coal reserves burning down, Spee rounded Cape Horn and entered the Atlantic to begin a final run for Germany. In London the Battle of Coronel, the Royal Navy's first defeat in more than century, finally stung the First Lord of the Admiralty, Winston

Churchill, into effective action. Two of *Australia*'s half-sisters, HMS *Invincible* and *Inflexible* (which belonged to the earlier Invincible-class battle cruisers) were despatched under the command of Vice Admiral Doveton Sturdee to hunt down Spee. The Admiral took his squadron south to the Falkland Islands to begin the search. When Spee attempted to raid Port Stanley on the morning of 8 December Sturdee, who was harbouring there, was caught unawares. Recovering quickly, he set off in pursuit. Giving chase with his two battle cruisers and five light cruisers, the British squadron wreaked its revenge in a running fight that saw *Scharnhorst, Gneisenau, Nürnberg* and *Leipzig* sunk, with only *Dresden* escaping. Spee, along with more than 1800 German sailors, including his two sons, was lost with the ships. The demise of Spee's squadron effectively removed any substantial threat to the Australian occupation of New Guinea.

HMAS Una, formerly KGS Komet (AWM H17517).

The only German naval asset still at large in New Guinea waters was the yacht *Komet*. *Komet* narrowly avoided interception during Patey's first expedition to the islands and thereafter Haber put the yacht at Spee's disposal to serve as a supply vessel for his auxiliary cruisers. *Komet* operated for two months from the north coast of New Britain at Talassia, a small plantation approximately 270 kilometres south-west of Rabaul. *Komet*'s anchorage was unofficially known as Komet Harbour (*Komethafen*).

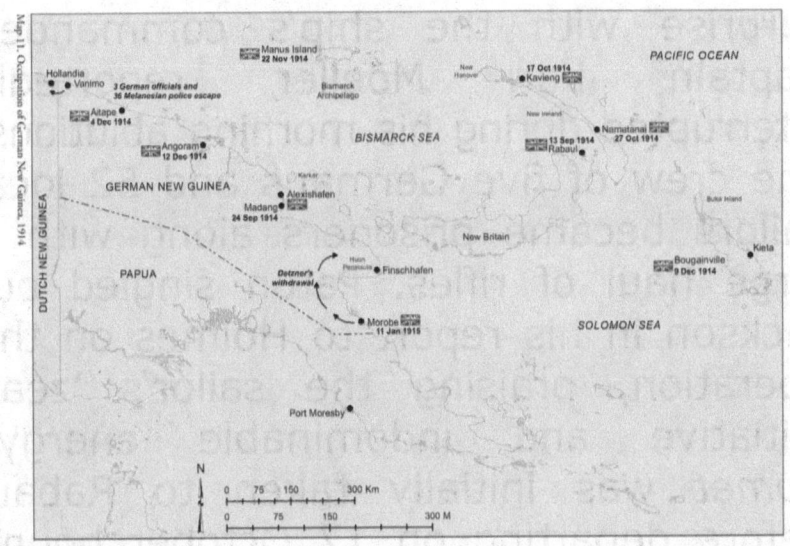

Map 11. Occupation of German New Guinea, 1914

The ship's presence was eventually reported to Holmes at Rabaul. In response he despatched Lieutenant Colonel John Paton with a party of troops aboard HMAS *Nusa* to capture the vessel. The armed steam yacht *Nusa* had been captured some weeks earlier, recommissioned as an RAN ship and was now captained by Lieutenant Commander John Jackson, RN. At dawn on 11 October, after a stealthy approach by Jackson, Paton and his latter-day buccaneers boarded *Komet* at anchor and captured the vessel in a bloodless coup. So surreptitious was their approach and boarding action that *Komet*'s crew was caught completely by surprise with the ship's commander, Captain Karl Möeller, reportedly interrupted during his morning ablutions. The crew of five Germans and 52 local sailors became prisoners along with a large haul of rifles. Paton singled out Jackson in his report to Holmes on the operation, praising the sailor's 'zeal, initiative and indominable energy'. *Komet* was initially taken to Rabaul before departing on 17 October bound for Sydney. Following a refit at Garden Island, the prize was recommissioned as HMAS *Una* and sent back to the islands.

While word spread of the surrender in New Britain, it took time for the news to filter to the more remote outstations and some of the isolated settlements remained unaware of the turn of events for some weeks. Gradually however, Holmes occupied the main German centres of the Old Protectorate. After Madang was secured, New Ireland was occupied over the period 17—27 October, Nauru on 7 November, Manus in the Admiralty Islands group on 22 November, Bougainville on 9 December, and

Morobe on New Guinea last on 11 January 1915.

During this period Holmes was to face mounting criticism in Australia over the Terms of Capitulation he negotiated with Haber. It began on 23 September as he and Patey were on their way to Madang. In the morning Patey stopped the convoy and requested Holmes to come aboard *Australia* to discuss an important message received the previous evening from Pearce. In the signal Pearce disclosed that the 'Commonwealth Government considers the terms stated [in Holmes' message of 17 September] unduly advantageous to the enemy.' Holmes was immediately forced to defend his actions, while Patey quickly made it clear that he had nothing to do with the negotiations.

Even though Haber had surrendered, not all Germans were prepared to give up. In the interior of New Guinea Lieutenant (*Oberleutnant*) Hermann Detzner was oblivious to the state of hostilities when war was declared. The experienced *Schutztruppe* officer was leading a German expedition tasked with checking the work of the 1909

Anglo-German Border Commission which had begun the task of delineating the conterminous border between New Guinea and Papua. As Haber signed the Terms of Capitulation, Detzner was operating out of Morobe with a party that comprised a German *polizeimeister*, 25 police, 45 porters, two servants and an interpreter. Only learning of the state of war at the beginning of October, Detzner refused to submit, although his force quickly evaporated as some were captured and others deserted. By the end of March most of the other Europeans in the colony had acquiesced to the surrender or been captured, while a handful fled west into neutral Dutch New Guinea where they were interred by the authorities. Undeterred, Detzner led his dwindling force to the Huon Peninsula. Eventually he found his way to the vicinity of the Lutheran Neuendettelsauer Mission at Sattelberg, above Finschhafen. Although the local German missionaries were supposed to remain neutral they agreed to keep his presence a secret and built him a house, supplying him with food, books and newspapers. There, among the local villagers Detzner, with the support of the missionaries, avoided contact with the Australians.

LIEUTENANT HERMANN DETZNER
THE LAST HOLDOUT

Captain Hermann Detzner after his return to Germany and promotion. In this post-war photograph, Detzner wears a Schutztruppe 1897 grey home uniform with a Sudwester slouch hat in grey felt, probably with collar, cuffs, hatband and piping in green for New Guinea. As a Bavarian officer, he wears his two Bavarian Military Merit Orders ahead of his Prussian Iron Cross 2nd Class on his medal bar. He also has the Colonial Service Medal for his pre-war assignments in Cameroon. He wears the Iron Cross 1st Class badge on his lower left chest (Detzner, Vier Jahre unter Kannibalen, 1921).

Hermann Detzner (1882—1970) was a Bavarian army officer who, by 1914, was a seasoned colonial soldier and explorer. He was born at Speyer in the Rhineland-Palatinate of Germany and was educated at the local Gymnasium before joining the Pioneer Corps of the Bavarian Army in 1901. He became a surveyor in the *Schutztruppe,* completing two tours in German Cameroon (*Kamerun*) in 1907—09 and 1912—13, before being sent to German New Guinea to check on the border markers placed by the 1909 Anglo-German Border Commission that had begun establishing and marking the border between German New Guinea and Australian Papua.

In late 1914 he heard of the German surrender on New Britain and he refused to capitulate. After the only other European in his party was captured, the pugnacious Bavarian led a diminishing band of Melanesians to the vicinity of the Lutheran mission of Christian Keysser above Finschhafen. According to Keysser,

Detzner rejected the Australian demand for his surrender because he considered such an act irreconcilable with his honour as an officer. With the aid of the German missionaries, he survived in the interior, out of sight, maintaining a largely token, non-violent presence. In his post-war memoir he claimed that he led his troops, marching through the bush singing 'Watch on the Rhine' and flying a German imperial flag made from dyed loincloths. In four years he led several expeditions attempting to escape into neighbouring Dutch territory. Because he did not seek to fight and remained hidden, the Australian garrison was unable to track him down and it is doubtful if they were even aware of this one-man resistance movement.

The only other German who remained at large in German New Guinea was Hellmuth Baum. After learning of Haber's surrender, the solitary German civilian retreated into the mountains beyond the Wau-Bulolo

Valley into an area later named 'Baum country'. This area lies south of Wau in New Guinea, roughly between the villages of Kudjeru and Bulldog over the border in Papua. Like Detzner he effectively disappeared for the duration of the war.

As the Australians extended their control over the territories of the Old Protectorate, Japan entered the war, invoking the Anglo-Japanese Treaty. Japanese involvement in the Pacific was a disturbing development from an Australian perspective, although there was nothing that the Commonwealth could do. On 7 August Britain requested Japanese assistance in hunting German raiders in Chinese waters. Sensing an opportunity to expand its influence in China, Japan sent Germany an ultimatum on 14 August which went unanswered. Consequently, on 23 August Japan declared war. As Vienna refused to withdraw the Austro-Hungarian protected cruiser SMS *Kaiserin Elisabeth* from Qingdao, Japan declared war on the Austro-Hungarian Empire on 25 August. On 2 September, as the ANMEF was leaving Palm Island for Port Moresby, the first of some 24,500 Japanese troops landed to besiege Qingdao. Supported by a British contingent of 1500 troops, the Japanese siege intensified during October as the Imperial Japanese Navy seized most of Germany's island colonies north of the Equator including the Marianas, Carolines and Marshall Islands. The campaign ended with the surrender of the German and Austro-Hungarian forces on 7 November, the same day the Australians occupied Nauru.

With the demise of Germany's Pacific territories, Holmes' role changed from that of expeditionary commander to military administrator. He now faced the enormous responsibility of governing the expansive island group. Legge's orders to him before leaving Australia contained no precise instructions on how to act once the Germans capitulated or how he was to administer the territories he occupied. His instructions simply directed him to 'carry out the objects set out ... in such manner as may be best.' On 18 August, just as he was preparing to depart Sydney, the Governor-General received a further cable from the Secretary of State for Colonies reiterating Holmes' task:

In connection with the expedition against German possessions in the Pacific, British flag should be hoisted in all territories occupied successfully by His Majesty's forces and suitable arrangements made for temporary administration. No formal proclamation of annexation should however be made without previous communication with His Majesty's Government.

Although given considerable latitude, Holmes had to comply with international law, specifically the 1907 Hague Agreement on Occupied Territories. This particular convention attempted to curb some of the excesses of past military occupations and restricted an occupier's ability to make legal or administrative changes to those arising from its responsibility for public order and safety and those of military necessity. To assist in the transition, Holmes and Haber agreed, under the Terms of Capitulation, that a number of German officials would be held over for a period in an advisory capacity with pay. Any other German businessmen, missionaries and planters who took an oath of neutrality were allowed to continue their normal activities.

Back in Australia, once the terms were made public, Holmes was roundly criticised by both the newly installed government and the press. An ill-informed government and populace, roused by claims of German atrocities in Europe and fanned by a jingoistic media, were less concerned with the facts and Holmes was forced to defend his actions to the government. Few, including Pearce, appeared to understand that his terms were consistent with international law and the instructions issued to him by his British and Australian superiors.

Despite the furore at home, Holmes pushed on with his task of governing and it quickly became apparent how enormous an undertaking this was. Among his immediate challenges were the establishment of an interim government complete with a treasury and a means of promulgating his directives; the maintenance of the existing civil infrastructure including ports, roads and railways; re-establishing law and order; and providing transport and supply for the main settlements and outlying garrisons. While many of the existing German systems could be adapted, Holmes had to make clear to the civil population (German and Melanesian) that it was 'no more 'um Kaiser', now it was 'God save 'um King'.

Holmes quickly reconfigured his brigade to provide the various garrisons for the scattered territories and allotted new responsibilities to those officers and men who held the requisite skills set. He had already given this matter some thought on the voyage north, issuing preliminary instructions on the subject on 10 September, and allocating supernumerary tasks to particular officers. He was fortunate that the diversity of his force provided men with different backgrounds, allowing him to cobble together a government from the resident talent. Of his headquarters staff, Francis Heritage was appointed Military Secretary, taking over all personnel management functions in addition to his duties as Brigade Major. From October 1914 to March 1915 he was also appointed Deputy Administrator under Holmes. Travers remained as Intelligence Officer and was employed during the Madang landings to take ashore the letter announcing the surrender to the German garrison. Basil Holmes was retained as Orderly Officer to his father, although both he and Travers became Holmes' goto officers over the coming months.

Other key appointees filled out the nascent government. Captain Walter Fry, who served briefly as Adjutant for the ill-fated 2nd Battalion and was a warehouseman in civilian life, was appointed Colonial Treasurer. Lieutenant Bede Goadby, the former Brigade Quartermaster, was appointed Director of Lands and Survey, allowing him to combine his military engineer training with his passion for botany. Lieutenant Guy Manning, a former plantation manager in Papua, was appointed Commissioner of Native Affairs. Lieutenant Keith Heritage, who in civilian life was a manger with the Union Steamship Company of New Zealand, was appointed Supply and Transport Officer for the Administration and Government Storekeeper. Lieutenant Jens Lyng, a Danish-born German linguist and draftsman, was appointed Government Printer and Interpreter. He became responsible for producing the *Government Gazette*. Some of Beresford's officers were also seconded to government posts. Lieutenant James Whittle, RANR, became Director of Works; Lieutenant Oscar Gillman, RANR, became King's Harbourmaster at Rabaul; and Lieutenant Commander Augustus Livesay, RN, was appointed Supply Officer ANMEF.

Officers' Mess ANMEF, September 1914. After the German surrender the Australian occupation took on many of the characteristics of a peacetime colonial garrison. Back row, left to right: Lieutenant (formerly Sergeant) Alan Anderson; Captain Errol Kirke (Garrison Adjutant, Rabaul); unidentified; Lieutenant Guy Manning (Native Affairs); Lieutenant Keith Heritage (Supply and Transport Officer and Government Storekeeper); Lieutenant Reginald Norman; Lieutenant John Westgarth; Lieutenant Commander Augustus Livesay, RN (Supply Officer ANMEF); Lieutenant Ivan Sherbon; Lieutenant (formerly Sergeant) William Penly; Captain Charles Manning (Assistant Judge Advocate General); mess waiters. Second row: Mr Jolly; Lieutenant Robert Partridge; Captain Lionel Ravenscroft (Provost Marshal); Lieutenant John McDowell; Lieutenant Victor Sampson; Captain James Harcus (OC Number 1 Machine-gun Section); Major Robert Beardsmore (OC A Company); Lieutenant (formerly Colour Sergeant) Herbert Bruce; Lieutenant Harold Johnson; Lieutenant Rupert Sadler; Lieutenant Patrick Quinn; Captain Alexander Ralston (OC G Company); unidentified; Lieutenant Collins; mess waiters. Front row: Captain Thomas McPherson (OC D Company); Captain Reginald Travers (Staff Captain and Intelligence Officer); Major Francis Heritage (Brigade Major, Military Secretary and Deputy Administrator); Colonel William Holmes DSO, VD (Administrator); Lieutenant Colonel John Paton (Second-in-Command 1st Battalion); Lieutenant Colonel William Russell Watson (CO 1st Battalion); Major Frederick Maguire (PMO); Captain Cyril Lane (Adjutant 1st Battalion);

Lieutenant Basil Holmes (Orderly Officer); Lieutenant Strasbourg, RAN (AWM A03234).

Away from the seat of government at the larger settlements distant from Rabaul, Holmes appointed District Officers to command the local garrison and attend to the civil administration. Major Edward Martin was landed at Madang on 24 September with a garrison of 160 men and two months' provisions as the District Officer for New Guinea. Captain Richard Grant Thorold became the District Officer at Kavieng (*Käwieng*) for New Britain.

Law and order was the most pressing matter as the German surrender had created a power vacuum following the disintegration of the police force. Reports were soon received of unrest among the local inhabitants and a number of outlying plantations were burned or looted. Under the Terms of Capitulation, former Melanesian *polizeitruppen* were re-enlisted in the service of Australia, and ANMEF NCOs appointed to command the constabulary detachments. The other half of the law and order issue was the establishment of a judiciary. Under the provisions of the Hague Conventions, the civil law of the former power had to be maintained where this was not inconsistent with the occupation. This meant that Holmes was required to take over the existing court system. However, as a military governor acting on behalf of His Majesty's Government, he could not allow the Germans to continue to administer that system. Among his officers Holmes had recently promoted Captain Charles Manning who was a barrister-at-law from New South Wales. Manning was initially appointed Holmes' legal adviser on 12 September, then on 10 October he became Judge of the Colony and, five days later, he was appointed Assistant Judge Advocate General. In this final role he was responsible for advising Holmes on all military and civil legal matters, as well as acting as Judge of the District Court. Manning held the appointment until April 1915 when he returned home.

The infamous flogging incident. In retaliation for the beating of a British missionary, Holmes had five of the German assailants flogged. The summary punishment was carried out in the presence of the German male residents of Rabaul and members of the ANMEF. No photographs were supposed to have been taken, but even before mobile phones, Facebook and Twitter, it was almost impossible to keep such a public event secret. At least one enterprising individual turned his photograph into a postcard for sale (AWM A02630A).

One of the first challenges to Holmes' administration was the physical assault of a British civilian by a number of Germans. On 26 October 1914, just a month after the German surrender, six German civilians, inflamed by a heady mix of patriotic fervour and alcohol, seized and flogged the Reverend W.H. Cox, a British missionary at

Namatanai on New Ireland who they accused of being a British spy. Among those involved and regarded as the ringleader, was the local doctor, Maximillian Braunert. After Cox made his way to Rabaul and Holmes learned of the incident he decided the matter required swift and unequivocal action.

Holmes had Captain Charles Manning, as Assistant Judge Advocate General, investigate the matter and he prepared a report for Holmes in which he recommended that the individuals be arrested and brought to civil trial. Holmes despatched Captain Alexander Ralston with a platoon of 25 men to arrest those involved. Ralston managed to apprehend five of the six perpetrators and bring them back to Rabaul. Once the culprits were in custody, Holmes ignored Manning's recommendations and opted for quick extrajudicial punishment in line with Hammurabi's code of an eye for an eye. On 30 November the five Germans were assembled in front of the Rabaul garrison and the European male civilians. With due solemnity, the assailants were flogged in turn, while stretched across a large travelling trunk.

Although cameras were prohibited from the scene, a number of photos were taken and these were reproduced, achieving wide circulation.

At first the Australian government concurred with Holmes in his handling of the affair but, as news leaked out, the action caused a minor commotion. When the British government learned of the punishment it was concerned that this might prejudice the treatment of British citizens held in German custody. The immediate outcome was that some of the German colonial officials who remained in the colony to assist with the transfer of power resigned in protest and Holmes had them removed to Sydney.

Given the international implications, Holmes was criticised by the British government at the time and later by historians who decry his lack of political acumen in the handling of such a politically sensitive matter. On the other hand, he was trying to impose a firm, fair regime in a newly occupied territory where some German civilians, including a large number of paroled army reservists, were tacitly resisting his administration. From London his actions appear naive but, from where Holmes sat, the swift punishment of a bunch of drunken Teutonic thugs sent an unequivocal message to those who remained in the colony that violence towards British subjects and resistance to the occupation would not be tolerated. When the Australian government sought legal advice on the matter, Professor Pitt Corbett, Emeritus Professor of Law at Sydney University, concluded 'the action by the Officer in Command was justified as an indispensable measure of military precaution, coming fully within the exceptions to the ordinary rule of the applicability of territorial law, contemplated both by Article 9 of the Terms of Capitulation of the 17th September 1914, and by Article 43 of the Regulations annexed to the Hague Convention, No.4 of 1907.' Thereafter the controversy subsided, the remaining German residents remained peaceful and the action appears to have had no longer term implications. The same cannot be said of the poor behaviour of a handful of Holmes' troops.

Once the fighting was over, a darker side of the ANMEF's character emerged. In the weeks following the German surrender a crime wave swept the main garrisons, especially at Rabaul. The crimes committed by Holmes' troops included breaches of the Hague Conventions, atrocities against Melanesians, looting, ongoing drunkenness and various disciplinary infractions. Some of these crimes were committed in ignorance and reflect the inexperience of many of the officers and NCOs, others because no-one in authority stepped in to stop them, and still others because those who should have been responsible for ensuring good order and military discipline participated in the crimes. It is a fine line that prevents military units from descending into anarchy to become an armed mob. Holmes, in common with a number of his AIF counterparts, failed an early test to bring his troops under control and keep them there.

To Holmes' credit he quickly realised that he had problems within the ranks of the ANMEF, advising Legge and the Minister for Defence that he was endeavouring to find and severely punish the guilty. By November he would lament that:

> ...it is now only too apparent that some men who enlisted for the Expedition had unenviable records in Australia, and, owing to the fact that the force had to be despatched within a week ... there was no opportunity of making enquiry into previous character. It was, therefore, only to be expected that a leaven of men of evil reputation would detrimentally influence many men of previous character, but of weaker wills and poor individuality.... At first several minor cases occurred; in some the perpetrators were undiscovered while in others the offenders were somewhat leniently dealt with by summary punishment. This leniency, no doubt, gave confidence to those who were evilly disposed.

Drink, boredom and antagonism between Australian soldiers and German civilians only added to Holmes' problems.

Brigadier General Sir Samuel Augustus Pethebridge, Australian Commissioner for the Pacific Islands. Pethebridge replaced Holmes in the islands and is shown here wearing service dress with the Tropical Force colour patch on his left shoulder. After returning to Australia he died at his residence on 25 January 1918 and was buried with full military honours in the Box Hill General Cemetery, Victoria (AWM A02667).

As the expiry date for the six-month term of enlistment for his soldiers approached, Holmes reminded the Australian government that their term of service was due to end and that both his battalions would need to be relieved. Eventually a replacement was found for

Holmes—Colonel Samuel Pethebridge. An Australian-born public servant and RANR officer, Pethebridge had served as Acting Secretary of the Department of Defence from 1906 to 1910 and thereafter as the Secretary of the Department until appointed Australian Commissioner for the Pacific Islands. On 8 January 1915 he succeeded Holmes as Administrator of German New Guinea.

The force Pethebridge brought with him to replace Holmes' battalions was the 3rd Battalion ANMEF. This body, also known as Tropical Force and the North West Expeditionary Force (and derisively nicknamed the Coconut Lancers), was raised in October 1914 and originally destined for the relief of those Japanese forces garrisoning the former German island territories north of the Equator. When Britain struck an agreement with Japan, allowing the Japanese garrisons to remain for the duration of the war, Pethebridge's force was left without an immediate task. Having already departed aboard SS *Eastern* on 28 November, Pethebridge was initially directed to conduct a fruitless expedition up the Sepik River in search of a non-existent secret German base. Once the Australian government was advised of the accord between Britain and Japan, it decided to redirect Pethebridge and employ his battalion to replace Holmes' garrisons.

On 9 January 1915, Holmes, Watson and 250 members of the ANMEF departed for Sydney leaving Paton and the remainder of the force to follow on. On 10 February the last of the original ANMEF left the islands and in March the force was disbanded. Thereafter many of the members of Australia's first expeditionary force re-enlisted in the AIF alongside Holmes.

Pethebridge and his successors continued to administer the occupied territory until 9 May 1921. On that date the last military Administrator of New Guinea handed over to the new Australian civil administration established to govern the mandate on behalf of the League of Nations. Although New Guinea became a backwater during the last four years of the war, Lieutenant Hermann Detzner still held out in the jungle where he had defiantly withdrawn in 1914. In late November 1918 he heard of the Armistice in Europe from a worker at the Sattelberg Mission. He wrote a letter to the Australian commander at Morobe offering to surrender. On 5 January 1919, attired in his carefully preserved dress uniform, the Bavarian officer surrendered at the Finschhafen District Headquarters and from there he was shipped to Australia and then repatriated to Germany. Herman Detzner holds the distinction of being the last German Army officer to surrender in the Great War.

As Detzner was making his way home, the Australian Prime Minister, William 'Billy' Hughes, was in Paris attending the Versailles Peace Conference. Against the wishes of Britain, Hughes successfully argued for separate dominion representation at the conference so that the self-governing territories could state their own case for compensation and a division of the German overseas territories. The irascible, gnome-like Hughes quickly earned the ire of American president Woodrow Wilson. Wilson, a professor of jurisprudence and a former president of Princeton, had joined the war reluctantly and late. His 'Fourteen Points' delivered in 1918 reiterated that the war was being fought for a moral cause and for post-war peace in Europe. Wilson envisaged a peace based on decolonisation, disarmament and the League of Nations.

Australia's wartime Prime Minister, William Morris Hughes visiting Australian troops in Belgium in February 1919. At the Versailles Peace Conference Hughes' irreverence and impish humour made him something of an enfant terrible to more dignified delegates, especially American President Woodrow Wilson. Hughes concentrated on three questions that he considered vital to post-war Australia: reparations from Germany, control of German New Guinea and the exclusion of a race equality clause in the covenant of the League of Nations. By the time he signed the treaty on 28 June

1919 he had gained the lion's share of what he sought. He returned home to a hero's welcome (AWM E04366).

For Australia, Wilson's fifth ideal of readjusting colonies fairly fell on Hughes' deaf ear. The main bone of contention was the fate of German New Guinea. Wilson wanted the former protectorate declared a trustee territory of his proposed League of Nations. To Hughes this was Australia's strategic front door and, now that Australia had wrestled it from German hands, he had no intention of handing it over to any other body. Hughes believed that the blood price Australia paid during the war to defeat Germany was sufficient justification and the size of the Australian casualty list, which was greater than that of the United States, entitled the Commonwealth to outright ownership. 'Am I to understand that Australia is prepared to defy the opinion of the whole civilised world, Mr Hughes?' Wilson demanded. Hughes fiddled with his hearing aid and pretended not to have heard. Wilson repeated the question. 'That's about the size of it,

Mr President', Hughes eventually replied. Doubt has been cast on this anecdote and Donald Horne suggests that 'it may even have been concocted in the Wilson camp' but it does encapsulate Hughes' nationalist stand. On 28 June 1919, exactly five years after the assassination of Archduke Franz Ferdinand, the plenipotentiaries assembled in the Hall of Mirrors to affix their signatures and seals to the Treaty of Versailles ending the state of war between Germany and the Allied powers.

To meet Australia's demands over German New Guinea a special C class mandate was created. Although not technically a colony, Australia was granted the 'full power to administer [New Guinea] ... as an integral part of the Territory of the Commonwealth'. This meant Australia could apply its own immigration and trade laws. International control of New Guinea and the inclusion of a 'racial equality' clause in the League of Nations' covenant, Hughes declared in his highly nasal style, would have meant the end of the White Australia policy and opened a door for a potential enemy, but now 'national safety [was] assured, as far as 5,000,000 people can assure it'. For Australians, German New Guinea was a prize of war and a gesture of compensation for those 60,000 Australians who had died for the Empire.

CHAPTER 7

AN AFFAIR OF CONTINUOUS GOOD LUCK?

The Australian naval historian, Arthur Jose, viewed the action at Bita Paka as 'an affair of continuous good luck'. In identifying what had won the day for the Australians, he believed 'Bowen's bluff..., Bond's audacity..., and the happy accident which prevented the explosion of the road-mine, were the decisive features.' Seaforth Mackenzie, on the other hand, considered the 'capacity of the Australians to fight in bush' and 'escaping the mines' as the key to their success. While luck and good tactics certainly played a role in the outcome of the battle, and on the back of this success Holmes was able to quickly conclude the New Guinea campaign, just how much was the Australian success due to these tactical advantages? Or were there other factors—strategic and operational—that shaped Australia's first victory of the Great War?

Recent Australian accounts of the New Guinea operations, following the lead of the *Official Histories,* generally focus on the day of the battle and take a cautiously glowing view of Australian tactical performance. In these standard histories, the swift and successful conclusion to the operation chronologically positions Bita Paka as a neat preliminary to the great AIF enterprises to follow on Gallipoli. Eight of the naval personnel involved in the action, including five officers and three ratings, were recommended for bravery awards. Bowen's recommendation for the DSO spells out the importance of his early success:

> By his disposition of skirmishers [he] discovered what was virtually an ambush, and by capturing the 3 Germans in command, utterly demoralised the native police and probably averted a disaster to the small party of Naval Reservists. Later on, the scheme of attack drawn up by him & Lieutenant Hill

proved to be sound, [and] eventually brought about the surrender of the trench.

Doubts over the legality of some of Bowen's actions probably led to the downgrading of his recommendation to an MID. Not so Bond, and, even though he too committed a war crime, he eventually received the DSO for:

...conspicuous ability and coolness under fire in leading his men through most difficult country and enforcing the terms of surrender whilst drawing off an attack by another body of the enemy. He showed great daring, when accompanied by only one officer and one man, in suddenly disarming 8 Germans in the presence of 20 German native troops drawn up under arms, all of whom were then marched off and held prisoners. Later he personally captured 5 armed natives.

Bowen became the first Australian officer decorated during the war. Elwell, Hill, Palmer and seven other navy personnel received MIDs. Pockley's sacrifice tending the wounded portends the same selflessness displayed by the more famous John Kirkpatrick Simpson (and his donkey) and he received a posthumous MID, while Travers was commended for services in action. The public recognition fits very neatly with the view that the men of the ANMEF were Australia's heroes before Gallipoli. Such is the accepted narrative, although the story is more complex and multi-layered.

At the operational level the two Australian services deserve considerable credit. At the top, the two senior commanders—afloat and in the field—were surprisingly capable given their lack of experience in joint operations. This is all the more notable since they were administered by distinct government departments, they operated on separate chains of command and neither service had operated so intimately together before. The success of navy-army relations, with little of the inter-service friction often prevalent in joint operations, probably stems from the personalities involved and the integrated command structure. Patey performed well juggling his dual responsibilities as Rear Admiral Commanding the Australian Squadron and joint expedition commander. Equally important, Patey and Holmes appear to have maintained a professional, cordial relationship. Holmes referred decisions to the Admiral when appropriate, while at their first meeting Patey made it clear that he intended to let soldiers run operations ashore without interference from him. The appointment of Stevenson as both *Berrima*'s captain and Holmes' naval Chief of Staff undoubtedly assisted matters, providing Holmes with an immediate adviser on issues such as shipboard routine, landing operations, naval gunfire support and the peculiarities of service culture that could easily have become a problem in such an extemporised organisation, especially since the brigade was only united for the first time when the contingents boarded *Berrima* in Sydney.

The navy's performance certainly warrants greater recognition than it has received up to now. Pearce's, Creswell's and especially Deakin's determination to make the RAN a reality was in

Australia's strategic interest. Without Patey and the fleet unit, the New Guinea (and Samoan) expeditions could not have been completed so promptly. That New Zealand had to rely on Australian warships to escort its expedition says much about the decision to build an Australian fleet versus paying Britain a subsidy to build additional British vessels that were notionally 'Australian'.

In actual fact the operational aspect that probably predetermined the successful outcome of the campaign was logistics. The pre-positioning of war stores by the RAN allowed Patey to quickly prepare his ships and despatch them to their war stations. The swift mobilisation of the ANMEF, with most classes of supply, was an equally significant achievement, especially since no specific preparations had been made by the army prior to the war. Against the overall success, it should be noted that there were no pre-positioned stocks earmarked for such an expedition and so compromises were necessary. This included the substitution of the army mess tins and the shortage of signalling equipment already noted. Despite these shortfalls *Aorangi* departed Sydney with two months' provisions for the force and its fresh rations were supplemented at Palm Island. Potable water was provided from *Berrima* until the force was established ashore and it could source water locally. Ammunition expenditure was limited during the small number of engagements at Bita Paka and Toma, so Holmes was able to establish his force ashore with what was on hand. Thereafter, with the demise of the German raiders, resupply was effected from Australia by regular steamer runs from Sydney. New Guinea may therefore add another 'first' since it was the only theatre in which Australia relied on its own logistic resources to fully supply its forces. On Gallipoli, in Egypt and Palestine, and on the Western Front the AIF was largely dependent on British logistics support and industry.

One particularly crucial facet of logistics was medical support. The early loss of Pockley aside, medical arrangements for the ANMEF were sound, despite the absence of any tropical medicine specialists and pre-positioned stocks of tropical medical stores. In this case Howse was fortunate to be able to procure drugs such as quinine from chemists in Queensland on the voyage north. Furthermore, the medical system performed very well under tight timelines and, in fact, Howse's staff did better than the much larger AIF staff in weeding out ineffective soldiers prior to Gallipoli. Howse's initiative was crucial and even something as simple as ensuring there was a dentist with the force saved a material amount of disability, inconvenience and suffering. The *Official History of the Australian Medical Services* records that, between August 1914 and December 1915, the force dentist 'performed some 108 extractions, 160 fillings, and some 50 dental dressings for abscess'. On his return to Australia in 1915 Maguire submitted a strongly worded report on the need to provide effective dental treatment in the field. As a result, dental surgeons were eventually appointed to the AIF, although a separate dental corps was not raised until 1943.

The ANMEF's tactical performance, however, has been inconsistently judged. Australian accounts, including the official histories and recent popular accounts, are for the most part positive. In contrast, German historian Herman Hiery offers a disparagingly negative interpretation, finding it 'quite astonishing that ... a hastily assembled indigenous troop of former plantation labourers and half-trained policemen, numbering just under forty together with five Germans, could hold four hundred Australians armed with machineguns at bay for five hours.' He makes much of the ANMEF's difficulties in subduing the defenders, implying it was incompetent. Underpinned by a stout defence, he opines, Haber managed to wring liberal surrender terms out of Holmes. Given the clear divergence of opinion there is a need to reassess the performances of both sides.

In assessing Holmes, we have to be cognisant of the two tasks given to him. The first was the capture of the wireless station and the occupation of the German territories. The second was the establishment of a viable temporary occupation administration. His second task was mostly administrative in nature and, aside from the distant outcries over the flogging incident and indiscipline among his troops, Holmes managed to create and implement an effective administration.

In completing his first task, Holmes had the advantages of considerable command experience and some prior operational service. While his experience on the veldt was geographically different from the operations he supervised in New Guinea, the Australian commander had been exposed to all the latest battlefield technologies including smokeless powder rifles, machine-guns and quick-firing artillery and he knew how these impacted on tactical operations. He also appreciated the importance of leadership and that defeating an enemy was as much a psychological endeavour as it was physical. His only real error was in discounting the enemy's vote in these proceedings and this began with a plan that dismissed the possibility of German resistance.

Despite the relatively accurate intelligence provided by Legge, Holmes decided he would face no opposition. Just how he came to such a conclusion becomes clear from a reading of his 'Appreciation of the Situation'. Although few historians pay much attention to military staff work, the problem is that, without taking sufficient account of the planning process and what commanders did and didn't know at the time, it is all but impossible to make a balanced and fair assessment of their ability. Troops and supplies do not magically appear on the battlefield and enormous effort is required to marshal forces and deliver them to the right point, at the right time, and in a condition to fight. Any appraisal of why naval and military organisations succeed or fail has to take into account not only what transpired but what was planned and how it was executed. Then, as now, competent commanders begin planning with an assessment of the task and the various factors that may influence its accomplishment. Holmes did just that on 1 September aboard *Berrima*. In his appreciation he wrote, 'I do not anticipate any opposition to landing, or occupation at either place.' His reasoning is laid out later where he notes that Patey's earlier landings on New Britain in August met with no resistance and such an assessment could only have been reinforced by Patey's later Samoan mission, which was achieved without a shot being fired. In weighing the evidence, Patey and Holmes were both lulled into thinking that the Germans would just give up and, from that miscalculation, stemmed many of the initial problems ashore.

Having made their assessment Patey and Holmes gave the plan form so that their intentions could be passed unambiguously to those subordinates tasked with their execution. Based on their evaluation two small landing parties from No.4 Naval Company were sent ahead to execute the task of seizing the two suspected wireless sites, while the main body occupied the major German settlements. This was the gist of Holmes' verbal orders on the afternoon of 9 September and his confirmatory instructions published the following day. The problem was that the initial landing groups were under-strength and lacked immediate support. Patey and Holmes needlessly exposed them to possible defeat or even annihilation if the Germans opposed them.

Miscalculation by the senior commanders thrust great responsibility onto the shoulders of their junior officers who had to execute the plan. At this level, leadership proved to be of mixed quality. Most of the junior naval officers performed competently and some, notably Bond, Bowen and Elwell, were outstanding. Likewise, a number of army commanders were noted for their diligence and emerge with the respect of their men, although none was really tested, other than Travers. The more senior leadership however, did come in for criticism during the battle. When Bowen found himself facing unexpected opposition and requested urgent support, there was no control over the flow of reinforcements, resulting in the despatch of Hill's disparate (and probably desperate) crew who provided little in the way of combat power and really only provided the Germans with additional targets. Once ashore the rapidly developing situation meant that there was no clear chain of command and the passage of information was poor. Elwell was left to grope his way forward. Moving up in support, he was uncertain where Bowen's troops were and he very nearly launched an attack on those he was sent to reinforce.

There are also cases in which the available weapons were not employed to best effect and this is certainly the case in the handling of the machine-guns. Beresford's battalion was allocated one of the machine-gun sections, though whether due to their weight or a lack of familiarity with their capabilities, the guns were relegated to the rear and only came forward behind Elwell. Hence they played no active role in clearing the German positions. In fairness, machine-guns at that time were viewed essentially as a defensive weapon and their capabilities in attack were underrated, except perhaps by the machine-gunners themselves. Private Axtens was certainly vocal in his criticism of what he perceived as the under-utilisation of the guns and, in his view, if the section had been sent forward earlier it could have covered the assault on the trenches and spared some Australian casualties.

Soldiers' rumours at the time related that, after the battle, Holmes rebuked Beresford for his handling of the operation. Soldier gossip aside, Beresford can certainly be accused of exercising little control over his troops before he landed and, once ashore, he appears to have been willing to despatch junior officers to perform tasks he probably should have undertaken himself. While it was a widely held opinion in army ranks that the naval troops had blundered, the problems all lead back to Patey's and Holmes' faulty assessments rather than to any failing of the sailors and their immediate officers. In the wake of the Great War, military theorist J.C.F. Fuller observed that:

> Intelligent obedience is but another name for initiative, and of all the qualities a soldier must possess, initiative will prove the most useful or the most dangerous

according to its application. Initiative is really obedience without orders, that is, obedience with reference to the general plan and object of the operations as governed by the conditions of the moment.

There can be little doubt that the naval troops on the Bita Paka road and in subsequent operations performed as well as their superiors could expect of them using their initiative under trying and novel conditions. In doing so they saved their seniors from a potentially dangerous reverse.

On the negative side, there are strong indicators of poor standards of individual training among the Australian troops, despite Holmes' earlier claims from Palm Island. Fire discipline was an issue that plagued the force, with one sailor recording two separate incidents of unauthorised discharges—the first when a rifle was accidentally fired while being loaded during the battle; the second involved his commander negligently discharging his pistol at night and causing a false alarm. There is also evidence that a number of ANMEF casualties were probably caused by Australian fire rather than German Mausers. Able Seaman William Lane described just how easily this could occur: 'Shooting going on all around us. Not knowing whether it was the enemy or our own men. Not knowing the German uniform and not knowing they had natives fighting for them we were in danger of shooting our own men or being mistaken for the enemy.' There was plenty of indiscriminate shooting during and after the battle, with accidental discharges, friendly fire and cases of fire directed at alleged snipers who turned out to be misidentified civilians.

Bandsman Bollard recorded one fatal accident in which a friendly Melanesian was shot by an Australian sentry. The Melanesian was working as a messenger for the Australians at Rabaul on the day of the surrender. He had been given the password to ensure that he could deliver his messages unmolested. Regrettably, when challenged by the sentry he forgot the password, panicked and tried to flee. In the confusion the sentry shot him in the back. Bollard merely acknowledged that it was a shame as the native was popular. Similar cases occurred on Gallipoli, notably when the partially deaf CO of the 2nd Battalion (AIF), Lieutenant Colonel George Braund, failed to hear the challenge of a sentry at night and was shot dead by one of his men.

It is equally true that three of the Australian casualties occurred during the attempted prisoner escape when it is unlikely that any of the German prisoners were armed. In this instance it appears possible that some, if not all, of the Australian losses can be attributed to friendly fire. Able Seamen Street, Sullivan and Tonks were all hit during the crossfire, Street's wounds proving mortal. If all three men were victims of friendly fire, it means that 16% of Australian fatalities and 50% of the wounded were due to friendly fire, overall a third of the ANMEF casualties sustained on 11 September.

Such evidence can be presented as an indicator of incompetence, as Hiery suggests, although it more accurately reflects the confused nature of jungle fighting involving novice troops.

Disorientation and uncertainty is inevitable under such conditions and consistent with historical trends for troops engaged on terrain where visibility is restricted, engagement ranges short, and positive target identification difficult. In fact it is highly likely that some of the German casualties were also fratricides but no-one bothered to record these Melanesian losses.

If the ANMEF's tactical performance was not as adroit as Australian accounts usually imply, it was certainly sustained and adaptable. The Germans clearly expected their opponents to march down the Bita Paka road where they would be clear targets for their entrenched riflemen and mines. The evidence on both sides is explicit: the naval troops used flankers and worked through the jungle to avoid the obvious fire lane of the road. When in contact, they manoeuvred using a mix of flanking moves and direct assault. For first-time jungle fighters they did well.

Then there is the German performance to consider. War is not a sporting contest where sometimes the best team loses. Battlefield results are brutal but arbitrary and, by definition, only the best team wins. German performance in the campaign has to be considered at both the operational and tactical levels. Operationally, Spee was the German main effort and, when it came time to weigh his options, he was caught in a quandary. He knew he was expected to wage commerce warfare against Allied maritime trade and yet he had a poor opinion of such a course. He was a proud man, an Admiral in the Imperial German Navy and the commander of the only remaining German squadron outside Europe. He gave little thought to wasting *Scharnhorst* and *Gneisenau* as commerce raiders and furthermore he demonstrated his poor opinion of the value of trade warfare by summoning his dispersed light cruisers to join him in the central Pacific, thereby concentrating rather than scattering the combat power of his squadron. In the end, he had a wager each way, unleashing *Emden, Cormoran* and *Prinz Eitel Friedrich* to raid, while taking the bulk of the squadron on a dash across the Pacific. In the process he won one action at Coronel and lost another at the Falklands. His raiding cruisers, notably *Emden,* enjoyed short, illustrious careers before being destroyed or interned.

Spee would probably have achieved more by embracing the commerce plan. *Emden* wreaked havoc across the Indian Ocean on its own and the other light cruisers may well have spread mayhem across the Indo-Pacific region. At the very least, the British would have been forced to deploy more assets to hunt down these rogue cruisers. At best, Spee's two big ships might even have been able to score a victory against the odds if they had intercepted one of the expeditionary force convoys bound for Samoa, New Guinea or Europe. While Spee did cause worry and some delay in the despatch of the first Australian and New Zealand troop convoy, in the final analysis he didn't achieve his mission and his fleet was lost for little gain.

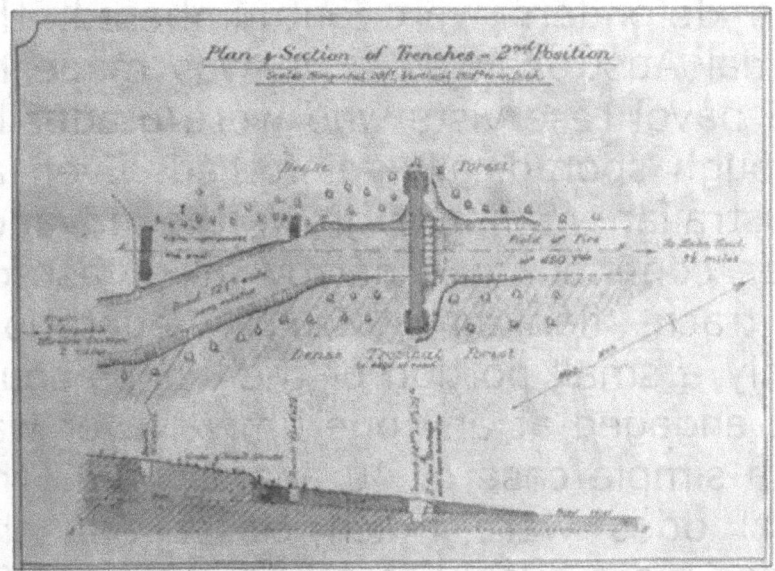

Detail from the map produced by Lieutenant Bede Goadby (Director of Lands and Survey) of the Bita Paka road after the battle. This plan of the second German trench shows how well-sited and formidable the German defences were. Unfortunately for Klewitz his subordinates failed to make the most of the German tactical advantages (author image, detail from AWM G8140.S65).

On land German tactical performance was equally deficient. While Hiery offers a sanguine portrayal of a plucky German defence against the odds, implying the Germans were the better side even though they lost, such an assessment is clearly fatuous when the evidence is examined. On his claim that the defenders were outnumbered, the initial Australian advance was made by 25 naval reservists who were gradually, though sporadically reinforced. Even as Australian numbers grew, the advance was confined to a narrow front astride a track, flanked by thick vegetation. Only a small portion of the troops could be engaged at any one time. Never was it a simple case of 40 against 400. The real odds were much closer and the sides more evenly matched. Around 200 Australian sailors and soldiers were involved in the fighting on 11 September. German combatants amounted to around 140 by German count, with at least 107 becoming casualties—killed, wounded or taken prisoner. The Germans also had significant advantages in that they were acclimatised, they knew the ground, and they fought from prepared positions.

In theory, the German tactics were sound and Klewitz produced as good a plan as possible within the political constraints he faced; in practice they proved unworkable. Klewitz's plan aimed to withdraw those detachments facing a superior force, while employing unengaged groups to counter-attack exposed flanks. He combined this with good use of field defences and makeshift mines. If there is a deficiency in his concept, it stems from a reluctance to directly oppose the Australian landing parties. With his sizable covering force, Klewitz could have inflicted early casualties on either or both parties as the exposed sailors disembarked. Thereafter his troops could have beat a quick retreat into the relative safety of the jungle. His decision to discount this option was probably based on three factors. First, there was an erroneous assumption that any landings would be made by short-term raiders rather than long-term invaders. Second, he was concerned about the firepower of the naval guns if he lingered near the coast. While such a fear is understandable, Gallipoli was to demonstrate that both the Germans and British overestimated the effectiveness of shipboard guns against entrenchments. Third, and looming large in German political calculations, was the fear of property damage. If resistance was offered close to the coastal settlements, German government and civilian property would be destroyed in any bombardment, an outcome Haber and the German population were desperate to avoid.

Self-imposed constraints aside, whatever miscalculations Klewitz made in drafting his plan, the real problem lay with the execution. As a professional soldier with considerable colonial experience he should have considered Carl von Clausewitz's approbation that war on paper is not war in reality. However he appears to have underestimated the demoralising effect of 'friction'. This concept, first proposed by the great Prussian theorist, occurs when 'countless minor incidents—the kind you can never really foresee—combine to lower the general level of performance, so that one always falls far short of the intended goal.' Its general effect Clausewitz described in the well-known phrase: 'Everything in war is very simple, but the simplest thing is difficult.' Clausewitz stressed that friction, accompanied by fear and fatigue, defines war and distinguishes war in theory from war in the flesh.

Although Klewitz's plans were sound on paper, once the fighting commenced, they quickly unravelled. He and his subordinates underrated their foe and failed to capitalise on their advantages: the early German local numerical superiority was squandered; Wuchert's force failed to detonate the mines; Mayer mistimed the counter-attack; and, worst of all, most of their trained leaders quickly surrendered, culminating in eight of them being disarmed by a single, determined naval officer. German tactical performance was simply poor. Haber later admitted as much to Midshipman Stan Veale stating, 'his defence arrangements were a week too late, and ... [the ANMEF] arrived a week to[o] soon.... He said although [his German troops] ... were all trained Army reservists, they were not too much good as soldiers.'

German prisoners of war and internees, Sydney, 1914 (SPC-A).

Given that popular opinion has cast the German Army in both world wars as a formidable fighting machine, it appears anomalous that resistance in New Guinea was so ineffective. Certainly most Germans who surrendered claimed that the native police were responsible for the quick capitulation. Indeed most accounts stress how poorly the Melanesian troops performed and how their training was substandard. This claim is undermined, at least in part, by witnesses who observed the police and commented on their fine bearing, especially when they paraded at Kokopo to lay down their arms. Of course, good drill at a surrender ceremony is hardly irrefutable evidence of a well-trained army; however it does indicate that the police may have become the scapegoat for defeat in much the same way as the Imperial German Army would later claim it was 'stabbed in the back' by the civil populace in 1918. Even if the Melanesian police performed as poorly as the Germans claimed, surely that fault lies with those who trained and led them—as the old military adage affirms, there are no bad soldiers only bad officers.

Only Haber appears to have accepted responsibility for his role in the affair and he apportioned at least some of the blame to his German troops. Australian participants agree. Veale judged 'that if the German troops had been more boldly led ... our losses must have been greater.' It was a lack of leadership and resolve that undid the Germans, not the myth of perfidious police. Interpretations aside, what cannot be disputed is the outcome. The radio transmitter was put out of action in one day, the Germans capitulated in less than a week, surrendering all their forces and territory within 10 days of the Australian landing. The ANMEF achieved its mission at an acceptable cost and, in war, victory is always the final determinant of success.

EPILOGUE

For some of the protagonists the New Guinea campaign was their brief moment of glory before they disappeared into obscurity, for others it was a springboard to greater achievements and for a handful it was a prelude to further tragedy. After his success commanding the Pacific expeditions, Patey was promoted to vice admiral on 21 September 1914. However, the rest of his war was something of an anticlimax as he missed the great fleet action at Jutland and was instead commanding the North American and West Indies Cruiser Squadron in the western Atlantic. Promoted admiral in 1918, he retired in 1919 and passed away in 1935 aged 76.

John Stevenson saw further sea duty with the RAN during and after the war until he retired as a rear admiral in 1931. His first son, who was a Spitfire pilot in the Royal Air Force, was killed over Dunkirk in 1940 while his second son, Captain John Phillip Stevenson, followed his father into the RAN and was the ill-fated CO of HMAS *Melbourne* when his ship collided with the American destroyer USS *Frank E. Evans* in 1969.

ANMEF officers of the Rabaul garrison, 1914. Identified, back row, standing (left to right): Second Lieutenant (formerly Warrant Officer Class Two, later Major) Harold Johnson; Lieutenant (later Major) John Maughan; Lieutenant (later Major) Ivan Sherbon (killed in action in France); Lieutenant (later Major) Victor Sampson (killed in action in France); Lieutenant (later Major) John Westgarth; Lieutenant Patrick Quinn; Second Lieutenant (formerly Sergeant, later Major) Alan Anderson; Lieutenant (later Major) John McDowell; Second Lieutenant (later Major) Robert Partridge; Lieutenant (later Colonel) Rupert Sadler; Lieutenant (later Major) Herbert Bruce; Second Lieutenant (formerly Sergeant, later Lieutenant) William Penly. Front row, seated: Lieutenant Lionel Ravencroft;

Captain (later Lieutenant Colonel) Alexander Ralston; Lieutenant Colonel (later Major General) John Paton; Captain (later Major) Sydney Goodsell; Captain (later Major) Charles Manning (killed in action in France). Of these 17 ANMEF officers, only Partridge did not serve with the AIF (AWM H15065).

Billee Holmes arrived home to an acrimonious welcome. Undeterred by an ungrateful nation he quickly joined the AIF and, on 16 March 1915, he took command of the 5th Infantry Brigade (AIF). He led his brigade on Gallipoli and the Western Front, before being promoted to command the 4th Australian Division in France in January 1917. On 2 July he was escorting the Premier of New South Wales on a tour of the Messines battlefield where the 4th Division had recently fought. Moving on foot along a usually safe track behind Hill 63, the party was bracketed by a salvo of German artillery fire. Holmes was the only member of the party hit. He was quickly evacuated to the nearest medical station but died. In 1919, in recognition of his distinguished service, the New South Wales government named the newly opened two-lane road linking Ramsgate and Mascot, in Sydney's eastern suburbs, General Holmes Drive.

Officers of the 1st RAN Bridging Train. Back row (left to right): Sub-Lieutenant Barrow; Sub-Lieutenant Mandeville Barker, RANR; Warrant Officer Henry Smithers; Sub-Lieutenant Alexander Cameron; Captain Griffiths (acting Medical Officer). Front row: Lieutenant Hansley Read, RANR; Lieutenant Commander Leighton Bracegirdle DSO, RAN (CO); Lieutenant Reginald Buller, RANR. Read, Bracegirdle and Buller served with the ANMEF before joining the RAN's second shore battalion—the Bridging Train (AWM A01267).

Most of Holmes' officers joined the AIF on their return from the islands. Colonel William Walker Watson commanded the 24th Battalion (AIF) on Gallipoli and the Western Front, while Watson's second-in-command, John Paton, rose to command the 6th

Infantry Brigade (AIF). Almost all of Watson's company commanders went on to distinguish themselves, including Colonel Robert Beardsmore, who commanded the 32nd Battalion in France; Brigadier General Edward Norrie, who commanded the 25th Battalion; Richard Grant Thorold, who joined the British Army and commanded the 18th Battalion of the Welch Regiment; Lieutenant Colonel Harold Morrison commanded the 4th Pioneer Battalion; Lieutenant Colonel Alexander Ralston, the 2nd Machine Gun Battalion; Brigadier General Edward Martin, the 5th Infantry Brigade; and former soldier Thomas Marsden rose to command the 5th Machine Gun Battalion. Rupert Sadler, who started the war as the ANMEF's Signalling Officer, finished in command of the 17th Battalion with a DSO and Military Cross. Frank and Keith Heritage joined one of their brothers already serving at the front, while a fourth served with the Canadian Expeditionary Force. Regimental Sergeant Major Inglis also signed on again, finishing the war as a major with the Military Cross and the French

Médaille Militaire. The ANMEF may have seen little action but its ranks proved a fruitful recruiting ground. According to the Australian *Official History*, 727 of 1073 army members of the 1st Battalion ANMEF re-enlisted in the AIF.

Nor was it only Holmes' soldiers who saw further service. After disbanding Beresford's battalion, the Naval Board offered to raise a bridging train for service in Europe. Designed to provide pontoon bridges for river and canal crossings and other maritime engineering tasks, the 1st RAN Bridging Train was raised in February 1915, comprising 292 all ranks, under the command of New Guinea veteran Leighton Bracegirdle, with Thomas Bond as his second-in-command and Midshipmen Reginald Buller and Charles Hicks. Diverted to Gallipoli, the unit served creditably at Suvla from August to December constructing piers and landing stages, assisting with the supply of water and other beach tasks. Eventually the unit was disbanded in March 1917 and most of its personnel returned to naval duties, although around a third volunteered to join the AIF.

As for the maligned Kennedy men, they may have been rejected by Holmes and dogged by a reluctant ship's crew, but that did not dampen the desire of many to serve. When *Kanowna* returned to Townsville on 2 September a large number of officers and men immediately volunteered for the AIF. Among the 12 officers aboard *Kanowna,* four—Hutton Armstrong, Hugh Quinn, John Walsh and Samuel Harry—were killed on Gallipoli.

Lieutenant Samuel Harry, a Philadelphia-born soldier who was one of the Kennedy Regiment 'youngsters' rejected by Holmes. Harry was 32 years old when he volunteered and had grown up on the goldfields of Charters Towers where he became the town clerk. Sam Harry, Hugh Quinn and John Walsh were boyhood friends and, after arriving back in Townsville from Papua, the trio travelled to Brisbane and joined the 15th Battalion (AIF) of John Monash's 4th Infantry Brigade. Harry was killed on Gallipoli while serving as the unit Adjutant (Rose Vivian).

After service in the islands, Neville Howse returned home early to secure an appointment with the AIF. By 1919 he had risen to become Director Medical Services AIF. From 1921 to 1925 he was the Australian Army's Director-General of Medical Services but resigned to contest the federal seat of Calare for the Nationalist Party in the December 1922 election. He won and subsequently held several ministerial portfolios, including Defence, Health, and Home and Territories before being defeated in the October 1929 election. In February 1930 Howse travelled to England for medical treatment for cancer only to die later that year.

Commander Joseph Beresford returned to Australia and continued to serve in the RAN. In 1916 he was Mentioned in Despatches for his services with the ANMEF. His only son joined the AIF and served in France where he was killed in 1918. The tragedy came as a double blow as Beresford only belatedly learned that his son had not been killed accidentally, as originally advised by the military authorities, rather the young sergeant had been murdered by another AIF soldier ('fragged' in the modern jargon). Beresford passed away in Hobart in 1952 at the age of 91.

Bowen recovered from the head wound he suffered at Bita Paka and returned to duty as a member of the naval staff in Melbourne in April 1915. When he left Beresford's command his CO rated him as 'a calm and capable officer under fire and most trustworthy.' However his wife Agnes died in October, leaving Bowen to raise their infant daughter. In 1916 he became the first State President of the Returned Sailors' and Soldiers' Imperial League of Australia (the forerunner to the RSL) and in 1917 he remarried. He was promoted to commander in 1919 and retired from the navy in 1936.

After commanding the RAN's Bridging Train, Leighton Bracegirdle continued his long and distinguished career. He retired in 1947 as a rear admiral having served for 16 years as Military and Official Secretary to the Governor-General. His posting spanned the tenure of three incumbents from the first Australian-born Governor-General, Sir Isaac Isaacs, the wartime service of Lord Gowrie and finally the Duke of Gloucester. He was knighted, created a KCVO in the New Year's Day Honours of 1947.

Following Haber's surrender, he was shipped to Sydney before being permitted to leave Australia in January 1915 to make his way back to Germany via the United States. In Berlin he continued as Acting Governor of the occupied German territories until December 1917 when he officially replaced Hahl, who was finally stood down. At the peace talks in 1919, Haber was appointed to the German delegation negotiating the C class mandates, but he resigned due to the hopelessness of the arbitration process. He survived World War II and died in 1947.

The two German regular officers captured in the islands spent the rest of the war as prisoners at the Berrima and Liverpool camps in New South Wales. Klewitz returned to Germany in 1919 and married the following year. Between the wars he held the brevet rank of major in the German Army Reserve while working in financial offices in Dresden. As a reserve officer during World War II he served on the army staff in Poland and France, retiring as a lieutenant colonel in 1941. He died in 1945.

German prisoners of war at Holsworthy, 1916. Left to right: Lieutenant Georg Mayer, Colonel Robert Sands (Australian Commandant Holsworthy Camp) and Captain Carl von Klewitz (AWM P00595.066).

Herman Detzner's determination was rewarded when he arrived back in Germany in 1919. He was awarded the Iron Cross (First Class), promoted captain and later presented with an honorary doctorate from the University of Cologne. Adding to his post-war fame was his autobiographical account of his four-and-a-half-year adventure in the islands, dramatically titled *Among the Cannibals: In the Interior of German New Guinea under the Imperial Flag, from 1914 until the Armistice.* In his book he vividly described his life on the run including a number of expeditions of exploration and unsuccessful escape attempts. After enjoying early commercial success in the 1920s, parts of the book were discredited and, in 1932, he publicly admitted that he had mixed fact and fiction in creating his ripping yarn. Thereafter he eschewed public life. During World War II he was called up for duty and served in a bureaucratic capacity in the logistics branch of the military administration. He lived to the age of 88, passing away quietly in 1970.

The other German holdout, Hellmuth Baum, did not fare so well. He wandered barefoot during the war years among the untamed tribes, learning their ways and languages and prospecting for gold. After the Armistice he reported himself to the Australian authorities but was permitted to remain in New Guinea and so returned to his wanderings and prospecting. Reported as 'a gentle and just man' he was killed in 1931 by Kukukuku tribesmen he had welcomed into his camp.

In 1922 memory of the New Guinea campaign was briefly revived as the British armies sought to recognise units that had served with distinction in the Great War through the traditional allocation of battle honours. In 1927 the final list for Australian Army units was published and the battle honour 'Herbertshöhe' was authorised to acknowledge the fighting along the Bita Paka road. The two original ANMEF battalions (naval and military) were both entitled to claim this honour although both had disappeared long before the deliberations were finalised. Instead, through a numerical sleight of hand, the 1st and 2nd battalions of the AIF inherited the ANMEF's only battle honour and through the AIF this was passed to the militia's 1st Battalion (City of Sydney's Own) and the 2nd Battalion (The City of Newcastle Regiment). Following the major reorganisation of the Citizen Military Forces in the 1960s 'Herbertshöhe' was inherited by the 1st/19th and 2nd/17th battalions of the Royal New South Wales Regiment.

The RAN took a little longer to recognise the role of its ships and crew. It was not until 2009 that the navy decided to make an overdue evaluation of the allocation of campaign and battle honours for its ships and units. As a result, the Governor-General eventually gave approval for a number of new battle honours including recognition of the 1914 campaign. Among the RAN's new battle honours was 'Rabaul 1914', granted to the 18 vessels directly involved in the New Guinea operations: *AE1,AE2, Aorangi, Australia, Berrima, Encounter, Grantala, Koolonga, Melbourne, Murex, Parramatta, Protector, Sydney, Upolu, Waihora, Warrego, Whangape* and *Yarra.* The RAN Naval

Brigade was the nineteenth recipient, along with its entitlement to the battle honour 'Herbertshöhe'.

Today the waters of the Bismarck Archipelago still lap gently against the shores of Blanche Bay. To the north-east the looming peaks of 'Mother' and her two daughters still dominate the skyline around Simpson Harbour. Standing on the rocky breakwater at Kabakaul it does not take too much imagination to place oneself there a century ago when Bowen's small band landed and set off inland into the unknown in search of the elusive wireless transmitter. Taking a short detour off the bitumen that now paves the old dirt road to Bita Paka, it is easy to empathise with Palmer and Eastman as they struggled through the tangle of secondary growth until they encountered Mauderer and his Melanesian charges. Further along the road is the quiet cemetery close to where the wireless station once stood. Although the radio transmitter and its towers are gone, looking back down the road in the gathering gloom of a balmy tropical night, it takes little imagination to conjure an image of Bond, Travers and Eitel striding forward with their gaggle of prisoners to seize their objective and, in that one bold move, sealing the fate of German New Guinea. They might have been forgotten, but theirs was Australia's first victory of the Great War.

APPENDIX 1

CHRONOLOGY

1883	Queensland raises the British flag at Port Moresby on 4 April and unilaterally annexes the non-Dutch half of New Guinea. Britain quickly disavows the Queensland action.
1884	
3 November	German New Guinea Company raises the German flag at Matupi Harbour, New Britain.
6 November	Commodore J. Erskine proclaims a British protectorate over the south coast of New Guinea (to become Papua).
19 December	Germany officially informs Britain of its actions in New Guinea.
1885	Imperial letter of protection over German New Guinea issued on 17 May.
1898	Reichstag ratifies the treaty officially placing Kiauchau, China, under German protection and establishes a naval base at Qingdao. German government takes over administration of New Guinea.
1899	Germany purchases the Carolines, Marianas, Marshalls and Palau islands from Spain.
1900	Germany claims Apia, Samoa.
1901	Australian colonies federate on 1 January to become the Commonwealth of Australia.

1902	Colonial Office transfers the Territory of Papua to Australia.
1906	Commonwealth accepts administration of the Territory of Papua.
1911	CNF retitled the RAN on 10 July.
1912	Vice Admiral M. von Spee takes command of the East Asiatic Squadron.
1913	RAN squadron, with HMAS Australia as flagship, arrives in Sydney on 4 October under the command of Rear Admiral G. Patey.
1914	
27 June	Commonwealth Federal Parliament dissolved.
28 June	Assassination of Archduke Franz Ferdinand of Austria.
3 July	Colonel J.G. Legge departs London for return to Australia as CGS designate.
28 July	Austria declares war on Serbia.
30 July	Australia places RAN at the disposal of the Admiralty.
1 August	Germany declares war on Russia.
3 August	Germany declares war on France, RAN placed under Admiralty orders for the duration of war.
4 August	Germany invades Belgium, Britain declares war on Germany, Australia departs Sydney for its war station. The 2nd Infantry (Kennedy Regiment) mobilised.

6 August	Britain requests Australia seize the German radio stations at Yap, Nauru and New Guinea; New Zealand to seize Samoa. Spee's squadron leaves Pohnpei.
8 August	Legge arrives in Adelaide and assumes post as CGS.
9 August	Legge arrives in Melbourne.
10 August	Colonel William Holmes accepts offer of command of ANMEF. Recruiting for the AIF opens. SMS Cormoran departs Qingdao.
11 August	Recruiting for the ANMEF opens.
12 August	RAN squadron under Patey raids Blanche Bay, New Britain. HMS Hampshire puts radio station at Yap out of action and severs the deep-sea cable to the island.
15 August	New Zealand Samoan expeditionary force sails. Japan sends ultimatum to Germany demanding evacuation of Qingdao.
16 August	Patey ordered to rendezvous with the New Zealand Samoan expedition.
18 August	ANMEF embarks on HMAS Berrima.
19 August	Berrima departs Sydney.
21 August	Berrima arrives in Moreton Bay, Queensland.
23 August	Japan declares war on Germany, Japanese fleet blockades Qingdao.
24 August	Berrima arrives off Palm Island.
25 August	Japan declares war on the Austro-Hungarian Empire.
30 August	New Zealand expeditionary force occupies Samoa.

2 September	Berrima departs Palm Island. Japanese troops land to attack Qingdao.
4 September	Berrima arrives at Port Moresby, Australia and Melbourne depart Samoa, Melbourne proceeds to Nauru.
7 September	SMS Nürnberg cuts the undersea telegraph cable at Fanning Island. Berrima and SS Kanowna depart Port Moresby, Kanowna's stokers mutiny and the ship returns to Australia with the 2nd Battalion ANMEF.
9 September	Australia rendezvous with Berrima at Rossel Island. Melbourne reports the Nauru radio station out of action.
10 September	Kanowna docks in Townsville. First raid in Bay of Bengal by SMS Emden.
11 September	ANMEF lands on New Britain. Action on the Bita Paka road, wireless station captured.
12 September	Rabaul occupied by ANMEF.
13 September	British flag hoisted at Rabaul.
14 September	HMAS Encounter shells Toma ridge, Lieutenant Colonel William Watson leads an advance on Toma, and Acting Governor E. Haber agrees to surrender. SMS Scharnhorst and Gneisenau arrive off Apia.
15 September	Surrender negotiations open at Kokopo between Holmes and Haber. Scharnhorst and Gneisenau depart Apia.

17 September	Haber signs Terms of Capitulation. Third Fisher government takes office in Melbourne.
21 September	Surrender of remaining German forces at Kokopo. Patey promoted vice admiral.
22 September	Scharnhorst and Gneisenau bombard Papeete, Tahiti, and sink the French gunboat Zélée along with a captured German freighter.
24 September	ANMEF occupies Madang.
26 September	Cormoran escapes detection in Alexishafen near Madang.
7 October	Japanese forces occupy the Caroline and Marshall islands.
11 October	ANMEF captures KGS Komet.
17 October	ANMEF occupies New Ireland.
1 November	Battle of Coronel. Australian and New Zealand convoy sails from Albany, Western Australia.
6 November	ANMEF occupies Nauru.
7 November	Japanese and British forces capture Qingdao.
9 November	HMAS Sydney defeats SMS Emden off Cocos (Keeling) Islands.
17 November	Former KGS Komet re-commissioned as HMAS Una.
19 November	ANMEF occupies Admiralty and Western islands.
28 November	Tropical Force departs Sydney.

4 December	Australian and New Zealand convoy reaches Egypt.
8 December	Battle of Falkland Islands, Scharnhorst, Gneisenau, Leipzig and Nürnberg sunk.
9 December	ANMEF occupies Northern Solomon Islands.
14 December	Cormoran interned at Guam.

1915

5 January	First 26 ANMEF troops depart Rabaul for Australia.
8 January	Colonel Samuel Pethebridge becomes Administrator of German New Guinea.
9 January	Holmes, Watson and 260 ANMEF troops depart Rabaul.
14 January	Another 53 ANMEF troops depart Rabaul.
10 February	Lieutenant Colonel John Paton and remaining 726 ANMEF troops depart Rabaul. Naval Battalion and 1st Battalion ANMEF disbanded on return to Australia.
11 March	SMS Prinz Eitel Friedrich interned at Newport News, United States.
14 March	SMS Dresden scuttled after being cornered by an RN squadron off the coast of Chile.
25 April	Australian and New Zealand Army Corps lands on Gallipoli.

1917

Cormoran scuttled by crew on 7 April following the entry of the United States into the war.

1918

16 March	Brigadier General George Johnston appointed Administrator of New Guinea and Commander ANMEF.
11 November	Armistice in Europe.
14 November	Hostilities cease in East Africa.
28 November	Kaiser abdicates.

1919

5 January	Lieutenant Herman Detzner surrenders at Morobe, New Guinea.
18 January	Peace conference opens at Versailles.
1 May	Brigadier General Thomas Griffiths appointed Administrator of New Guinea and Commander ANMEF.
28 June	Versailles Peace Treaty signed.

1921

1 April	AIF officially disbanded.
5 April	Griffiths' appointment as Administrator of New Guinea and Commander ANMEF terminated. Brigadier General Evan Wisdom appointed Administrator of New Guinea.
6 April	C class Mandate for New Guinea received by Australia from League of Nations.
9 May	End of military occupation of German New Guinea.

APPENDIX 2
NAVAL AND MILITARY RANKS

Naval Ranks (German Equivalent)	Army Ranks (German Equivalent)	Typical Employment (naval/military)
Commissioned Officers		
Admiral of the Fleet (Grossadmiral)	Field Marshal (Generalfeldmarschall)	Titular head of service
Admiral (Admiral)	General (Generaloberstt)	Major fleet command/army commander
Vice Admiral (Vizeadmiral)	Lieutenant General (Generalleutnantt)	Fleet command/army corps commander
Rear Admiral (Konteradmiral)	Major General (Generalmajor)	Independent naval squadron/army division commander
Commodore (Kommodore)	Brigadier General	Naval squadron command/senior staff officer
Captain (Kapitdn zur See)	Colonel (Oberst))	Major combatant CO/brigade commander

Commander (Korvettenkapitön or Fregattenkapitän)	Lieutenant Colonel (Oberstleutnantt)	Flotilla commander or ship CO/battalion CO
Lieutenant Commander (Kapitdnleutnantt)	Major (Major)	Destroyer/submarine CO/battalion second-in-command
Lieutenant (Oberleutnant zur See)	Captain (Hauptmann or Rittmeister in the cavalry)	As above/Company OC
Sub-Lieutenant (Leutnant zur See)	Lieutenant (Oberleutnant)t)	Half-company OC
Acting Sub-Lieutenant	Second Lieutenant (Leutnant)	As above
Midshipman (Fähnrich zur See)	(Fähnrich)	Officer under training or probationary officer

Warrant Officers		
Warrant Officer (Oberstabsbootsmann)	Warrant Officer Class One (Feldwebel-Leutnant)	Brigade Sergeant Major, Regimental Sergeant Major
Chief Petty Officer (Oberbootsmann)	Warrant Officer Class Two (Feldwebel)	Signal Boatswain/Company Sergeant Major

Non-Commissioned Officers		

No equivalent	Colour Sergeant or Staff Sergeant (Vizefeldwebel or Vize·wachtmeister in the artillery)	
Petty Officer (Stabsbootsmann)	Sergeant (Sergeant)	Yeoman of Signals/half-company sergeant
No equivalent	Lance Sergeant	Usually a corporal acting in a sergeant's position
Leading Seaman (Quartiermeister)	Corporal (Unteroffizer)	Section commander
No equivalent	Lance Corporal	Section second-in-command

Seamen/Privates		
Able Seaman (Matrose 1 Klasse.)	No equivalent	Stoker or Writer
Ordinary Seaman (Matrose 2 Klasse)	Private (Gefreiter)	Driver, gunner, rifleman, sapper, signaller or trooper

APPENDIX 3

AUSTRALIAN ORDER OF BATTLE

RAN Squadron
- Commander: Rear Admiral George Patey KCVO, RN, commanding His Majesty's Australian Fleet
- Battle Cruiser: HMAS Australia, Flag Captain Stephen Radcliffe, RN
- Light Cruisers: HMAS Encounter, CO Captain Charles Lewin, RN

  HMAS Melbourne, CO Captain Mortimer Silver, RN

  HMAS Sydney, CO Captain John Glossop, RN

  HMAS Pioneer, CO Commander Thomas Biddlecombe, RNR
- Destroyer Flotilla: Commander Claude Cumberlege, RN
- Destroyers: HMAS Parramatta, CO Lieutenant Commander William Warren, RAN

  HMAS Warrego, CO Commander Claude Cumberlege, RN

  HMAS Yarra, CO Lieutenant Stewart Keightley, RAN
- Submarines: AE1, CO Lieutenant Commander Thomas Besant, RN
  AE2, CO Lieutenant Commander Henry Stoker, RN

Submarine tenders	HMAS Protector
	HMAS Upolu

Merchant fleet auxiliaries

HMAS Berrima (formerly SS Berrima), CO Commander John Stevenson, RN

Hospital Ship VIII (formerly SS Grantala), Master Captain R.E. Brissenden

Merchant ships taken up from trade

SS Aorangi (fleet supply vessel)

SS Kanowna (transport)

SS Kaituna (collier)

SS Koolonga (collier)

SS Murex (oiler)

SS Telena (oiler)

SS Waihora (collier)

SS Whangape (collier)

French Squadron

Commander	Rear Admiral A.L.M. Huguet
Armoured Cruiser	Montcalm

ANMEF

Commander	Colonel William Holmes DSO, VD

Naval Battalion—503 all ranks
- CO — Commander Joseph Beresford, RAN
- Left Wing — Lieutenant Commander George Browne, RN
- OC No 1 Coy — Lieutenant Commander Richard Lambton, VD, RANR
- OC No 2 Coy — Lieutenant Clarence Read, RANR
- OC No 3 Coy — Lieutenant Oscar Gillman, RANR
- Right Wing — Lieutenant Commander Charles Elwell, RN
- OC No 4 Coy — Lieutenant Rowland Bowen, RAN
- OC No 5 Coy — Lieutenant Stewart Cameron, RANR
- OC No 6 Coy — Lieutenant Thomas Bond, RANR

1st Battalion—1073 all ranks
- CO — Lieutenant Colonel William Russell Watson VD
- OC A Coy — Major Robert Beardsmore
- OC B Coy — Captain Edward Norrie
- OC C Coy — Captain Richard Thorold
- OC D Coy — Captain Thomas McPherson
- OC E Coy — Captain Harold Morrison
- OC F Coy — Captain Edward Twynam
- OC G Coy — Captain Alexander Ralston
- OC H Coy — Major Edward Martin

2nd Battalion—500 all ranks
- CO — Major Arthur Aitken
- OC A Coy — Captain Hugh Quinn (possible)

OC B Coy	Captain John Walsh (possible)
OC C Coy	Lieutenant Samuel Harry (possible)
Medical Section	Captain Stuart Kay

Machine-Guns

OC No 1 Section	Captain James Harcus
OC No 2 Section	Lieutenant Thomas Marsden

Medical

PMO	Lieutenant Colonel Neville Howse VC

APPENDIX 4

GERMAN ORDER OF BATTLE

East Asiatic Squadron

Commander	Vice Admiral (Vizeadmiral) Maximilian von Spee
Armoured Cruisers	SMS Scharnhorst, CO Captain (Kapiton zur See) Felix Schultz
	SMS Gneisenau, CO Captain (Kapiton zur See) Gustav-Julius Maerker
Light Cruisers	SMS Dresden, CO Captain (Kapiton zur See) Emil Fritz Lüdecke
	SMS Emden, CO Captain (Kapiton zur See) Karl von Müller
	SMS Leipzig, CO Captain (Kapiton zur See) Haun
	SMS Nürnberg, CO Captain (Kapiton zur See) Karl von Schonberg
Sloop	SMS Cormoran (immobilised at Qingdao)
Auxiliary Cruisers	SMS Cormoran (formerly SS Rjosan), CO Captain (Korvettenkapitän) Adalbert Zuckschwerdt
	SMS Prinz Eitel Friedrich, CO Captain (Korvettenkapitän) Max Therichens
Survey Vessel	SMS Planet, CO Captain (Korvettenkapitän) Oswald Collmann

German New Guinea

Civil Governor	Doctor Albert Hahl (absent in Germany)
Acting Governor	Deputy Governor Eduard Haber

Naval Assets

Government yacht KGS Komet, Captain (Korvettenkapiton) Karl Moeller

Polizeitruppen—670 all ranks

Police Commander	Captain of Cavalry (Rittmeister) Carl von Klewitz
Rabaul Garrison	OC 'Luttich', Lieutenant (Oberleutnant) Georg Mayer
	OC 'Bebra', Captain (Hauptmann) Hans Wuchert
	OC 'Samoa', Lieutenant (Oberleutnant) E.E. Fieberg
	Various observation groups

APPENDIX 5

COLONEL WILLIAM HOLMES' APPRECIATION OF THE SITUATION

The most important points to seize and occupy are (First) Herbertshöhe and Rabaul, then Frederick Wilhelmshafen.

These should be garrisoned fairly strongly, particularly Rabaul, and positions entrenched.

It may be advisable to place small garrisons at one or two other points, or at least post an Officer and a Sergeants' guard at each to represent British authority.

The flag to be hoisted at each of the important places, with as much ceremony as possible, and British occupation duly and publicly proclaimed.

Detailed instructions to be issued to the Officer in command of the garrison at each place as to disarming inhabitants, protecting life and property, securing law and order among natives, continuing Native Police, protecting supplies, hospitals, wharves, stores, supplies, etc.

From information received to date, I do not anticipate any opposition to landing, or occupation at either place.

After garrisoning the two main places, it would be advisable to keep balance of the Force on board the *Berrima* at Simpsonhafen in preference to camping ashore, in order to minimise the effects of Malaria, which it may be expected will be troublesome later on in the Summer when the mosquitos [sic] become active. The force would act as a mobile reserve for use wherever required, and to act as reliefs to the garrisons when necessary. The troops would go ashore daily for training.

I consider the force at present at my disposal on the *Berrima* is sufficient, from the information now to hand, to accomplish what is required.

With regard to the detachment now on board the *Kanowna* at Port Moresby; these are, I understand, mostly young Trainees under the Universal Training System, who form part of the Garrison Troops of Thursday Island, probably immature men. My present impression is, that it will not be necessary or advisable to take them on any further, but allow them to remain at Port Moresby as a Reserve, and await developments.

I prefer, however, before coming to a definite decision, to await arrival at Port Moresby, and ascertain their physical condition, as I should not be surprised if there are a good many sick among them already, in which case they would be a hindrance rather than an advantage. The condition of their equipment, and state of efficiency and training must also be ascertained.

I quite realise that as long as the German Warships in these waters are unaccounted for, there is danger, but I assume that as soon as my force has been safely disposed of on German Territory, the Warships of the Australian and China Stations will at once search for and definitely locate the hostile vessels, which will clear up the whole situation.

When this is accomplished it would seem quite unnecessary to further retain any considerable force in the vicinity, and, beyond what is required for garrison duty, the troops might be utilized in some other part of the Empire, and the Detachment now on board the *Kanowna* at Port Moresby could be returned to Queensland.

In considering these operations I am keeping in view the idea that these possessions will be maintained as British Colonies with, no doubt, Rabaul as Governing centre, on account of its fine harbour and other natural and physical advantages.

I am assuming there are no guns mounted at either Rabaul or Frederick Wilhelmshafen, but should my assumption be wrong, and opposition be met with, the guns of the fleet would be required to cover the landing, as my force is composed of Infantry and four Machine Guns only—no Artillery.

Should the harbour front at Rabaul be defended, the maps indicate that a landing could be accomplished at Talili Bay, which is connected with Simpsonhafen by three good roads—distance about 4 miles.

In view, however, of the result of the reconnaissance of Blanche Bay made recently by H.M.A.S. *Sydney* and destroyers, it seems reasonable to suppose that no opposition will be met, unless, of course, the German ships have since returned to this place, which is improbable.

**(sgd) WILLIAM HOLMES, Colonel
BRIGADIER COMMANDING**
Tuesday, 1st September, 1914.

APPENDIX 6

ANMEF OPERATION ORDER NUMBER 1

AUSTRALIAN NAVAL & MILITARY EXPEDITION: OPERATION ORDER NO.1 BY.
Colonel William Holmes, D.S.O., V.D., Brigadier Commanding:

H.M.A.S. "Berrima"
10-9-1914.

	(1)	The Expedition will occupy the German Colonies of New Britain tomorrow.
	(2)	Little, if any, resistance is anticipated.
HERBERTSHOHE GARRISON: O.C.Comm. J.A.H.Beresford R.A.N. 4 Coys. Naval Contingent 1 M.G. Section 1st Infantry 1 Section A.A.M.C.	(3)	One Coy. Naval Contingent (less details) has been despatched by H.M.A.S. "Sydney" to seize the Wireless Station near Herbertshohe. Arrangements for transport of the Herbertshohe of Garrison will be communicated personally to Commander Beresford. 150 rounds of ammunition per rifle and 1 week's rations to be taken.
RABAUL GARRISON: O.C. Lt.-Col.J.Paton, V.D. 1st Infy. 1 Coy. Naval Conting't 4 Coys. 1st Infantry. 1 Section M.G. 1st Infy. Signallers 1stt Infantry Section A.A.M.C.	(4)	The Force detailed in the margin under the command of Lt.-Col. J. Paton, V.D. will, as soon as kit can be disembarked from H.M.A.S. "Berrima", occupy and garrison the seat of Government at Rabaul. 150 rounds ammunition per rifle and 1 day's rations to be taken.
	(5)	Detailed instructions have been issued separately to O.C. Herbertshohe and Rabaul Garrisons.
	(6)	Provost Marshal will seize all Government property. Regimental Police 1st Infantry are placed under his orders.
	(7)	Messages in first instance to H.M.A.S. "Berrima".

(Sgd.) Francis Heritage
Major.
Brigade Major.

(O.C. Naval Cont.
To- (O.C. 1st Infantry
(P.M.O. & Provost Marshal.
By-A.D.C

APPENDIX 7

TERMS OF CAPITULATION OF GERMAN NEW GUINEA

Made this seventeenth day of September, 1914, between Colonel William Holmes, DSO, VD, Brigadier Commanding the Australian Naval and Military Expeditionary Force, on behalf of His Most Gracious Majesty King George the Fifth of the first part, and Herr E Haber, Acting Governor of the German Possessions known as Deutsch Neu Guinea, on behalf of the Imperial German Government of the second part.

WHEREAS the principal centres of Deutsch Neu Guinea have been occupied by an overwhelming force under the command of the said Colonel Holmes;

And whereas the said Acting Governor has no authority to surrender any portion of the German Possessions under his administration, but in view of the said occupation by the said overwhelming force, the said Acting Governor is prepared to give assurance that all military resistance to such occupation in Deutsch Neu Guinea shall cease forthwith.

NOW, the following terms and conditions are solemnly agreed upon between the said contracting parties:-

1. The name Deutsch Neu Guinea (German New Guinea) includes the whole of the German Possessions in the Pacific Ocean lately administered from Rabaul by the said Acting Governor on behalf of the German Imperial Government, and the said Possessions are hereafter referred to as "The Colony."
2. All military resistance to the said military occupation of the Colony shall cease forthwith.
3. The armed German and native forces now in the field are to be surrendered at Herbertshöhe on the 21st day of September at Ten (10) o'clock in the forenoon. Military honours will be granted.
4. Upon the said Acting Governor giving his parole to take no further part directly or indirectly in the present war, no obstacle

will be placed in the way of his returning to Germany. Such parole shall not prevent the said Acting Governor from tendering to the Imperial Government at Berlin such advice as he may deem proper with regard to terms of peace.

5. Such officers of the said forces in the field as are officers of the German Regular Forces will be treated as prisoners of war in the usual manner. Such officers of the said forces as are not officers of the German Regular Forces, but whose usual occupation is civil, on taking an oath of neutrality for the duration of the present war, will be released and permitted to return to their homes and ordinary avocations, except where such avocations are official, in which case the provisions of paragraphs 10 and 11 hereof will apply.

6. As the said Acting Governor gives his assurance that none of the white Noncommissioned Officers and men now in the field belong to the Regular Forces of the

German Empire, such Non-commissioned Officers and men, upon taking the said oath of neutrality will be released and permitted to resume their ordinary avocations, except where such avocations are official, in which case the terms of paragraphs 10 and 11 hereof will apply.

7. As it is understood that the safety of the white population depends to an extent on the existence of a Native Constabulary, that portion of the armed native Constabulary which now forms part of the German Forces in the field, if found satisfactory, will be transferred to the Military Administration.

8. As the administration of the Colony during the military occupation will be conducted by the British Military Commander, all monies and properties of the late Administration are to be handed over to the said Colonel Holmes, Brigadier Commanding.

9. During the said military occupation the local laws and customs will

remain in force so far as is consistent with the military situation.

10. As it is intended that the administration shall be carried on under the control of British officers, subject to the succeeding paragraph, such only of the civil officials of the late German Administration as it may be considered necessary to retain in an advisory capacity will be continued in their offices. Officials so retained will be required to take the oath of neutrality and their former salaries will be continued. Officials not so retained, and those who refuse to take the said oath, will be deported to Australia, but will have no obstacle placed in the way of their returning thence to Germany as soon as possible.

11. For the protection of the white population against the natives, the German officials now in charge of outlying portions of the Colony will continue in their

official capacities until relieved by the Military Administration.

12. Any British subjects at present imprisoned, or held in duress in the said Colony, are to be released and returned to their homes and former positions forthwith. This does not apply to such persons (if any) who may be serving a sentence imposed by a Criminal Court of competent jurisdiction.

In witness whereof the said contracting parties of this first and second parts have hereunto set their hands this seventeenth day of September, 1914, at Herbertshöhe, New Britain.

E. HABER.

Witness to signature of E. Haber
Von KLEWITZ

WILLIAM HOLMES.

Witness to signature of William Holmes—
J.B. STEVENSON

APPENDIX 8

THE BATTLEFIELD TODAY

The New Guinea campaign played out in the littoral waters and islands of the Bismarck Archipelago and focussed on the Gazelle Peninsula at the northern end of the island of New Britain. The Bita Paka battlefield is located approximately 48 kilometres south-east of Rabaul (the old German capital) and about five kilometres south-east of Kokopo (previously *Herbertshöhe*) and today the provincial capital of East New Britain Province. The fighting is commemorated at the Rabaul (Bita Paka) War Cemetery, which is located near the site of the former German wireless station.

WHEN AND HOW LONG TO VISIT

PNG has a hot-wet tropical climate and Rabaul is subject to a distinct 'wet' or monsoon season and a 'dry' season. The 'time belong rain' lasts from

November to April with December to March the most likely time for cyclones. The best time to visit the Great War sites is September when a ceremony is held at the Rabaul (Bita Paka) War Cemetery to coincide with the battle's anniversary. A seven-day visit is recommended as there are many sites to tour and the scenery of New Britain is stunning. A suggested itinerary for a visit focussing on the 1914 campaign should include two days for travel to and from New Britain, a one-day orientation tour of the Gazelle Peninsula, a day to participate in the commemorative activities on 11 September, two days to self-explore the battlefield and related sites in and around Kokopo and Rabaul, and a rest day.

GETTING THERE

Australian-based airlines operate daily flights from all Australian capital cities and some regional centres to Port Moresby (POM), while PNG's airlines operate flights from Brisbane (BNE), Cairns (CNS), and Sydney (SYD). PNG domestic flights provide a daily connection from Port Moresby to Tokua Airport (RAB) on New Britain, with a flight time of around one and a half hours.

Tokua Airport, one of PNG's largest domestic airports, services Kokopo and Rabaul and is located on the north-east tip of the Gazelle Peninsula. The airport is 10 kilometres east of Kokopo and around 15 minutes' drive on a sealed road. Rabaul is 40 kilometres by road from Tokua, which is some 45 minutes' drive from the airport depending on the road conditions and the weather. A number of the Kokopo hotels offer free airport transfers, while those in Rabaul usually charge a fee because of the greater distance.

WHERE TO STAY

East New Britain is a popular tourist destination, although it is better known for its diving, fishing and World War II sites than its World War I connection. There is a range of accommodation choices at Rabaul and Kokopo. For convenience it is better to stay at

Kokopo as this bustling town, with an estimated population in excess of 26,000, is the provincial capital and is closer to both the airport and the main Great War sites. Alternatively, there is accommodation in the former capital of Rabaul, which is still recovering from the devastating volcanic eruption of 1994 that destroyed most of the town and left few vestiges of its colonial past.

GETTING ORIENTED

If visiting New Britain for the first time or if unfamiliar with PNG it is recommended that visitors take an orientation tour to familiarise themselves with the Gazelle Peninsula. There are a number of tour companies and some lodges provide accommodation and tour packages. All travellers, even those who are experienced, are advised to check the Australian Department of Foreign Affairs smart traveller website (smartraveller.gov.au) for up-to-date travel advice and to register travel and contact details. In general however, New Britain does not have the same security concerns as Port Moresby and other urban locales in PNG as the people of New Britain (local Toali and expatriates) are invariably friendly and helpful.

A typical escorted all-day Gazelle Peninsula tour will include the Rabaul (Bita Paka) War Cemetery, remnants of the Japanese World War II occupation, and major historical and ecological sites. Of note in Kokopo is the East New Britain Historical Centre, which holds a range of war relics and some information on the German and Japanese occupations. In and around Rabaul there are various World War II memorials, the Namanulla tunnels and Admiral Yamamoto's command bunker. Opposite Yamamoto's bunker is the remaining intact building of the historic and sometimes infamous New Guinea Club. Originally founded in 1919 in the premises of what was then the ANMEF's NCOs' Mess, the New Guinea Club's membership once included Errol Flynn during his pre-Hollywood days. The current clubhouse was rebuilt in 1949 after being heavily damaged during the Japanese occupation, and was again extensively damaged following the 1994 eruption. Today, the building has been partly restored and is home to a small museum operated by the Rabaul Historical Society. Check opening times in advance.

Once oriented, take another day or two to examine the World War I sites more closely, either as a self-guided tour or with a local guide. Some resorts will tailor a tour for you if you prefer to have a local driver and guide, although visitors should be aware that some guides will know little of the history of the Great War operations and their only knowledge will be related to Bita Paka cemetery. A number of car rental companies operate from Kokopo and, although it can be difficult to pre-arrange a booking, local hotel staff can assist once you are there. A four-wheel drive vehicle is recommended and, although car rental is relatively expensive, the distances are not great and most sites can be accessed comfortably in a couple of days.

PREPARATION

Before visiting New Britain some prior planning and preparation will enhance the experience. Aside from this volume, at a minimum you should read Seaforth Mackenzie's *Official History*, especially Chapters I to XI. This volume, and the others of Charles Bean's *Official History*, can be accessed online at the Australian War Memorial's website. In addition, it is worthwhile acquiring two topographical maps of the Kokopo-Rabaul area. The two most relevant maps are the Papua New Guinea 1:50,000 topographical survey (T703)—1997, sheets Kokopo 9389-II and Rabaul 9389-IV. These maps should be pre-ordered as it might not be possible to obtain them in Rabaul.

When exploring the battlefield you should dress in comfortable, 'breathable' clothes with stout walking shoes or hiking boots. Long pants and long-sleeved shirts are recommended if you intend exploring off the beaten track. A day pack with water, high-energy snacks, mosquito repellent, sunscreen, and toilet paper are essential. A prismatic compass and topographical map are highly recommended additions for your tour kit.

THE BITA PAKA BATTLEFIELD

The Bita Paka battlefield is relatively easy to find along the road south from Kabakaul and it is one of the few tourist sites that is well signposted. To get to Kabakaul from Kokopo, drive east along the sealed Kokopo-Tokua Road, as if returning to the airport. The turn-off to the cemetery is 7.5 kilometres from the Kokopo market and this should take about 10 minutes to drive. The turn-off is a crossroads with Kabakaul along an unsealed road to the left (north) and the cemetery along the sealed road to the right (south).

Before proceeding to the cemetery, take a short detour to the landing site where Bowen and his party came ashore on the morning of 11 September 1914. The beach is to the left (north-east) just one kilometre from the crossroads, along a rutted dirt track. There are some additional buildings today between the crossroads and the landing site, but otherwise the topography is largely unchanged. At the end of the track is the stone and concrete pier jutting out into Blanche Bay. While the pier has been improved since 1914, this is where the Australian landing party disembarked from the destroyers' boats just after dawn.

Having examined the pier, retrace your steps to the crossroads and proceed through the intersection heading south for one kilometre. As you proceed south you will observe a large cleared area to the right (west). This area was a coconut plantation in 1914 but was cleared during World War II and was the site of a Japanese airfield. Also note that there has been some urban encroachment and the palm plantations are now larger and more numerous than they were in 1914, but otherwise the ground is little changed. Bowen's advance followed the road with his flankers moving through the jungle fringe.

A kilometre south of the crossroads the road bends to the left (to the south-east) and today there is a sand quarry on the right-hand side of the road (to the west) just past the bend. Stop where it is safe to do so and park on the left-hand verge. If you turn around and face north, you are looking back at the approximate site of the first clash between Bowen and the Germans. Looking back along the road (to the north), around 200 metres from the bend, was the approximate site of the first German mine. There was a track (since disappeared) off to the left (running north-west) along which Mayer's force approached from Takubar intending to ambush the Australians. The site of the encounter between Petty Officer Palmer and Sergeant Major Mauderer is also off to the left (to the north-west). This area is now plantation but in 1914 it was jungle.

If you turn around and face back in the direction you were driving (south), the first German trench was beyond the bend in the road some 500 metres to the south. When Elwell and Gillman arrived with reinforcements at around 1.00pm they manoeuvred through the scrub on either side of the road—Elwell on the right and Gillman on the left. Elwell was killed leading a bayonet charge on the trench. It was there that Kempf surrendered.

Return to your vehicle and continue driving south for three kilometres. Remember that today the road is two-lane, sealed and mostly flanked by palm plantations; a century ago the track was single-lane, dusty and lined with thick bush. Three kilometres from the last stop the road veers right (to the south-west). Stop here and park on the left-hand verge. If you turn around and face north you will looking over the site of the second German trench where the bulk of the Germans surrendered. The trench was around 300 metres to the north of the bend and cut completely across the track. This is the site of the attempted prisoner escape. Sergeant Franz Ritter, the only German fatality, and more than a dozen police were killed, and Able Seamen Street, Sullivan and Tonks were wounded, Street fatally.

Return to your vehicle and continue south along the road to the village of Ratavul. The Bita Paka (Rabaul) War Cemetery is on the southern edge of the village, eight kilometres from the crossroads. The cemetery is on the left (east) side of the road. The old wireless station was located on the higher ground around 200 metres before the cemetery on the right (west) side of the road. Today a number of local government buildings stand on the former transmitter site, but none dates from 1914. While the buildings that comprised the wireless station are long gone it is still possible to appreciate its commanding position.

The original graves of Able Seaman Billy Williams and Captain Brian Pockley at Kokopo, 1914 (SPC-A).

The second graves of Able Seaman Billy Williams (front left), Captain Brian Pockley (front right) and Able Seaman Harry Street (right rear), circa 1915—16. Street was originally buried alongside the Bita Paka Road where he was killed, but was exhumed along with Pockley and Williams and reinterred in another cemetery on the edge of Kokopo during the war. In 1919 the three were moved again and reinterred in the AIF section of the Rabaul Cemetery. In 1950 the ANMEF graves were transferred to Rabaul (Bita Paka) War Cemetery. The grave to the left rear is that of Able Seaman Herbert Willans, another member of the ANMEF. Willans died from the effects of malaria at Kokopo on 24 December 1914; he too was moved to Rabaul (Bita Paka) War Cemetery in 1950 (SPC-A).

RABAUL (BITA PAKA) WAR CEMETERY

Park your car in the visitors' carpark in front of the Bita Paka cemetery. The Rabaul (Bita Paka) War Cemetery was established by the Army Graves Service in 1945 and was taken over by the Commonwealth War Graves Commission in 1947. It contains the graves of those who lost their lives during the operations in New Britain and New Ireland, or who died in the area during both World Wars. The cemetery contains 1120 Commonwealth burials of World War II, 500 of them unidentified. It contains 29 Commonwealth burials from World War I, including the graves of several Australian Great War veterans who died in New Guinea after the war. The World War I graves were brought in from Rabaul Cemetery in 1950 and from Kokopo Old German Cemetery in 1961.

The contemporary grave marker of Able Seaman Henry William Street in the Rabaul (Bita Paka) War Cemetery. Unlike the familiar Portland headstones used in France and Belgium, the individual graves at Bita Paka have low relief pedestal markers with a bronze plaque (SPC-A).

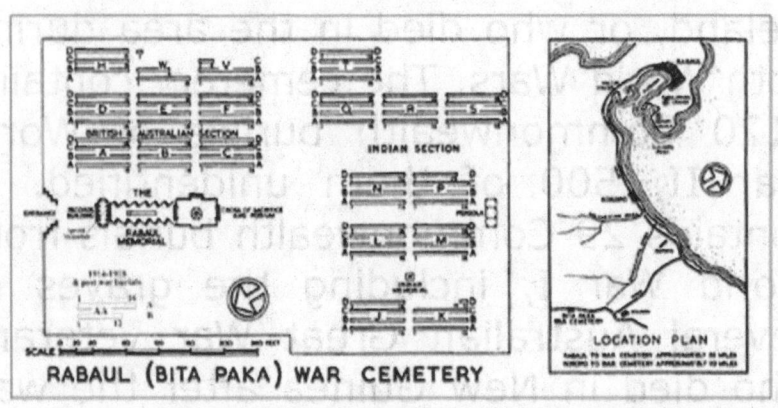

Map 12. Rabaul (Bita Paka) War Cemetery (Commonwealth War Graves Commission)

At the entrance to the cemetery are two bronze memorial plaques. One commemorates the Australian action on 11 September 1914 and the six Australians killed as a result. The other plaque commemorates the loss of the *AEI*. The World War I section is in the north-west corner of the cemetery, on the immediate right as you enter via the front gate. In all, 32 World War I servicemen are buried or commemorated in two rows including 27 ANMEF and one RN burial.

OTHER LOCATIONS ON NEW BRITAIN

Rabaul is located 20 kilometres north-east of Kokopo and was the capital of German New Guinea from 1910 to 1914. It remained the centre of the Australian military administration until 1921 when it transitioned to a civil administration. Thereafter Rabaul became the capital of New Britain Province and later capital of East New Britain. Following the twin volcanic eruptions in 1994 which devastated much of Rabaul, the capital was moved to Kokopo. Above Rabaul township is Namanulla Hill where the German Governor's residence once stood. The building was destroyed in 1994, although the foundations and cement steps of the mansion still mark its location on the sealed road to Namanulla lookout. On the way up to the lookout you pass the Japanese World War II memorial, the only one of its kind in the south-west Pacific area.

Another location worth visiting for the young and fit is the 'Mother' volcano where the Germans established an observation post after the declaration of war. Climbing 'Mother' takes about four hours. The views from the top are spectacular, offering a grand sweep over St George's Channel and Blanche Bay through which Patey's squadron approached Rabaul. It is recommended that you engage a local guide if you intend to make the climb.

The only other clearly identifiable feature from the Australian occupation period is Proclamation Square in the centre of Rabaul. Although the casuarina trees that lined the square when Holmes paraded the ANMEF are now gone, the outline of the once grassed square is still clearly identifiable, surrounded by a boundary of thick volcanic ash.

The village of Toma is located 12 kilometres west of Bita Paka and 13 kilometres south-west of Kokopo by road. Toma sits high on the Toma Ridge above Blanche Bay and, due to its elevation, was used as a rest station by the Germans before becoming the temporary seat of government following the outbreak of war in 1914. Later it was used by the ANMEF as a rest station. Today it is still a small, straggling village stretching along the ridge. The trip from Kokopo to Toma is 12.9 kilometres along a sealed road.

To get to Toma, start at the Kokopo market and drive north-west along the Kokopo—Rabaul road. After 2.2 kilometres there is a road to the left which is the Toma Road. The road climbs steadily for 10 kilometres and then forks. Take the left fork and this will take you to the centre of Toma village, which is 500 metres further on. This is the approximate route Webber took on the morning of 11 September, although he only went about halfway and turned around at the village of Gire Gire to return to Kokopo. It is also the route Watson followed on 14 September following the naval gunfire mission.

The other route to Toma is from Bita Paka. This is a longer trip of 18 kilometres. If you decide to travel this way, continue south from the Bita Paka cemetery for 2.7 kilometres to a 'T' intersection where a road enters on the right. Turn right (to the west) and follow this partially sealed road through the villages of Tabuna and Katakatai to Toma. This is a pleasant drive, although in 2016 parts of the road were in poor condition.

Toma commands views north towards Blanche Bay and south to the rugged interior and Baining Mountains beyond. The country south of Toma is where Lieutenants Victor Sampson and Ivan Sherbon journeyed to recover the buried German treasury.

SELECT BIBLIOGRAPHY

Brett, Judith, *The Enigmatic Mr Deakin*, The Text Publishing Company, Melbourne, 2017.

Burnell, Frederic Spencer, *Australia Versus Germany: The Story of the Taking of German New Guinea*, George Allen and Unwin, London, 1915.

_____ *How Australia took German New Guinea: An illustrated record*, Australasian News, Sydney, 1914.

Butler, Arthur G., R.M. Downes, F.A. Maguire and R.W. Cilento, *The Official History of the Australian Medical Services in the War of 1914—1918*, Vol. I, *Gallipoli, Palestine and New Guinea*, Australian War Memorial, Melbourne, 1930.

Connor, John, *Anzac and Empire: George Foster Pearce and the Foundations of Australian Defence*, Cambridge University Press, Melbourne, 2011.

Detzner, Hermann, *Four Years Among the Cannibals in the Interior of German New Guinea under the Imperial Flag, from 1914 until the Armistice,* Gisela Batt (trans), Pacific Press, Gold Coast, 2008.

Hiery, Hermann, *Neglected War: The German South Pacific & the Influence of World War I,* University of Hawaii Press, Honolulu, 1995.

Horne, Donald, *The Little Digger,* Macmillan, South Melbourne, 1979.

Hyslop, Robert, *Australian Naval Administration 1900—1939,* The Hawthorn Press, Melbourne, 1973.

Jane, Fred T., *Jane's Fighting Ships 1914,* David & Charles, London, 1968.

Jose, Arthur W., *The Official History of Australia in the War of 1914—1918,* Vol. IX, *The Royal Australian Navy,* Angus & Robertson, Sydney, 1928.

Kirkcaldie, Rosa Angela, *In Gray and Scarlet,* Alexander McCubbin, Melbourne, 1922.

Macdonald, Colin (ed), *The Caruse of the Kanowna: Frederick Macdonald's 1914 Diary,* Colin Graham Macdonald, Aranda, 2005.

MacKenzie, Seaforth S., *The Official History of Australia in the War of 1914—1918,* Vol. X, *The Australians in Rabaul,* Angus & Robertson, Sydney, 1927.

Meade, Kevin, *Heroes Before Gallipoli: Bita Paka and that one day in September,* John Wiley and Sons, Milton, 2005.

Pelvin, Richard, 'HMAS Australia' in Bruce Taylor (ed), *The World of the Battleship: The Design and Careers of Capital Ships of the World's Navies, 1900—1950,* Naval Institute Press, Annapolis, 2018.

Pfennigwerth, Ian, *Under New Management: The Royal Australian*

Navy and the removal of Germany from the Pacific, 1914—15, Echo Books, West Geelong, 2015.

Piggott, Michael, 'Stonewalling in German New Guinea', *Wartime: The Journal of the Australian War Memorial,* Issue 12, April 1988.

Raffin, Gregg, *Australia's Real Baptism of Fire: Heroes Known Only to a Few,* Five Senses Education, Seven Hills, 2013.

Reeves, Signaller L.C., *Australians in Action in New Guinea,* The Australasian News Company Ltd, Sydney, 1915.

Rowley, Charles Dunford, *The Australians in German New Guinea 1914—1921,* Melbourne University Press, Carlton, 1958.

Stevens, David, *In all Respects Ready: Australia's Navy in World War One,* Oxford University Press, South Melbourne, 2014. Travers, B.H., *William Holmes, Secretary and Soldier: A first biography,* Echo Books, West Geelong, 2016.

Travers, Geoffrey, *William Holmes: The Soldiers' General,* Big Sky Publishing, Newport, 2020.

Tyquin, Michael B., *Neville Howse: Australia's first Victoria Cross winner,* Oxford University Press, South Melbourne, 1999.

Veale, Commander Richard Stanley, *Autobiographical Recollections of a Naval Reserve Officer 1893—1987,* John M. Wilkins (revised and edited), Navy League of Australia, Melbourne, 1997.

Worthington, Angus Hermon, *Our Island Captures: Being an account of the operations of the Australian Expeditionary Force in the South Pacific Ocean, 1914,* G. Hassell and Son, Adelaide, 1919.

BACK COVER MATERIAL

AUSTRALIA'S FIRST CAMPAIGN

***

THE CAPTURE OF GERMAN NEW GUINEA, 1914

The Australian campaign to seize German New Guinea in 1914 is one of the forgotten episodes of the First World War. Preceding the Gallipoli landings by seven months, this remarkably successful amphibious operation was the very first of its kind undertaken by the Royal Australian Navy and the Austrlian Army. The campaign was also everything the Gallipoli campaign was not: the New Guinea operations were planned and executed by Australian officers, the fighting was short, sharp and successful, and it was a highly effective use of military force, achieving its operational objectives at a remarkably low cost and serving Australian strategic interests in a direct and tangible way.

This volume of the Army History Unit's Campaign Series describes how a novice navy and army planned, mounted and launched a complex joint operation over 3300 kilometeres from their mounting base and defeated or forced the withdrawal of German naval and land forces posing a direct threat to Australia and New Zealand.

Australia's First Campaign presents a fresh examination of the evidence from a range of participants, providing a thoroughly researched and readable account of the Australian military's first joint operation. The volume is supported by more than 100 illustration and includes a useful guide for those wishing to visit the battlefield today.

Index

A
Abyssinia (1867-1868), *110*
Adam, A.D., *110*
Admiralty Islands (Admiralitäts-Inseln), *357*
AE1, *50, 67, 223*
  loss of, *325*
AE2, *50, 67, 223*
Aitken, Major Arthur, *90, 232, 239*
Alexishafen, *348*
Allen, James, *76*
ammunition, illegal, *314*
Anderson, Major Alan, *205, 372*
Anglo-Egyptian War (1882), *110*
Anglo-Japanese Treaty, *365*
Anglo-Sudanese War (1884-1885), *110*
Anglo-Zulu War (1879), *54, 110*
Annear, Able Seaman A., *274*
Antill, Lieutenant Colonel John 'Bull', *117, 126, 133*
Aorangi (SS), *205, 207, 213, 223, 239, 241*
Apra Harbour, *348*
Armstrong, Second Lieutenant Hutton, *239*
AIF service, army and navy culture, contrasted, *195, 197*
Army Medical Corps, *126*
Australia defence preparation, *40, 60, 63, 67, 71, 76, 223, 226*
  education, *148, 151*
  joint force with New Zealand, *76*

trade, international, *40, 46*
Australia (HMAS), *4, 49, 58, 60, 71, 306*
armaments, *50*
  commissioning, *50*
  crew, *50*
  joint conference aboard, *243*
  New Guinea, in, *173, 180, 249, 348*
  development of, *71, 195*
  discipline, *197, 200, 205*
Australian Garrison Artillery, *223, 239*
Australian Imperial Force (AIF), *83, 121, 145, 205*
1st Battalion, *103, 123, 133, 161*
1st Division, *126*
1st Infantry Brigade, *86*
4th Battalion, *103*
ANMEF, clashes with, *103*
ANMEF personnel who served with, *386*
Australian Intelligence Corps, *246*
Australian Naval and Military Expeditionary Force (ANMEF), *34, 43, 213, 249, 314*
1st Battalion, *103, 123, 133, 161*
2nd Battalion, *228, 232, 235, 239*
3rd Battalion, *386*
AIF, clashes with, *103*
artillery, *141*
awards and accolades,
battalion organisation, *123*
climate, adjusting to tropical, *223*
crimes during the occupation, *378, 382*
embarkation, *160, 161, 165, 184, 365*

equipment, *110, 126, 135, 213, 235*
establishment, *86, 90*
formal occupation, announcement of, *323*
headquarters (Rabaul), *100*
landing, *216*
leadership, *205, 248, 328*
medical section, *126, 133, 207, 210, 223, 248, 255*
morale, *248*
Naval Battalion, see Naval Battalion officers, *372*
operational performance, assessment of, parameters of mission, *184, 187, 191*
personnel, overview, *145, 148, 151, 155, 160*
return to Australia, *386*
structure, *90*
tactical performance, assessment of,
training, *135, 145, 184, 213, 219, 223*
uniforms, *135, 141, 235*
volunteers, *110, 117, 121, 133, 135, 228*
Australian Order of Battle,
Axtens, Lieutenant John, *205, 297, 304*
amputation, *274, 304, 314, 320*

B

Baining Mountains, *173*
Barker, Sub-Lieutenant Mandeville,
Barrow, Sub-Lieutenant,
battle honours,

battle of annihilation (vernichtungsschlacht), *37*

battleships,
see also cruisers, destroyers
battle cruiser concept, *58*
HMAS Australia, see Australia (HMAS)
Indefatigable class, *58, 60*
Invincible class, *58, 351*
strengths and weaknesses, *58*

Baum, Hellmuth, *365*
bayonet charge, *117*
Bean, Charles, *103*
Beardsmore, Colonel Robert, *121, 155, 372*
  AIF service,
Beaton, Chief Petty Officer, *110*
Bebra group (German Army), *249, 270, 306*

Beresford, Commander Joseph, *90, 110, 117, 145, 243*
Bita Paka, action at, *249, 255, 258, 270, 274, 278, 282, 286, 293, 304, 306, 308, 323*
  discipline, *205*
  post-New Guinea campaign, Rabaul, *323*
Beretawl station, *249*
Berrima (HMAS), *165, 180, 184, 205, 210, 213*
  evacuation of casualties, *274, 320, 321*
  landing troops, *216, 306*
  life aboard, *187, 191*
  New Guinea, in, *223, 239, 241, 246, 278, 323, 348*
  supplies, *207*
Besant, Lieutenant Commander Thomas, *67*

Bismarck Archipelago (Bismarck-Archipel), *76*
Bita Paka (Bitapaka), *4, 249, 255*
  road, *255, 258, 270, 293*
  timeline, *265*
  wireless station, *4, 27, 37, 249, 265, 293, 304, 306*
Blanche Bay, *173, 249, 255, 331*
  map, *178*
Boer War (1899-1902), *33, 110, 117, 145*
Bollard, Bandsman Arthur, *173, 180, 314*
Bond, Lieutenant Thomas, *110, 117, 265, 293, 297, 304, 306, 308*
1st RAN Bridging Train,
Bougainville Island (Bougainville-Insel), *357*
Bowen, Agnes Grace (nee Bell), *249*
Bowen, Lieutenant Rowland, *110, 117*
Bita Paka, action at, *249, 255, 258, 270, 274, 278, 282, 286, 293, 304, 306, 308, 323*
  decoration,
  map of New Britain, *243, 246*
  post-New Guinea campaign,
Boxer Rebellion, *110, 117*
Bracegirdle, Lieutenant Commander Leighton, *110, 117*
  1st RAN Bridging Train,
  post-war career,
Braund, Lieutenant Colonel George,
Braunert, Maximillian, *376*
Bridges, Colonel William Throsby, *73, 83, 86, 103, 126*
British Army discipline, *197*

British China Squadron, *173, 180*
Browne, Lieutenant Commander George, *110, 117*
Bruce, Lieutenant Herbert, *372*
Buchanan, Angus, *160*
Buchanan, Frank, *160*
Bulldog, *365*
Buller, Lieutenant Reginald, *110, 265, 270, 274, 278, 304*
1st RAN Bridging Train,
Burnell, Frederick, *145, 223, 235, 320, 338*
Burtinshaw, Sister Bertha, *210*
Bush, Bernard, *160*
Bush, Eric, *160*

C

Cameron, Lieutenant Stewart, *110, 117*
Cameron, Sub-Lieutenant Alexander,
Cape Gazelle, *249, 258*
Carolines (Karolinen), *4, 12, 37, 173, 365*
casualties, *308, 314, 320, 321*
  Bita Paka action, *265, 274, 278, 282, 293, 304, 306, 308, 320*
  British naval, *348*
  distribution of, *308, 314*
  evacuation of, *320, 321*
  friendly fire, *308*
  German naval, *351*
  gossip and rumour regarding, *314*
  prisoners, *297, 304*
chronology,
Churchill, Winston, *351*
Clouston, Sister Rachel, *210*
coal, *4, 67, 348*

Cock, Midshipman Charles, *110*
Coconut Lancers, *386*
Cocos (Keeling) Islands, *348*
Colless, Sister Stella Lillian, *210*
Collins, Lieutenant, *372*
Commonwealth Naval Forces (CNF), *46, 49, 195*
compulsory service scheme, *71*
Cook, Joseph, *40*
Cooper, Lieutenant Arthur, *200*
Corbett, Professor Pitt, *378*
Cormoran (SMS), *4, 37, 348*
Coronel, Battle of, *348, 351*
Courtenay, Able Seaman, *265*
Cox, Reverend W.H., *376*

Cradock, Rear Admiral Sir Christopher, *348*
Crater Peninsula, *173*
Creswell, Rear Admiral Sir William, *40, 46, 49, 54, 100*
Cripps, Driver Bernard, *228*
cruisers, *50*
  battle,
    see battle cruisers
  Challenger-class, *63*
  Chatham group of Town-class light, *63*
    Minotaur-class, *58*
    Pelorus-class, *63*
Cumberlege, Commander Claude, *67, 173, 274*

D

De Mestre, Matron Sarah, *210*
Deakin, Alfred, *43, 46, 49, 50, 71*

decentralised command philosophy, *191*
Deroubaix, Joseph, *160*
destroyers, *49, 50, 63, 67, 205*
   British Acheron class, *63*
Detzner, Lieutenant (Oberleutnant) Hermann, *357, 361, 365, 386*
   background, *361*
   post-war career, Direction Island, *348*
Donaldson, Captain John, *126, 246*
Dovey, Mary (nee Duncan), *155*
Dovey, Wilfred, *155*
Dresden, *351*
dum-dum rounds, *314*
Dutch New Guinea, *357*
deployment of medical personnel, *246*

E

East Asiatic Squadron (German), *4, 37, 54, 80, 348*
   reputation, *6*
Eastern (SS), *386*
Eastman, Able Seaman Leslie, *270*
Eitel, Private Conrad, *191, 265, 304*
Elwell, Lieutenant Commander Charles, *110, 117, 265, 348*
   Bita Paka, action at, *278, 282, 286, 289, 293, 308, 314, 320*
   recognition of service,
Emden (SMS), *4, 37, 60, 348*
   destruction of, *348, 351*
Encounter (HMAS), *50, 63, 213, 328, 331*
   armaments, *63*
   New Guinea, in, *173, 216, 223, 239, 241, 249, 325, 348*

shore bombardment, *325, 328*
Emden, encounter with, *348, 351*
 joint conference aboard Australia, *243*

F
Falkland Islands, *351*
Ferdinand, Archduke Franz, *4, 80, 173, 386*
Ferguson, Sir Ronald Munro, *80*
Fieberg, Lieutenant (Oberleutnant) E.E., *249, 255*
field guns, *141*
 7.85-centimetre (6 pounder) Krupp (Feldkanone C73), *27*
 12-pounder breech-loading, *141, 145, 304, 323, 325*
 37-millimetre Hotchkiss Revolving Cannon (3.7-zentimeter maschinenkanone), *27, 31, 37*
Finlayson, Lieutenant Commander John, *249*
Finlayson, Private George, *145*
Finschhafen, *8, 361, 365*
First Moroccan Crisis, *46*
Fisher, Admiral Sir John 'Jacky', *58*
Fisher, Andrew, *40, 49*
fleet units, *43*
flogging incident, *376, 378*
Fort Macquarie, *161, 165*
Foster, Colonel Hubert, *161*
Fowler, Ronald, *110*
Fox, John, *160*
Fox, Thomas, *160*
Frank E. Evans (USS),

Freeborn, John, see Plimer, John
Fry, Second Lieutenant Walter, *232, 369*
fuel, *4, 67, 205, 207, 348*
Fukoko Maru, *37*

G

Gallipoli, *117, 306, 314, 328*
Garsia, Lieutenant Rupert, *314*
Gazelle Peninsula, *173, 325*
  map, *173*
George V, King, *50, 80*
German Army, *37*
3rd Marine Battalion (III. Seebataillon), *6, 8*
  deployment to meet Australian landings, *249*
  operational performance, assessment of,
  reservists, *27, 249, 314*
  tactical performance, assessment of,
German New Guinea (Deutsch-Neuguinea), *243*
  defence, options for, *27, 33*
  indigenous police, see indigenous police (polizeitruppe)
  mobilisation, *180*
  occupation of, *354, 365, 369, 372, 376, 378, 382, 386*
  population, *6*
  post-war administration, *386*
  surrender, *328, 331, 334, 338, 348, 365*
German Order of Battle,
German police officer (polizeimeister), *8, 17*

German Samoa (Deutsch-Samoa), *76, 80*
Germany
expansionism, *46, 50*
Pacific trading and colonisation, *4, 6, 8*
Gillman, Lieutenant Oscar, *110, 117, 278, 282, 286, 293*
occupation, role in, *372*
Gire Gire, *306*
Glossop, Captain John, *63, 180, 223, 239, 241*
Gneisenau (SMS), *4, 37, 173*
sinking, *351*
Goadby, Honorary Lieutenant Bede, *100, 210, 369*
map of Bita Paka road,
Godley, Major General Alexander, *76*
Gooch, Private N.R., *255*

Good Hope (HMS), *348*
Goodsell, Captain Sydney, *100, 123, 210*
Gordon, Brigadier General Joseph, *76*
Grantala (SS), *207, 210, 246, 320*
Australian preparations, *40, 80, 83*
outbreak, *4, 37, 80*
Greco-Turkish War (1897), *54*
Green, Susan Ellen, *94*
Green Hill Fort, *226*
Gregg, Chief Petty Officer J., *210*
Griffiths, Captain, gunboats, *67*
German mission-type (auftragstaktik), *191*
German performance, assessment of,

H

Haber, Deputy Governor Eduard, *17, 27, 31, 33, 37, 180, 328*
  Australian forces, communication with, *249, 304, 306, 323, 325*
  post-war career, surrender, *328, 331, 334, 338, 357, 365, 369*
Hague Agreement on Occupied Territories (1097), *365, 369*
Hague Conventions, *348, 376, 378*
  breaches of, *270, 297, 378, 382*
  illegal ammunition, *314*
Hahl, Governor Dr Albert, *12, 17, 331*
Harcourt, First Viscount Lewis, *80*
Harcus, Captain James, *90, 265, 278, 297, 372*
Hardy, Alfred, *160*
Hardy, William, *160*
Harry, Lieutenant Samuel, *232*
  AIF service,
Hazlett, Warrant Officer Henry, *126*
Henderson, Captain John, *126, 155*
Henderson, Chaplain Charles, *210*
Henley, Captain Harold, *155*
Herbertshöhe battle honour,
Herero Rebellion, *14*
Heritage, Lieutenant Keith, *160, 369, 372*
  AIF service,
Heritage, Major Francis 'Frank', *90, 100, 121, 123, 160, 223, 246, 372*
  AIF service, occupation, role in, *369*
Hext, Sub-Lieutenant Avenal, *110, 117*

Hicks, Midshipman Charles, *117*
1st RAN Bridging Train,
Hill, Lieutenant Gerald, *265, 274, 278, 286, 293*
  recognition of service,
Hoffman, Petty Officer, *110*
Holmes, Colonel William 'Billee', *73, 86, 94, 100, 126, 160, 216, 241, 255, 357, 372*
  AIF service,
  ANMEF, raising, *86, 90, 100, 103, 135*
  assessment of situation, *239, 248*
  background, *94*
  Bita Paka, action at, *278, 304, 306, 320*
  embarkation of ANMEF, *165, 173, 210, 213*
  formal occupation, *323, 325,* *357, 365, 369, 372, 376, 378, 382, 386*
  German surrender, *331, 334, 338, 348, 365, 369*
  joint conference aboard Australia, *243, 246*
  Kennedy Regiment, *232, 235, 239*
  leadership, *205, 248*
  Legge, orders from, *184, 187, 191, 246, 365*
  Patey, relationship with,
  shore bombardment, *325, 328*
  tactical performance, assessment of,
Holmes, Lieutenant Basil, *100, 369, 372*
Horsfall, Acting Fleet Surgeon William, *210*

Hospital Ship VIII, *207, 210*
Howse, Lieutenant-Colonel Neville, *90, 123, 126, 155, 223, 232*
　AIF service,
Hughes, William 'Billy', *386*
Hunter, Signal Boatswain William, *110, 278, 282*
Huon Peninsula, *357*

I
Ibuki, *348*
Imperial Defence Conference 1909, *50*
Imperial German Pacific Protectorate, *173, 348*
　colonial protectorate troops (Schutztruppe), *6, 8, 12, 17*
　map, *17*
　occupation of, *354, 357, 365*
　population, *6*
Imperial Japanese Navy, *365*
Indefatigable (HMS), *60*
Indian Mutiny (1857-1859), *110*
indigenous police (polizeitruppe), *8, 12, 17, 357*
　casualties, *308, 314, 321*
　occupation, under, *376*
　prisoners of war, *297, 304, 321*
　training, *17, 33*
　uniform and equipment, *17, 27, 314*
Infantry Training manual, *219*
Inflexible (HMS), *351*
Inglis, Major, *205*
Inglis, Sergeant Major William, *103*
　AIF service,
　initiative, importance of,

Instance, Petty Officer, *110*
intelligence, *173, 246, 255, 270*
Invincible (HMS), *60, 351*

J

Jackson, Lieutenant Commander John, *357*
Japan, *4, 365, 386*
Jerram, Vice Admiral Sir Thomas, *180*
Jiaozhou Bay (Deutsch-Kiautschou), *161*
Johnson, Major Harold, *205, 372*
Jutland, Battle of, *60*

K

Kabakaul, *243, 246, 249, 293, 320*
   Australian forces, *249, 255, 265, 278, 304, 306*
   pier, *249*
Kabiu ('Mother'), *173, 180*

Kaiserin Elisabeth (SMS), *365*
Kaituna (SS), *205*
Kanowna (SS), *223, 226, 228, 232, 235*
   workers' strike, *239, 241*
Kavieng (Käwieng), *372*
Kay, Captain Stuart, *232*
Kearns, Arthur, *160*
Kearns, Edward, *160*
Kember, Stoker First Class William, *274*
Kempf, Lieutenant (Oberleutnant) E.E., *265, 274, 286, 293, 297, 304*
Kennedy, Edmund, *226*
Kennedy Regiment, *223, 226, 228, 235, 239*
Keysser, Christian, *357*
King, Major George, *232*
King-Hall, Admiral Sir George, *54*

Kirkcaldie, Sister Rosa, *210*
Kirke, Captain Errol, *372*
Kitchener, Field Marshall Lord, *71, 73*
Klewitz, Captain of Cavalry (Rittmeister) Carl von, *12, 14, 17, 27, 37, 270, 304, 306, 328*
  background, *14*
  defence strategy, *249, 255*
  post-New Guinea campaign, surrender, *331, 338*
  tactical performance, assessment of,
Kokopo (Herbertshöhe), *8, 173, 180, 243, 249, 321, 323, 331*
  German surrender, *328, 331, 334, 338*
  landing at, *249, 258, 265, 304*
  post office, *334*

Komet Harbour (Komethafen), *351*
Komet (KGS), *31, 37, 348, 351, 357*
  HMAS Una, as, *351, 357*
Koolonga (SS), *205, 239*
Kudjeru, *365*
Kulgoa (Sydney ferry), *165*
Kyriako, Arthur, *160*
Kokopo, at, *265, 306, 328*
Weihai (Port Edward), *37*
Westgarth, Lieutenant John, *372*
Whangape (SS), *205, 241*

L

Lambton, Lieutenant-Commander R.S., *117*
Lane, Able Seaman William,

Lane, Captain Cyril, *123, 223, 372*
Langtry, Company Sergeant Major Henry, *155*
Lawton, Sergeant Maurice, *155*
Leadbeater, Captain John, *155, 205*
League of Nations, *386*
Legge, Brigadier General James, *40, 73, 255, 331, 382*
  background, *73*
  orders for Holmes, *184, 187, 191, 246, 365*
  raising a force, *83, 86*
Lehmaier, Brigadier Lionel, *155, 160*
Leipzig (SMS), *4, 37*
  sinking, *351*
Lewin, Captain Charles, *63*
Livesay, Lieutenant Commander Augustus, *372*

logistics, *4, 205, 207, 210, 213*
Louisiades Archipelago, *180*
Lüttich group (German Army), *249, 255, 270, 306*
Lyng, Lieutenant Jens, *372*

M

medical knowledge, *248*
McDowell, Lieutenant John, *372*
machine guns
  .303-inch Maxim Converted, *129*
  crews, *219*
  Vickers, *129*
  Vickers-Maxim, *129*
MacLaurin, Colonel Henry, *86, 103*
McMillan, Sister Florence, *210*
Macnaghten, Major Charles, *103*
McPherson, Captain Thomas, *121, 372*

Madang (Friedrich Wilhelmshafen), *31, 348, 357, 372*
Maguire, Captain Frederick, *126, 155, 223, 246, 314, 372*
malaria, *248*
Manning, Captain Charles, *160, 372, 376, 378*
Manning, Lieutenant Guy, *160, 369, 372*
Manus, *357*
Maori Wars (1860-1864), *110*
Marianas (Marianen), *12, 365*
Marsden, Lieutenant Thomas, *90, 223*
   AIF service,
Marshall Islands (Marschall-Inseln), *12, 80, 365*
Martin, Brigadier General Edward, *121, 372*
Martin, Private John 'Jack', *314*

Matupi Harbour, *173*
Mauderer, Sergeant Major (Vizewachtmeister) Maurice, *255, 265, 270*
Maughan, Lieutenant John, *200*
Maxim, Sir Hiram, *129*
Mayer, Lieutenant (Oberleutnant) Georg, *12, 17, 33, 37*
   Australian landing, and, *249, 255, 265, 270, 278, 306*
medical forces
   ANMEF, *126, 133, 207, 210, 223, 248, 255*
   equipment, *126*
   hospital ships, *207, 210*
Meek, John, *160*
Meek, Leopold, *160*
Melanesian police, see indigenous police (polizeitruppe),
Melbourne (HMAS), *49, 50, 63, 71*

Emden, encounter with, *348*
New Guinea, in, *173, 243*
Merrett, Charles, *160*
Merrett, Frederick, *160*
military organisation, *123*
  army and navy, contrasted, *195, 197*
military ranks,
  army and navy, *195, 197, 200*
  German, *12*
militia, *71, 86*
2nd Infantry (Kennedy Regiment), *223, 226, 228, 235, 239*
  discipline, *200, 205*
mobilisation, *223, 226*
Millen, Senator Edward, *165, 173*
Milman Hill, *226*
mines land, *249, 265, 282, 286, 297*
  underwater, *241, 249*
Minotaur (HMS), *348*

Möeller, Captain Karl, *357*
Moffat, Signalman Robert, *265, 282, 320, 348*
Monmouth (HMS), *348*
Montcalm, *331, 348*
Montefiore, Charles, *160*
Montefiore, Leonard, *160*
Morobe (Adolfhaven), *37, 180, 357, 386*
Morrison, Lieutenant Colonel Harold, *121*
  AIF service,
Mount Sinewit, *173*
Müller, Captain Karl von, *37*
Murex (SS), *205, 239*
Murray, Judge Herbert, *239*
Mauser, *270, 304*

N

Namatanai, *376*
Namibia, *14*

Nauru (Pleasant Island), *4, 80, 180, 243, 357*
Naval Battalion, *103, 110, 117, 123, 145, 148, 205, 213, 216, 243, 249*
  No.3 Company, *265, 278*
  No.4 Company, *249, 255, 265*
  No.6. Company, *265, 293, 331*
Naval Board, *4, 54, 110, 126, 173*
  conversion of transports, *184*
naval brigades, *110*
naval guns,
  4-inch (10-centimetre) Mark VIII, *63*
  6-inch (15-centimetre), *63*
navy and army culture, contrasted, *195, 197*
  orders, giving, *248*
Neale, Sister Constance, *210*
Neuendettelsauer Mission, *361, 365*
New Britain (Nue-Pommern), *4, 357, 372*
  geography, *173*
  German deployment (map), *249*
  map, *243, 246*
New Guinea, *80*
  campaign battle honours,
  civil administration, *386*
  occupation government, *365, 369, 372, 376, 378, 382, 386*
New Ireland (Neu-Mecklenburg), *357, 376*
New Zealand forces, *76, 173, 180, 348*
  joint force with Australia, *76*
Norman, Lieutenant Reginald, *372*
Norrie, Brigadier General Edward, *121*

AIF service, North West Expeditionary Force, *386*
Nürnberg (SMS), *4, 37, 173*
  sinking, *351*
Nusa (HMAS), *357*

O

orders, giving, *248*
Open Bay, *173*
  ANMEF performance, assessment of, concept, *83*
  German performance, assessment of, navy and army culture, contrasted, *195, 197*
orders, giving, *248*

P

post-war career, Pacific operations (Great War), *80*
  map, *348*

Pacocha, Battle of, *54*
Paidas, Nicholas, *160*
Palm Island, *207, 213, 219, 223, 365*
Palmer, Petty Officer George, *110, 117, 265, 270*
  recognition of service,
Paparatava, *255*
Papeete, *348*
Parramatta (HMAS), *50, 63*
  New Guinea, in, *173, 239, 249, 325*
Partridge, Lieutenant Robert, *372*
Patey, Rear Admiral Sir George, *50, 54, 60, 213, 223, 255*
  background, *54*
  Bita Paka, action at, *270, 278, 304, 306, 320*
  Holmes, relationship with,

joint conference aboard Australia, *243, 246*
  leadership, *205, 248, 328*
  New Guinea, in, *173, 180, 239, 241, 243, 323, 348*
  post-New Guinea campaign, RAN squadron, creation of, *63, 67, 71*
  Terms of Capitulation, *357*
Paton, Lieutenant Colonel John, *100, 123, 323, 357, 372, 386*
  AIF service,
Pearce, George, *40, 43, 50, 73, 76, 331, 357, 369*
  background, *43*
Penly, Lieutenant William, *372*
Permanent Military Forces, *71, 103, 133, 232*
Pethebridge, Brigadier General Sir Samuel Augustus, *382, 386*

Pioneer (HMAS), *63*
pistols C, *223*
Plane, Alfred, *160*
Plane, Leslie, *160*
Planet (SMS), *31, 37*
Plimer, John, *121*
Pockley, Captain Brian, *126, 151, 155, 191, 246, 248*
  Bita Paka, action at, *270, 274, 304, 320*
  fatal wounding, *265, 274, 308, 314, 320, 321, 348*
  landing at Kabakaul, *255, 265*
  recognition of service,
Pockley, Francis, *348*
Pockley, Helen, *348*
Pohnpei (Ponape), *4, 37, 173*
Police Expeditionary Force (Polizei Expeditionstruppe), *12, 17*
  reservists, *27, 314*
  uniform, *27*

Port Moresby, *180, 223, 232, 239, 365*
Port Stanley, *351*
Prey, Lieutenant (Oberleutnant) Albert, *12*
Prinz Eitel Fredrich (SMS), *4, 37, 348*
prisoners of war casualties, *297, 304*
   German soldiers, *270, 293, 297, 304*
Protector (HMAS), *67, 223*

Q

Qingdao (Tsingtao), *4, 161, 365*
quinine, *248*
Quinn, Lieutenant Patrick, *372*
Quinn, Major Hugh, *232, 235, 239*
   AIF service,

R

Rabaul, *17, 27, 37, 173, 243, 321, 376*
   Australian forces in, *173, 180, 210, 249, 323, 348, 357*
   map, *178*
racial prejudice, *314, 321*
radio, *4, 180*
Ralston, Lieutenant Colonel Alexander, *121, 155, 372, 378*
   AIF service,
Ravenscroft, Captain Lionel, *372*
Read, Lieutenant-Commander C.H., *117*
Read, Lieutenant Hansley,
retaliation, *314*
rifle clubs, *226*
rifles 7.92 mm Mauser Model 1898 (Gewehr 98), *34*
   Mauser Model 1871 (Gewehr 71), *34*
   Mauser Model 1888 (Gewehr 88), *34*

Short Magazine Lee-Enfield, see Short Magazine Lee-Enfield (SMLE) rifle,
Ritter, Sergeant Franz, *293, 297, 304, 308*
Rossel Island, *180, 223, 243*
Royal Australian Naval College, *43*
Royal Australian Naval Reserve (RANR), *110, 195*
Royal Australian Navy (RAN), *43, 50, 71, 173, 195*
1st RAN Bridging Train,
   establishment of local naval forces, *49, 50*
   training exercises, *71*
Royal Marine Artillery, *110*
Royal Marine Light Infantry, *110*

Royal Marines, *103, 110*
Royal Military College, Duntroon, *43, 103*
Royal Naval Reserve (RNR), *195*
Royal Navy (RN), *4, 103, 195*
   discipline, *197, 200, 205*
   naval brigades, *110*
Ryan, Colonel Charles, *126*
Ryazan (SS), *37*

S

Sadler, Lieutenant Rupert, *121, 123, 372*
   AIF service,
St George's Channel, *173*
Samoa, *4, 180, 213, 223, 348*
Samoa group (German Army), *255*
Samoan Expeditionary Force, *173*

Sampson, Lieutenant Victor, *334, 372*
Sands, Colonel Robert,
Sanford, Squadron Leader Frederick, *155*
Sattelberg, *365, 386*
Scharnhorst (SMS), *4, 37, 173*
sinking, *351*
Second Ashanti War (1873-1874), *110*
Shepherd, Sergeant William, *314*
Sherbon, Lieutenant Ivan, *334, 372*
Sherbon, William, *103*
shore bombardment, *141, 325, 328*
Short Magazine Lee-Enfield (SMLE) rifle, *34*
.303-inch, *135, 140*
.303-inch Mark I, *140*
.303-inch Mark III 67, *140*
Silver, Captain Mortimer L'Estrange, *63*
Simpson, John Kirkpatrick,
Simpson Harbour (Simpsonhafen), *173, 241, 249, 320*
Skillen, Able Seaman Daniel, *265, 282*
smallpox, *133*
Smithers, Warrant Officer Henry,
Spee, Vice Admiral (Vizeadmiral) Maximilian von, *4, 6, 37, 60, 80, 135, 173, 348, 351*
  operational performance, assessment of,
Staines, Able Seaman Sidney, *270*
Stevenson, Captain John, *184, 205*

joint conference aboard Australia, *243*
leadership, *205*
post-New Guinea campaign,
Stevenson, Captain John Phillip,
Stiefvater, Herman, *160*
Stirling, Midshipman James, *110*
Stoker, Lieutenant Commander Henry 'Harry', *67*
Strasbourg, Lieutenant, *372*
   German battle, *37*
Street, Able Seaman Henry 'Harry', *265, 304, 320, 348*
Street, Geoffrey, *103*
Sturdee, Vice Admiral Doveton, *351*
submarine telegraph cables, *4, 180, 348*
submarines, *50, 63, 205*
   E class, *67*
Suez Canal, *46, 76*
Sullivan, Able Seaman Timothy, *265, 304*
Sumatra (SS), *180*
Sydney (HMAS), *49, 50, 60, 63, 173, 213, 323*
   Emden, encounter with, *348, 351*
   New Guinea, in, *180, 223, 239, 241, 248, 249*
   shore bombardment, *141, 325, 328*
Szabowski, Julian, *160*

T
tactics,
   adaptation of military doctrine, *216, 219*
   ANMEF performance, assessment of,
   decentralised command, *191*

Takubar, *249, 255, 265, 278*
task organisation, *83*
Tavurvur (Matupit Crater), *173*
Telena (SS), *205*
Terms of Capitulation, *331, 338, 357, 369, 376, 378*
Thorold, Captain Richard Grant, *121, 372*
  AIF service, Thursday Island, *226, 228, 232, 239, 249*
Titania, *37*
Tobera, *255*
Toma, *180, 249, 255, 265, 270, 306, 331, 338*
  shore bombardment, *325, 328*
Tonks, Able Seaman James, *265, 304*
torpedoes, *67*
18-inch (46-centimetre), *63*

Tovanumbatir ('North Daughter'), *173*
Travers, Captain Reginald 'Jack', *100, 135, 246, 265, 372*
  Bita Paka, action at, *278, 293, 297, 304*
  occupation, role in, *369*
  recognition of service,
Travers, Dorothy (nee Holmes), *135*
treasury, surrender of German, *331, 334*
Treaty of Versailles,
Trickey, Leslie, *110*
Trinca, Dr A.J., *210*
Tropical Force, *386*
Turagunan ('South Daughter'), *173*
Twynam, Captain E., *121*
typhoid (enteric fever), *133, 223*

U

Universal Training Pattern uniform, *135, 228*

Universal Training Scheme, *71, 226*

Upolu (SS), *67, 223*

V

Valparaiso, *348*

Veale, Midshipman Richard 'Stan', *110, 117, 306, 314, 328*

Versailles Peace Conference, *386*

Victoria Barracks, Paddington, *117, 126*

Vulcan, *173*

W

Waihora (SS), *205, 241*

Walker, Able Seaman John, *278, 320, 348*

Wallace, Arthur, *160*

Wallace, Ernest, *160*

Wallace, Frederick, *160*

Wallack, Colonel Ernest, *86, 90, 117, 126*

Walsh, Captain John, *232, 239*
  AIF service,
war crimes, *304*

Ward, Captain J., *228*

Warrego (HMAS), *50, 63, 67, 71*
  New Guinea, in, *173, 239, 249, 265, 274*

warships,
  see by name,

Watriama, Sergeant William, *160*

Watson, Lieutenant Colonel William, *90, 100, 103, 121, 123, 155, 235, 243, 328, 372*
  AIF service,
  discipline, *205*
  Kokopo, at, *265, 304, 306, 323, 325*

Wau-Bulolo Valley, *365*

Webber, Sub-Lieutenant Charles, *110, 117, 249*

White, Major Cyril Brudenell, *83*
White Australia policy,
Whitlam, (Edward) Gough, *155*
Whitlam, Margaret (nee Dovey), *155*
Whittle, Lieutenant James, *372*
Wide Bay, *173*
Wilkinson, Staff Sergeant Major William, *100*
Williams, Able Seaman William 'Billy', *145, 148, 265, 274, 320, 348*
Willian, Midshipman Henry, *110, 117*
Wilson, Chief Petty Officer A., *210*
Wilson, Woodrow, *386*
wireless telegraphy, *4, 80, 173*
Worthington, Able Seaman Angus, *191, 246, 248, 297, 304*
Wuchert, Captain (Hauptmann) Hans, *249, 265, 270, 278, 306*

Y

Yap, *4, 80, 180*
Yarra (HMAS), *50, 63, 71*
 New Guinea, in, *173, 239, 249, 274*
Young, Warrant Officer Gunner, *110*

Z

Zambezi (SS), *173*